Dear Reader:

The book you are about to read is the latest bestseller from the St. Martin's True Crime Library, the imprint the *New York Times* calls "the leader in true crime!" Each month, we offer you a fascinating account of the latest, most sensational crime that has captured the national attention. St. Martin's is the publisher of bestselling true crime author and crime journalist Kieran Crowley, who explores the dark, deadly links between a prominent Manhattan surgeon and the disappearance of his wife fifteen years earlier in THE SURGEON'S WIFE. Suzy Spencer's BREAKING POINT guides readers through the tortuous twists and turns in the case of Andrea Yates, the Houston mother who drowned her five young children in the family's bathtub. In Edgar Award-nominated DARK DREAMS, legendary FBI profiler Roy Hazelwood and bestselling crime author Stephen G. Michaud shine light on the inner workings of America's most violent and depraved murderers. In the book you now hold, WITHOUT A TRACE, Marion Collins takes a close look at the case of Robert Durst—a case that has grabbed recent national headlines.

St. Martin's True Crime Library gives you the stories behind the headlines. Our authors take you right to the scene of the crime and into the minds of the most notorious murderers to show you what really makes them tick. St. Martin's True Crime Library paperbacks are better than the most terrifying thriller, because it's all true! The next time you want a crackling good read, make sure it's got the St. Martin's True Crime Library logo on the spine—you'll be up all night!

Charles E Spicer

Charles E. Spicer, Jr.
Executive Editor, St. Martin's True Crime Library

"Hey, Dad, there's a body over there."

David and his two kids had spent the afternoon fishing off a breakwater in Galveston, Texas, less than a block from their home. He was stretched out lazily enjoying the last rays of the downing sun near his daughter. His 13-year-old stepson James had wandered off to troll the rocks with a net looking for small fish to use as lures.

He called over to the youngster. "I could use some help with these lines."

"Okay. I'm coming," James replied and started back along the shore. Suddenly, he stopped. Over by the pier, there was a shapeless, pinkish object bobbing in the waves. The teen stared at it for a few seconds, barely able to comprehend what it was. Slowly, his eyes widened as his brain processed the gruesome sight; the gory lump used to be a living creature which now was very, very dead. Recoiling in horror he cried out, "Hey Dad, there's a body over there."

"Don't kid around," David told him without looking up. "Don't tease your sister."

"I'm not," the boy protested. "It really is a body."

David dropped his line and rushed to the boy's side. "Is it a pig?" asked James, gazing down at the bloated mass of bloodied flesh.

"No," said his stepfather, shaking his head. "No it's not." David worked as a surgical nurse and he knew exactly what the youngster had found.

It was a human body. . . . or at least, what was left of it. What remained was the clearly naked trunk of a man. The head had been severed, the legs and arms chopped off. . . .

WITHOUT
A TRACE

MARION COLLINS

St. Martin's Paperbacks

WITHOUT A TRACE

Copyright © 2002 by Marion Collins.

Cover photograph courtesy Rex USA / *New York Post*.

ISBN: 0-312-98502-9

Printed in the United States of America

St. Martin's Paperbacks edition / November 2002

10 9 8 7 6 5 4 3

WITHOUT A TRACE

CHAPTER I

MURDER IN TEXAS

THE night before, the thirty-two-mile-long island strip had been lit up by growling thunderstorms and the temperature plummeted, but on that last Sunday of September 2001 the 58,000 inhabitants of Galveston, Texas, were basking in a seasonable 78 degrees. The folks in the blue-collar port city are used to sudden squalls that blow in and fizzle just as quickly. They also know that anything the angry sea doesn't swallow, it spits back up.

David Avina and his two kids had spent the afternoon fishing off a breakwater where Channelview Drive intersects 81st Street, less than a block from their home in the row of beach houses that rim the bay and look out over the Texas City Ship Channel. He was stretched out lazily enjoying the last rays of the downing sun and fending off his daughter Elyse who was pelting him with questions only an eight-year-old could ask as he impaled some bait on a hook for her. His 13-year-old stepson James Rutherford had wandered off to troll the rocks with a net looking for small fish to use as lures.

He called over to the youngster. "I could use some help with these lines."

"Okay, I'm coming," James replied and started back along the shore. Suddenly, he stopped. Over by the pier, there was a shapeless, pinkish object bobbing in the waves. The teen stared at it for a few seconds, barely able to comprehend what it was. Slowly, his eyes widened as his brain processed the gruesome sight; the gory lump used to be a living creature which now was very, very dead. Recoiling in horror he cried out, "Hey, Dad, there's a body over there."

"Don't kid around," David told him without looking up. "Don't tease your sister."

"I'm not," the boy protested. "It really is a body."

David dropped his line and rushed to the boy's side. "Is it a pig?" asked James, gazing down at the bloated mass of bloodied flesh.

"No," said his stepfather, shaking his head. "No, it's not." David Avina worked as a surgical nurse and he knew exactly what the youngster had found. It was a human body, or at least, what was left of it. What remained was the clearly naked trunk of a man. His head had been severed, his legs and arms had been chopped off.

Gathering up his kids and the gear as fast as he could, Avina ran for help. A few minutes later the Galveston cops and the beach patrol arrived and roped off the area to keep the growing gaggle of curious onlookers from getting in the way of the forensic team. When the preliminary on-site measurements were completed, and the area swabbed for evidence, the torso of what appeared to be an elderly man was loaded into an ambulance and removed to the police morgue.

There the medical examiner determined that the body hadn't been in the water for long and the dismemberment had been executed, not by a frenzied lunatic who'd gone berserk with an ax, but by someone with chilling clinical expertise. The killer, he concluded, was a cold-blooded butcher who knew what he was doing.

For the next several hours, the Sunday quiet of the sleepy bay was transformed into a hive of police activity. Cops fanned out along the half-mile stretch between the recently renovated pier and the old stone pier near the humpbacked railroad bridge. Once, the only way onto the island was by boat or rail; Galveston didn't join the rest of the country until the span carrying the I-45 over the 2-mile-wide Intercoastal Waterway was built.

Some of the folks who lived across the street told the cops that they'd seen garbage bags floating in the bay that morning, but paid them no attention, thinking that some antisocial slob had tossed his trash in the surf. As darkness fell floodlights lit up the area where police divers got ready to wade into the shallow water, then trawl the floor of the bay. Floating just offshore about eighty feet from where the body had washed up were three black plastic bags. In them were hacked-off arms and legs, which were dispatched to the morgue to be united with the rest of the victim. Scouring the shoreline, the cops found four more silver and black bags. But the poor devil who lay as cold as a fish on the mortician's slab was still without his head.

It was Galveston Police Officer Gary Jones's job to sift through the bags and make an inventory of the contents. He found two arms and two legs, one of them with two Band-Aids on it, but no head. They also contained a cash register receipt dated September 28 for trash bags and a drop cloth from Chalmers Hardware, a cover for a Green Thumb $6.99 bow-saw, with the store identification number attached, bloodstained towels, a flip-flop sandal, a red zori shower shoe, a piece of tan fabric that looked like it had come from a tool apron, blue plastic cups and paper towels. Officer Jones also discovered a Metamucil packet with the identification number NDC37000-024-09 on the top and another number, (L)1128XD06, on the back. In one of the bags was a copy of the weekend edition of *USA Today* with a delivery address sticker still on it. A pair of men's underpants and a blue bedsheet were recovered near where young James Rutherford had stumbled on the headless, limbless body.

Reading Officer Jones's report, Cody Cazalas, the burly, mustachioed detective assigned to the case, decided that although the killer was undoubtedly vicious, he was either incredibly sloppy or downright stupid to leave such a trail of evidence. He was also unlucky. If thunderstorms hadn't cleared the air on Saturday night, allowing the sudden cold front to move in, this poor sucker would likely have sunk to the bottom of the bay and never been heard of again. His butcher would have gotten off scot-free. As it was, the sudden change in temperature had made the corpse rise to the surface and the churning tides brought it back.

Officer Jones had obtained a set of fingerprints from the limbs that had been found in the trash bags and ran them through the police computer. He got a perfect match. The victim of this stomach-churning homicide was 71-year-old Morris Black, a white male born on the 21st of October, 1929.

Cazalas knew they were looking for an out-of-towner, someone who didn't know about the tides. That left plenty of suspects: people pass through Galveston like water through a sieve. There are the sailors who man oil tankers the size of New York city blocks, berthed two and three deep, their diesels humming, waiting to lade with the one million barrels of oil that are pumped to the docks 24/7 through gurgling pipelines from refineries forty miles away in Houston. And there's the low-rent trade that follows them—two-bit motels, greasy-spoon diners and whores, especially whores, of every shape, size, color and preference. Whoever dubbed the bustling seaport "Queen City of the Gulf" had a wicked sense of humor.

It's also an easy town to leave. Every year, hundreds of these massive vessels ferry their cargoes of black gold to destinations in Europe, South America and Asia. Yet more ships carry grain, cars and the city's newest bulk export, the 150,000 vacationers who crowd onto luxury cruise liners headed for resort paradises in Mexico or the Caribbean.

The day after the body was found, Cazalas went to Chalmers Hardware. The clerk looked at the receipt and confirmed that both it and the ID sticker on the bow-saw had come from the store. On October 2, Jones and Cazalas headed over to 2213 Avenue K, the delivery address on the newspaper that had been in the bag with the saw, the same address that had popped up on the computer for Morris Black.

It turned out to be what realtors call a fourplex: an unremarkable beige-and-brown–painted wood-frame house with gingerbread trim and storm shutters that had been restored and converted into four small apartments. Both the house and the area of downtown where it was located had seen better days. But old cottonwood trees and swaying palms lined the street, and St. Joseph's Catholic Church on the corner gave the neighborhood a kind of faded gentility of its own.

Cazalas, who'd been a Galveston police officer for thirteen years and was currently assigned to the Criminal Investigation Division, walked around to the back of the house, where the garbage cans were stashed in the narrow alley, and lifted the lids. Bingo! Officer Jones tipped up the first bin and started sorting through the contents. Inside was an empty trash bag box that matched the bags found at the crime scene, wrapping from a drop cloth, paper towels which were the same brand as the ones in the recovered trash bags, blue plastic cups, discarded food and food containers, packaging from a four-inch knife with a Chalmers Hardware sticker, an empty Metamucil packet with serial numbers that corresponded to the one in a bag pulled out of the bay and a bloody sock.

The contents of the second trash can were even more interesting to Cazalas and Jones. When it was upturned, among the spilled-out contents they retrieved a .22-caliber pistol and the casing of a spent shell (a check disclosed the gun was bought in Houston), a Band-Aid, underpants the same make and size as the ones recovered next to the corpse, a crumpled-up eviction notice that had been sent to the tenant of apartment #1, Morris Black, and a receipt for an eye exam from a Galveston optometrist, Dr. Ray Matocha, and made out to a Robert Durst, who'd given his address as 2213 Avenue K #2.

Cazalas went looking for the landlord, Rene Klaus Dillman. He said that Black had rented apartment #1 from him, but, no, he had no tenant on his property named Robert Durst.

"Who lived across the hall from Morris Black, then?" Cazalas asked.

It was a woman, Dillman told him, a nice middle-aged lady whose name was Dorothy Ciner. She hadn't rented the place herself, he added. About a month after Black arrived in October of 2000, Dillman had gotten a call from a man who asked if he could rent an apartment for his sister-in-law, Mrs. Dorothy Ciner, who suffered from a throat condition; several operations on her larynx had left her mute. That's why he was calling, the man explained, since she couldn't talk for herself. He told Dillman that Mrs. Ciner would be prepared to pay a year's rent in advance.

OK, Dillman had told the caller, it's yours.

When Mrs. Ciner moved in she communicated with him by writing notes. She'd been alone when she'd arrived at the $300-a-month apartment and written that she would be traveling a lot. Mrs. Ciner didn't have a phone, Dillman told Cazalas. Why would she? She couldn't speak.

They'd arranged that Dillman would check on her apartment when she was out of town and she'd given him a note saying that her brother-in-law, a botanist, would also look in occasionally and sometimes stay over—was that okay? she'd asked. Dillman said he hadn't seen Mrs. Ciner since the first of the year.

Dillman also told Cazalas that he had met the man, but he had never actually seen them together. One of them would go into the apartment and the other would leave shortly afterwards. He had spoken to him once, and yes, he could have said his name was Robert Durst. By the time Morris turned up dead, the brother-in-law had been staying in Mrs. Ciner's apartment on and off for six months, a situation, Dillman added, that was causing him headaches.

Morris, he explained, was a crabby old man with a foul temper. He never had any visitors and the other tenants had complained to him about the rows that frequently took place between him and Mrs. Ciner's brother-in-law across the hall.

"They yelled at each other a lot," he said. They argued

about turning the TV up too loud, and sometimes the air had been blue with curse words flying back and forth across the hallway. Morris could swear like a sailor.

He was also miserly. He shut the lights off at night because he convinced himself he was being charged extra for them, never switched on the air-conditioning, slept in the kitchen and picked fights with everyone. Eventually Dillman had had enough. Fed up with the endless gripes from his other renters, he'd told Morris that his lease was not going to be renewed when it expired on October 6. He'd better start looking for somewhere else to live.

Officer Jones checked out the dead man's apartment. It had been completely cleared out. There was blood in the kitchen sink, the shower, the washbasin in the bathroom and on the carpeting; more in the hallway between apartments #1 and #2; and he noticed that the hallway floor had been recently mopped. He also found blood outside the house.

On October 3, Cazalas stood outside while Dillman performed a "safety check" on Mrs. Ciner. From his stance at the doorway Cazalas could see a drop cloth spread out on the floor and a box of trash bags the same type and size as the ones at Chalmers Hardware. He noted that the box still had its store tag. Dillman told him he'd found the front section of the weekend edition of *USA Today*.

That was enough for Cazalas. The next morning, he was back with a warrant. The search of what few belongings she had offered few clues about the strange itinerant woman who'd lived there for nearly a year, or of her alleged brother-in-law. The sparsely furnished efficiency contained only a futon bed, a table and a television. The stove was unused, no one had so much as boiled an egg on its burners. But the apartment itself offered up lots of information. Inside it Jones and his team found a bloody four-inch knife and bloodstained boots. There was also blood on the front door and on the brown carpeting. Jones also noticed a tear in the kitchen linoleum which had been recently scrubbed clean. When he lifted it, he could see that blood had seeped onto the wooden boards underneath.

Samples of the blood were collected and tested to see if they matched that taken from the corpse of Morris Black. Those preliminary tests came up positive. Cazalas then talked to the occupant of apartment #3, Maria De Hernandez. On Sunday night, she told him, she'd seen Durst loading black plastic trash bags into a silver station wagon. Armed with this description, Detective Cazalas checked back with headquarters to get the vehicle identification number (VIN) of any automobile registered to a Robert Durst. Then he contacted Deputy Mike Creech from the Galveston County Auto Crimes Task Force and gave him the VIN that the search had coughed up. Creech ran an AutoTrack check which showed the number belonging to a silver Honda CRV.

The hunt was on. An all-county alert to apprehend Robert Durst went out. Knowing that the cops had to be on his tail, it seems incredible that he did not flee the state, if not the country. Instead, he tended to his one piece of unfinished business. The receipt from the eye doctor that had been in the trash bag with Morris Black's hacked-off limbs was for eyeglasses. In their wildest dreams the cops couldn't have imagined that anyone would risk his life and liberty over something he could pick up anywhere. What they couldn't have known was that a cheapskate like Bobby Durst would never have skipped town without collecting lenses he'd already paid for.

In the event that he might still be in the neighborhood, cops began keeping an eye on both the apartment house and the doctor's office. Dr. Matocha had told them that the suspect had visited him on October 1, the day after the body of Black had been found, and had made a lunchtime appointment for October 5. Cazalas told the optometrist to beep him if Durst showed up. The day came and went, and he never appeared.

Deciding that he was long gone from the area, the cops pulled their surveillance of the optometrist's premises.

Three days later Bobby turned up. As soon as he had left with new contact lenses, Dr. Matocha telephoned the police.

The next day, October 9, Officer Gary Jones spotted the silver Honda CRV cruising along the beachfront near 13th Street and Broadway, just a mile and a half from Avenue K, and flashed him to pull over. As the driver rolled down the window, Officer Jones came face to face with the suspected killer. He asked for ID. The driver produced a Holiday Inn Express hotel card with the name Jim Turss.

Officer Jones made a search of the car, and found a 9-millimeter gun that a subsequent check revealed had been bought in Tyler, Texas, in 1993, a bow-saw, marijuana and a receipt from a dry cleaner in New Orleans. He told Durst to get out, place his hands on his head and turn around to face the vehicle. He didn't look like a crazed butcher, Jones thought. The suspect was a slightly built man, he couldn't have weighed more than 130–140 pounds and was no more than 5' 8" tall, with receding gray spiky hair that could use a visit from a comb.

Bobby didn't put up a fight, he meekly obeyed Jones's demand to put his hands on the car and spread his legs. After patting him down to make sure he wasn't armed, Jones read him his Miranda rights, handcuffed him and brought him in. His colleagues back at the cop shop were milling about the lobby as Jones arrived with his perp; it's not every day you nab a guy who's sliced another human being into barbecue-size chunks. Something else caught their attention: he didn't seem at all bothered by his predicament.

Looking tired, but unnervingly defiant, dressed in shorts and a faded gray sweatshirt, he posed for his mugshot. Then he turned to Cazalas. "How do I get out of here?" he asked.

"The D.A. is going to ask for three hundred thousand dollars bail. You pay ten percent down, and you walk," the cop told him. "You got thirty thousand dollars?" he asked.

"Not on me," Bobby replied coolly. Cazalas stared at

him. What on earth do we have here? he asked himself silently.

A few hours later, Bobby was charged with the murder of Morris Black. Despite the horrific nature of the crime, Assistant District Attorney Kurt Sistrunk asked for bail to be set at $300,000, $250,000 for the murder charge and $50,000 on possession of marijuana.

On the face of it, it seemed a reasonable request, since the suspect could show no visible means of support and was obviously a transient. Judge Susan Criss also took into account that he had no criminal record. Not that she had any choice but to impose bail. In Texas, only people charged with capital murder—the killing of a cop or federal official—or committing murder while in pursuit for another crime (rape, robbery, etc.) can be held without bail.

Bobby asked to make a call. He phoned a New York number. "I'm in trouble, I need you to wire me some money and get a lawyer," he told the person at the other end of the phone. He spent the night in a holding cell dozing fitfully while his New York connection went to work. An overnight wire transfer of $30,000 would be enough to get him out of there, and he knew that would pose no problem for his contact. The next morning, he didn't even try to suppress an arrogant smirk as he posted the cash and walked out the door—a move that caught the Galveston police completely off guard.

"We had no idea who he was," police spokesman Lieutenant Michael Putnal says. "Here was a man living in a $300-a-month apartment, who didn't have a telephone and who wouldn't have looked out of place standing on the corner outside the Salvation Army."

Bobby hired Galveston lawyer Mark Kelly to represent him at his upcoming arraignment, which had been set for October 16, and promptly skipped town. Kelly was appalled by his client's flight, and publicly, the police shrugged off the fact that they had no idea where he'd gone. A.D.A. Sistrunk became aware of how big a fish had slipped through his fingers when he got a call from *New*

York Post reporter Larry Celona, who had been tipped off by a police source. Since Durst's get-out-of-jail money had come from New York, Sistrunk's office had asked the N.Y.P.D. to find the moneybags who had bailed him out.

"This Robert Durst you have in custody, could he possibly be our Robert Durst?" asked Celona and filled in the blanks for the dumbstruck A.D.A. Robert (Bobby) Durst was 58 and the eldest son of the late New York real estate baron Seymour Durst, whose company, the Durst Organization, was worth $1 billion. Nearly twenty years before, his beautiful young wife Kathie had vanished without a trace. Her body was never found, and no one was ever arrested in connection with her disappearance. The investigation had never been aggressively pursued and had been buried in the graveyard known as the Missing Persons File ever since, until recently, when the case had been reopened. Bobby had been the major suspect.

There was more, Sistrunk learned. There was the unsolved case of Susan Berman. She had been a writer, the only child of the gangster Davie "The Jew" Berman, and she'd been Bobby's best buddy since their college days. She'd been discovered slain, execution-style, in her Los Angeles home on Christmas Eve, 2000, just weeks after the Westchester, New York, District Attorney Jeanine Pirro had ordered the search for Kathie Durst revisited. Bobby had been questioned in that case too. So, was this the same Bobby Durst?

Sistrunk groaned. This had all the signs of turning into an enormous headache for him and his staff. Galveston was used to trouble—in 1900, the booming city with fortunes built on cotton, banks, mercantile houses, flour and grain mills, railroads and shipping, was pounded by the worst storm in U.S. history that left 6,000 souls dead and a further 8,000 people homeless. The bodies, which were buried at sea, had been swept back into the bay by the tides then too. Sistrunk had a sinking feeling that he was about to be hit by a tempest no less cataclysmic.

He also hadn't a clue as to what had brought Bobby to town. It wasn't the sort of place where the rich hang out, it was more of a jumping-off spot to get to somewhere better. At the height of the summer, around 60,000 visitors swamped the island, but, to tell the truth, the locals were just as glad to see them leave, and were fiercely proud of their B.O.I tag—Born On the Island—which they wear like a badge to differentiate themselves from their fellow Texans.

The next morning the fugitive millionaire was front-page news all over the country and the Galveston A.D.A. had egg on his face. On October 25 the red-faced Sistrunk went to Judge Susan Criss and Bobby's bail shot up to a billion dollars, making him Galveston County's first ever billion-dollar fugitive.

Back East, Bobby's upper-crust friends and family could scarcely believe their eyes as they unrolled their morning papers and were met by the picture of the scruffy-looking real-estate heir and read the horrific charges against him. How, they asked, as they poured their first cups of coffee in their luxurious Fifth Avenue apartments and their million-dollar suburban mansions, had it come to this? Bobby Durst was one of them, born into wealth, and his already huge family fortune had more than doubled in the last twenty years. He'd had a first-class education and had been blessed by a good brain, above average looks and a lively intelligence. Hadn't he married that pretty young wife, and whatever happened to her, anyway?

How could he possibly have killed an old man and then hacked off his head and his limbs? His mugshot was decorating the New York papers, and worse, he'd gone on the lam. Now his face was on the FBI's wanted list and displayed in post offices. How did he sink to this?

CHAPTER 2
BOBBY

IF there was ever anyone destined for success it was Bobby Durst. The man who had been charged with the incomprehensible murder of Morris Black had been born in New York on April 12, 1943, with not just a silver spoon but the whole canteen of cutlery in his mouth.

The day itself wasn't particularly memorable, but across the nation, many families feared for the safety of their sons. World War II was grinding inexorably on across three continents; the U.S. 8th Army was in Africa, the Brits were jubilant over the downing of 88 German planes, the Russians were thrashing Hitler and Mussolini's Axis troops in Kharkov and American forces had driven the Japanese out of Guadalcanal. At home, 3,000,000 previously exempt married men aged between 20 and 30 woke up to find themselves upgraded to 1-A status and nervously awaited their invitation to the dance from Uncle Sam, while up in the Bronx, the Dodgers had humiliated the mighty New York Yankees by sweeping them in their own ball field.

The new infant's father, Seymour B. Durst, was 29 and beginning to claw his way up the ladder in the cutthroat world of commercial real estate. Three years before he had joined the business founded by his father in 1927 and had quickly proved himself a worthy lieutenant to the old man. He and his pretty dark-haired 25-year-old wife, the former Bernice Herstein, were overjoyed at the birth of their first child, and called the little boy Robert Alan Durst. As they stood over his blue-trimmed crib, they couldn't, in their worst nightmares, have imagined the impact that this helpless baby would grow up to have on the lives of Morris

Black, Susan Berman and Kathleen McCormack.

The family had gone from rags to riches in just two generations. By the time young Bobby made his debut, the name Durst was a force to be reckoned with in New York. His paternal grandfather, Joseph Durst, had emigrated from Austria in 1902 with, according to family lore, just $3 sewn into the lapel of his shabby overcoat. For the next thirteen years he toiled in the garment trade until he'd saved enough cash to put down a deposit on his first property.

Joseph quickly figured out that midtown was where money was to be made, in the square mile between New York's two great railroad terminals, Grand Central and Pennsylvania Station, which every day spewed hundreds of thousands of commuters from the suburbs of Westchester, Long Island, Connecticut and New Jersey onto the surrounding streets.

Like many ambitious immigrants before and since, Joseph had worked all the hours God gave him and saved every cent he could. By 1915, he had scraped together enough to buy a property on 34th Street and 12 years later, he incorporated the Durst Organization. Fueled by his vision of a growing business center which would fan out from the two transit hubs, the company embarked upon an ambitious plan of snagging every available lot that came up for grabs. During the Depression, he'd bought mortgages and leases on commercial properties and made sure his children had a good education. By the fifties Joseph had built his first skyscraper at Third Avenue and 42nd Street and began his relentless march uptown.

He'd sent Seymour and his brothers, who'd been born in the Washington Heights section of the city, to Horace Mann School in suburban Riverdale in the southern tip of the Bronx just over the Hudson River from the top of the island of Manhattan. From there Seymour went on to attend the University of Southern California where he graduated with a degree in accounting in 1935.

His father's genius had been to foresee the insatiable demand for office space as the city's manufacturing base declined. Seymour's business smarts had been to acquire parcels of land around Rockefeller Center in choice locations west of midtown. One of the towering blocks that rose from a razed tenement lot was 1133 Avenue of the Americas, which became the impressive headquarters of the Durst Organization.

Joseph had lived by the rule: "Don't buy anything you can't walk to," he'd tell his sons, the message implied being, "Don't waste money on unnecessary luxuries like limousines." Seymour was listening. When he turned his attention to the underdeveloped West Side, he'd take the subway. As powerful in his day as Donald Trump is now, he was as low-key and tightfisted as Trump is flamboyant and ostentatious; extravagance was repugnant to him. But like Trump, Seymour was an expert at the art of the deal, which he preferred to seal with a handshake. A century after Joseph landed on American soil, the family fortune stands at at least $1 billion.

Back in the forties, not only were Seymour's real estate holdings rapidly multiplying, his family was growing too. Bobby's birth was quickly followed by the arrival of his sister Wendy and his brothers Douglas and Thomas.

With his family expanding and profits soaring, Seymour began looking for a larger home in which to raise his brood. He settled on a spacious house in Scarsdale, in Westchester County. It was one of the wealthiest and oldest of the New York suburbs, some twenty-two miles north of Manhattan. It was a perfect spot to raise a large family, he decided. The charming little town looked like a misplaced English hamlet complete with mock Tudor public buildings; it had practically no crime, fine schools and, with a train every half hour, easy access to his office in midtown Manhattan.

It was also a neighborhood awash with money. "We were the richest community in the country at that time," says Maxwell Weissen, a realtor who now lives in Greenwich, Connecticut, another enclave of the fabulously rich, who went to Scarsdale High School with Bobby. His family were neighbors of the Dursts. "Every billionaire you read about was there: the Millsteins—the banking and real estate family who at that time . . . were making linoleum floor covering—they were our neighbors. The Tisches [who owned the Loews theaters and a hotel chain] lived across the road from us. All the Jewish millionaires and billionaires, the richest Jews in the world, lived in that part of Scarsdale."

The manse Seymour and Bernice had picked out at 27 Hampton Street was in the Fox Meadows section of town. It had a large yard with plenty of room for the children to romp and grow. The house itself was a foreboding structure; built of dark gray stone with small paned windows and steeply pitched roofs, it wouldn't have looked out of place in *The Addams Family*. From the front it looked like a two-story dwelling with attics, but the property dipped way down at the back, and the house was twice as big from the rear. Most of the homes on the gracious street were built on a rise with open driveways that showcased them in all their architectural glory, framed by sturdy oaks so tall that the branches, even in full leaf, didn't obscure them from passersby. The Durst house was sunk into a hollow with dense trees and shrubs crowding the front door. It was not the home of a man who'd greet the neighborhood Welcome Wagon with a smile.

Nor was it much brighter inside. The walls in the downstairs reception rooms were lined with wood paneling, and an impressive oak staircase led from the dimly lit hall to the upstairs rooms. It was a puzzling choice for a young couple with four lively children, but possibly perfect for a bookish man like Seymour, who spent what little spare time he had away from work poring over historical tomes in his library.

Many of the neighborhood children avoided it like the plague. "We lived on Brite Avenue and the Dursts lived just around the corner. But I didn't play at the house when we were kids because his father was very weird," says Weissen. "It was a great big dingy, huge Tudor house—I just remember it being dank and dark and dreary and depressing. It was very eerie and I never wanted to go there."

Bobby's cousins, Stephen and Lesley, the children of Seymour's brother Roy and his wife Shirley, were also neighbors, says Weissen. "They lived in a much more cheerful house on Wayside Lane and their parents were friendly with my parents. But my mother was also very friendly with Bob's mom."

One kid who did brave the forbidding house was Robert Quasman, who now lives in Lutherville, Maryland. "I met Bob at Fox Meadows Elementary School. Throughout second, third and fourth grades we were best friends, and then we drifted apart. We lived four or five blocks away and I played at the house often, and had sleepover dates many times. Bob had a bedroom to himself upstairs. I remember it being basically dark."

At first the young Dursts seemed like any other affluent family that had fled the city to raise their kids in leafy suburbia, but behind the shades, there was something dreadfully amiss.

Having four children in quick succession had taken its toll on Bernice. Marooned in a home, no matter how grand, and coping with four youngsters under the age of seven while her driven husband was in Manhattan from early morning until night seemed to sap her energy and deflate her spirit. Bobby, her intuitive oldest child, sensed the sadness and turmoil in the mother he adored, but he was much too young to understand, never mind do anything to help her. And anyway, given the times, when families kept their darkest secrets to themselves, it's doubtful that anyone but Seymour knew the real depth of her misery, and he too seemed powerless to lift her mood.

On a miserable winter night in 1950, a distraught and disheveled Bernice was discovered teetering on a narrow ledge above the steep roof of the garage. Seymour, mortified by the spectacle and unable to find the words to soothe her troubled soul, tried to coax her, implore her, then order her down. She stood rooted to the spot, unable to move, her nightdress clinging to her shivering slender frame in the soaking rain. The disturbance attracted the attention of the neighbors, who'd spilled out of their homes to gape horrified at the drama unfolding 50 feet aboveground. A young nanny tried to comfort the wailing younger children out of sight, but Bobby had squirmed out of her clutch and watched in stupefied silence.

Bernice's New York doctor and the emergency services were sent for. When help arrived in the shape of the Scarsdale Fire Department, a ladder was put up against the garage and fireman Thomas Langan began to climb. But just as he reached the top rung and stretched out to grab Bernice, she slid by him and plunged to the driveway, crushing her skull on the pavement.

She was rushed to White Plains Hospital in a police ambulance and pronounced dead shortly after. She was just 32 years old. The medical examiner, Dr. Victoria Bradess, ruled the February 8 death an accident and said that Bernice had been taking medication for severe asthma and somehow had become deranged or disoriented enough to clamber up onto the tiled roof of the garage. Unsteady under the influence of sedatives, she had missed her rescuer's outstretched hand and thudded headfirst onto the driveway below.

The Scarsdale Inquirer faithfully reported the official line, but everyone who saw the tragedy knew the real truth was even sadder, says Weissen. "She killed herself," he says. "She wasn't on the garage roof. The master bedroom had a wrought-iron balcony that was a couple of floors above the driveway which went steeply down at the side of the house, and that added depth and hardness to her fall. She jumped off the balcony and fell onto the driveway. The local paper didn't say she killed herself, because they didn't understand depression at that time. They said she slipped, that she was walking on wet leaves—it was a rainy night. I was very young when it happened, just 6 or 7, but I remember my mom was very upset. Mrs. Durst was very sweet and sensitive, and my mom had really liked her.

"She was probably manic-depressive and suffering from all that postpartum stuff that nobody knew about in 1950. They didn't have drugs to treat depression then either. People didn't really deal with it. They didn't really deal with anything," he says.

Weissen says that behind the veneer of wealth and privilege, girls like the former Bernice Herstein were pushed into arranged "good" marriages and then left to flounder, with no career to fulfill them and scant sympathy for their frustrations.

"If you were a woman in that era, you just got married at 18 or 19, you had no other role. My own mother is one example," he says. "She was a very intelligent woman who married someone her parents picked and had children with someone who she probably never loved, and lived a life of quiet desperation. She was actually made happier when she was finally a widow. Terrible but true. Even she is shocked how meaningless her life was, but it was typical of how that generation of women like she and Bernice Durst lived.

"And Jewish women didn't even have the outlet of liquor—it wasn't their custom. We were all too close to the Old Country." It didn't help either, says Weissen, that Scarsdale in the fifties was a cultural desert.

"Anyone would be depressed living there," he says. "As soon as we all left home, my parents sold the big house on Brite Avenue to Bernard Nussbaum, President Clinton's White House counsel, and built a smaller house on Wigg Road. But after a couple of years they finally gave up and moved back to the city. They just hated the suburbs, the quiet of it."

Much later, and years after the medical profession had begun to recognize the depth and destruction of postpartum depression, Durst family members acknowledged that Bernice had hurled herself to her death in a fit of the post-baby blues. And if anything could have made it worse, it was that 7-year-old Bobby had witnessed the whole wrenching incident. He'd seen the desperation in his mother's face, heard the sickeningly dull thud when she landed a few feet from where he was standing, and watched the blood ooze from her head as she lay sprawled on the wet ground. The little boy was too shocked to scream, and it was a scene he relived over and over again.

While his children struggled to take in the cruel fact that their mother was gone forever, Seymour began making funeral arrangements. Services for his lovely young wife were held at Scarsdale Jewish Community Center on Friday, February 10. She was buried hours later at the Mount Pleasant Cemetery in Valhalla New York.

The sight of his pretty mother in a coffin was to haunt Bobby for the rest of his life. His 7-year-old brain could not take in that he would never see her again; he tried to hold on to her, by physically doing just that. At the funeral, as Bernice's casket was being lowered into the grave, he threw himself on top of it and had to be yanked off by his father.

Seymour went back to work, and hired help to run his home. Although he had four young children to raise, the quiet-spoken, mild-mannered Seymour never married again. His only passions, it seemed, were building skyscrapers and collecting memorabilia about old New York; his only vice, a fondness for the foul-smelling cigars on which he constantly chomped. Bobby and Wendy returned to their classes at Fox Meadows Elementary School and found themselves the objects of curiosity and pity.

"We had just moved to Scarsdale when his mom died," says Bobby's childhood friend Peter Freydberg who now lives in Odessa, Florida. "We'd moved into a house on Horseguard Lane and the Dursts were three blocks away. Bobby is supposed to have seen it—she jumped off the roof, is what I heard. After that, the children were looked after by housekeepers."

Not unnaturally, his mother's death had a devastating effect on the whole family. Seymour never really understood why Bernice, with her splendid home, her children and a husband who provided for them royally, would end her life in a way that had brought shame and scandal to his doorstep. Dour and unsociable when she was alive, he now withdrew to his library and buried himself in his books. His oldest child became unreachable and aggressive and his battles with his younger brother Douglas became so uncontrollable that he sought counselling for both boys. Bobby in particular never seemed to come to terms with the horror of that night. His mother's death drove a wedge between him and his remote father and distanced him from his younger siblings, whose tender age had spared them the worst memories.

The incident also seemed to leave the shy youngster with an odd way of talking. "He spoke with a drawl, long pauses punctuated his speech as if he were struggling to spit out the words," writer Julie Baumgold, whose family celebrated birthdays and shared vacations at Elberon on the Jersey shore with the Dursts, told the New York *Daily News*.

By the time he got to Scarsdale High School, where teenage girls dressed like suburban matrons in pleated skirts and sweater sets and the guys wore the kind of outfits their fathers donned on Saturdays to wash the car—chinos, khakis, plaid shirts and sports coats—he faded into the student body of 3,100. And though he was to become a household name in the worst possible way after the murder of Morris Black, Bobby went through school without causing a ripple. Teachers and classmates describe him as quiet, a loner, whom nobody loved to death or heartily disliked either. In the same class was his cousin Stephen, who was better looking, more outgoing and altogether more popular. Bobby tried to fit in, and with Steve he joined the Aviation and Spanish Clubs; he also belonged to the Camera Club, the Projection Club and the Leaders Club and played Junior Varsity soccer.

In the Leaders Club he met a pretty and popular brunet named Dorothy (Dottie) Ciner who was also in the Latin, French and Science Clubs, the Junior Red Cross, the Usherettes and the Future Teachers of America Club.

"We hung out together in school, doing the things that

kids do, like smoking behind the school buildings, oh, God, yes," says Freydberg. "But Bob was pretty quiet, he kept to himself a lot. I don't remember him ever having a girl-friend in school."

Like many of his classmates, Sam Koret, who now lives in Raleigh, North Carolina, can barely remember him. "I looked at the photograph of him in the yearbook after I'd seen pictures of him after his arrest and thought, 'Do I really know this guy?' I said, 'Jesus, it's him.' We had a thirty-fifth reunion several years ago and his name never came up—that's how much of an impression he made."

Even his childhood pal Robert Quasman barely knew him any longer. "I really had no contact with him in high school. There were 300-odd in the class and he was just a kid who was there. But he struck me as different, yet if you were to ask me in what way I couldn't tell you."

Maxwell Weissen says Scarsdale High School was a tough fit for a lot of kids, but especially for an introverted boy like Bobby. And it wasn't made easier by their over-achieving parents' wealth and success. "I hated Scarsdale. Just hated it. It was a dreadful, horrible place to raise a child," he says. "It gave you totally unrealistic expectations of reality, and if you weren't an incredible athlete or gor-geous or, you know, so brilliant that you got solid A's, then you were just nothing. That raised all sorts of insecurities—at least in me.

"It was totally cliquey. There were the athletes and the brains—everyone else was a shlepper. It was impossible to shine unless you were absolutely extraordinary."

The non-shining Bobby graduated from Scarsdale High School in June 1961. Beside his senior year picture, the *Brandersnatch* (the school yearbook) wrote:

We DURST not criticize this Bob,
Whose activities make him stand out from the mob.

His cousin, the dashing Steve, in whose shadow Bobby had always paled, earned a more glowing tribute:

This brilliantly practical carefree guy
Chose "Pay as you go" over "Pie in the sky."

To rub salt in the wound, Steve was also dubbed "most likely to succeed." *Brandersnatch* sub-editor Dottie Ciner, who made a lasting impression on Bobby, although she didn't know it at the time, was dubbed:

> Tween the serious student
> and the fun-loving flirt,
> Dot sails a midcourse,
> cheerful and pert.

Halfway through Bobby's last year at the school, there was an ugly incident which left scars on the whole community. Each Christmas, the Scarsdale Golf Club played host to the Holly Ball, where the town's upper-crust debutantes put society on notice that they were no longer girls, but beautiful young women fast approaching marriageable age.

This "coming out" was the highlight of every affluent 18-year-old girl's calendar. Weeks before the event, the debs and their mothers would descend on Saks Fifth Avenue and Bergdorf Goodman to shop for white ball gowns. Corsages and limousines were ordered, escorts picked and invitations mailed out.

One of Bobby's classmates, Pam Nottage, had asked former student Michael Cunningham Hernstadt, a 19-year-old sophomore at the University of Colorado at Boulder, to be her date for the night. But when the golf club learned who Pamela planned to have on her arm at the Holly Ball, she was told in no uncertain terms that Mike Hernstadt was not welcome. Humiliated and angry, Pamela canceled her debut.

The problem was Mike's Jewish father. In 1961, the snooty Scarsdale Golf Club saw nothing wrong with its bigotry. Jews and non-Jews just didn't mix socially. The Jews had their own perfectly fine golf club, they just weren't accepted as members at S.C.G., and they certainly

weren't supposed to escort their daughters to their show-
case social event of the year.

If anything could have made the shameful situation
worse, it soon became clear that the Scarsdale Golf Club
had discriminated against one of their own. Although his
dad was indeed Jewish and his mother Roman Catholic,
Mike was a card-carrying Episcopalian. Both parents,
mindful of the prejudice against any kind of mixed marriage at the time, had decided not to inflict their religious
beliefs on their three sons, but to let them choose their own
spiritual affiliations when they were old enough.

Mike had chosen to become an Episcopalian at age 17
and had been baptized by Reverend George French Kempsell, Jr., rector at the most fashionable church in Scarsdale,
the Protestant Episcopal St. James the Less.

The whole nasty business might have been swept under
the carpet if it hadn't reached the incredulous ears of Reverend Kempsell. "The next Sunday, he gave a big sermon
about how horrible it was, how disgraceful," says Max
Weissen, who remembers the shock waves the incident sent
through the little town and the high school.

"Prejudice should be stopped at its beginning," thundered the priest. "Any act of discrimination against the Jews
because of their blood gets more dangerous, more powerful,
and ultimately can result in, as in Nazi Germany, a desire
to destroy the Jewish people." Then he announced from the
pulpit that he would withhold communion to any church
members (three of them were on the Holly Ball committee)
who had been responsible for the decision to ostracize
young Mike.

The ugly incident triggered a huge scandal which divided the wealthy community. For the next couple of
weeks, the rich commuters on the 8:02 A.M. to Manhattan
found that their dirty linen was being aired not only in *The
Scarsdale Inquirer*, but on the pages of *The New York
Times*, even in *Life* magazine. On the morning ride to the
city, they talked of little else.

The Holly Ball committee and the president of the club

at first kept a stoic silence, convinced that the whole thing was a storm in a teacup and would just blow away since, they reckoned, there was no great local outcry to change the status quo.

It was a miscalculation that dragged the club's reputation through the mud and kept op-ed writers busy for weeks. The civil rights issue was threatening to explode across the south, but here in New York was a case of prejudice and exclusion tailor-made for ambitious young hacks to sink their teeth into.

What's more, the pesky priest wouldn't shut up. He not only railed Sunday after Sunday from his own pulpit at St. James the Less, but became a star guest speaker at heavily attended religious meetings across the city.

Eventually, the club members, appalled by seeing themselves being pilloried in the press as bigots, pressured the committee to change its ruling. On January 23, the Scarsdale Golf Club issued a grudging letter of "clarification of future guidance" in which it announced that any of their 750 member families could henceforth invite anyone they wanted to use the club's facilities.

The matter was settled, but the powerful club mavens simmered with rage at the meddlesome priest who had forced this unwelcome change of rules on them. Quietly, they began to wield their extensive clout. Reverend Kempsell soon learned that wealthy people don't get mad, they get even. He found himself transferred to a parish in Texas.

The ugliness of the Holly Ball scandal wasn't lost on the Dursts or any of the other Jewish families who suddenly felt less welcome in the town. All over the land the times were, as Bob Dylan was soon to announce, a-changing. The younger generation had put the country on notice that the existing social order needed updating. Little did the parents of Scarsdale or in any other comfortable community know that their cosseted offspring were about to join a revolution that would question their whole *Leave It to Beaver* lifestyle, which, until the sixties, had epitomized the American Dream.

But Bobby had yet to find his rebellious feet. After high school, Seymour's son and heir appeared to be a chip off the old block. He opted to study business and economics at Lehigh University near the steel town of Bethlehem, Pennsylvania, a decision his father had warmly encouraged. The way he saw it, Bobby could enjoy four years of comparative freedom before he was reined back in to the family fold. Seymour, with his old-world values, his fascination for history and his determination to consolidate his father's empire-building dreams with hard work and business acumen, couldn't have foreseen the drastic upheaval about to take place in American society either.

Change was in the air in 1960 when John F. Kennedy was elected and suddenly the White House no longer belonged to old men with dowdy wives hell-bent on keeping the status quo, but was occupied by a vivacious and youthful family. Young people everywhere had heard his exhortation to "Ask not what your country can do for you; ask what you can do for your country," and joined the Peace Corps in droves. While Kennedy gingerly pushed his domestic agenda for a more equal society at home, he unflinchingly sent troops to Asia to combat the growing threat of communism in the region.

But when his successor Lyndon B. Johnson escalated the fray and the teenage soldiers sent to Vietnam "on an advisory basis" started coming home in body bags, universities across the nation seethed with dissent; their undergraduates, all of whom, incidentally, were excused from the draft as long as they remained in higher education, threw themselves into protesting the war; that is, when they were not checking out the latest shipment of dope or trading in their textbooks for guitars.

The sheer exhilaration of the youth movement swept Bobby up in its tide. Rebelliousness was the order of the day and "Do your own thing" was the mantra of everyone under 30. For Bobby, it provided moral support for his reluctance to go to work in the family business. Too boring, he told his father, he'd pass.

His decision didn't sit well with Seymour; a life of shunning responsibility was not what he'd intended for his oldest son. As his heir, Bobby was expected to follow in his father's footsteps and carve out a new era of his own for the Dursts. They were builders and developers; Joseph had developed midtown, and under Seymour's watch the Avenue of the Americas had been transformed from a ho-hum sprawl of dingy tenement blocks to become the headquarters of the country's top investment, legal and publishing corporations.

None of this was of any interest to Bobby, who was rapidly becoming a true child of the sixties, more interested in sex, drugs and rock 'n' roll, especially drugs. Sure it was nice to be a rich kid, with plenty of cash to indulge his whims. But he was an artist, he had soul, and he wasn't about to hide his sensitive nature under a three-piece suit and spend his days with boring corporate types. He repeatedly told his father that he had no interest in working for him.

"When I was growing up, it was the days of long hair and marijuana. In terms of announcing that you were going into the family business, that was extremely uncool," he explained. In 1965, with a degree in economics and business under his belt, he announced that he'd enrolled at the University of California in Los Angeles where many of its students, like others across the country, were majoring in radical social disobedience and anti-establishmentarianism.

CHAPTER 3

SUSAN

AT U.C.L.A. Bobby met a strikingly sexy girl blessed with masses of shiny black hair which she wore with bangs that fringed a pair of inquisitive brown eyes. She had a mischievous wraparound grin and although at 5'4" she wasn't tall, she had inherited her ex-dancer mother's shapely legs and confident stride. He found out that her name was Susan Berman, she was 21 years old and a journalism student. Despite the mutual attraction they never became sweethearts. Theirs was a deeper bond. The relationship was founded on the recognition that they had some ghosts in common and they struck up a genuine, loving friendship that was to endure for over thirty-five years. To the orphaned Susan, Bobby was the big brother she'd never had.

At first glance, they were an unlikely duo. To their fellow students, the skinny, introspective New Yorker was a loner with a somewhat convoluted sense of humor and several antisocial habits; he belched and farted in company, but the words "Excuse me" never escaped his lips. He had the kind of nondescript good looks that went unnoticed in a crowd and a startlingly gravelly voice that underscored an intense personality that was a bit too edgy for some of them. His family might have scads of dough, but Bobby had been drilled by his conservative father to keep it quiet. Seymour himself was devoid of flash; he had great wealth, but worked diligently, gave to charities and led a life of modest luxury. His name rarely appeared in the gossip columns, and since his wife's death, his personal life was a closed book. He had tried to instill these same values of restraint, selflessness and self-discipline in his children.

And so it was hardly surprising that Bobby was fascinated by his exotic new friend. Susan was the flamboyant daughter of gangster Davie Berman, the legendary Bugsy Siegel's right-hand man and business partner who began life in crushing poverty on a Jewish farming settlement in North Dakota and ended up as the King of Las Vegas.

Susan, Bobby soon discovered, was as outspoken and opinionated as he was reticent and self-contained. She had an infectious musical lilt to her voice; Bobby rasped everything he had to say in his cynical, throaty bark. In company he seemed to brood, rarely contributing to the conversation; Susan never shut up.

Like Bobby, Susan had been raised in luxury, but while he'd come from bricks-and-mortar money back East, her family's fortune was the ill-gotten kind wrung from the gaming tables of Las Vegas after Siegel, Berman and Meyer Lansky's Jewish Mafia reinvented the desert town as a magnet for punters. An only child, she had been adored by her handsome and glamorous parents.

Therein lay the attraction. Both of their fathers were immensely powerful. But while Seymour Durst built his empire block by block, buying and selling tracts of valuable land and redeveloping entire sections of Manhattan, Davie Berman ruled through intimidation, thievery and brute force. To get their own way, both specialized in evictions: Seymour used legal coercion, the power of the courts, the smell of hard cash and the sheriff's officers to oust people from property that stood in the way of his ambitions; Davie's evictions tended to be permanent—anyone brave or misguided enough to thwart him was simply removed from the face of the earth.

Both Bobby and Susan had been dealt their fair share of smarts, but while Bobby had more than an inkling about the wheeling and dealing that went on in his father's business, when they met, Susan hadn't a clue about how her father's fiefdom had really operated. Sure, she'd heard stories about his Mob connections, but as clever and curious as she was, she had consigned them to the PENDING tray in her brain.

While Bobby was struggling through childhood without his mother at the gloomy Westchester mansion, Susan was growing up surrounded by love and warmth in Las Vegas, which was little more than a dusty truck stop when mobster Bugsy Siegel hit on the idea of turning it into a gambling mecca.

In 1829 a Mexican scout looking for water on the Old Spanish Trail to Los Angeles stumbled on the desert oasis and found it blessed with an abundance of artesian springs. Twenty-five years later Mormon leader Brigham Young ordered some of his followers to colonize the valley in order to secure the post road from Utah to California, but they quit two years later and went home. It wasn't until the San Pedro, Los Angeles and Salt Lake City Railroad thundered into the valley in 1905 that Las Vegas began to look anything like a town.

It remained a quiet settlement of a few thousand inhabitants who mainly catered to the needs of railroad employees until the late twenties when construction began on the massive Hoover Dam, bringing Depression-weary laborers and their bedraggled families into the area. To entertain them, and relieve them of their hard-earned cash, two casinos sprung into operation. The El Rancho, which opened in 1941, was located just off the main highway, and with a swimming pool in the middle of its huge parking lot, it was a roaring success. The Hotel Last Frontier followed a year later.

With the outbreak of WW II, the Las Vegas Aerial Gunnery School, now the Nellis Air Force Base, was built on 3 million acres north of Las Vegas where land went for $1 an acre. It became home to a fleet of B-17 and later, B-29 U.S.A.F. bombers and their young crews.

By the time Siegel and Berman blew into town, the war was just over and servicemen were returning home in droves. The country was in a rebuilding mode; industries that had churned out tanks, armaments and warplanes were retooling their plants to provide the nation with the consumer goods that were considered the spoils of peace. There would be jobs and money in bucketloads, Siegel figured. It would be like taking candy from babies. He'd provide a resort with more pizzazz than anything in town, where the newly flush workers could throw their money away at his gaming tables. All he had to do was build it, and they would come.

The vision of opulence that swirled in Bugsy Siegel's head escaped Susan's mother when she first arrived in Vegas. Gladys Evans, who'd been born Betty Ewald, was one half of a tap-dancing act called The Evans Sisters (her partner was her cousin Lorelei) when she caught Davie's eye. At thirty-five he was a confirmed bachelor. For a guy who could kill with impunity, when it came to girls, he had the morals of a monk. Despite the opportunities he never philandered, he didn't drink or gamble, and wouldn't swear in front of a woman. He'd first noticed her in 1939 when his brother Chickie took him to the Paradise Club in Minneapolis where Gladys was appearing. He was so blown away by this whirling specter of loveliness, her long black hair flying as she tapped and spun, her gold dress glinting in the lights, that after the show he marched up to her and announced: "I'm Davie Berman and I want to marry you." To Florence, her ever-present, domineering stage mother, he said, "You have the most beautiful daughter in the Twin Cities."

Gladys had plenty of men after her; Groucho Marx had been smitten with her when she'd bumped into him earlier that year on a sight-seeing trip to MGM Studios. But Davie would not be deterred. For months he plied her with flowers and gifts and courted Florence as much as her daughter. When he did surprise her with a diamond ring on November 29 and she agreed to marry him, he didn't give her time to change her mind. He whisked her off to Northwood, Iowa, famous for its quickie weddings, where they were

married a few hours later by a justice of the peace. Chickie
and the lawman's wife, in her nightdress, were the witnesses.

After a luxurious honeymoon in Miami Beach they
moved into a house Davie bought for his bride on Bryant
Avenue. She thought she'd landed in a blast furnace when,
in 1945, she stepped off the train from Minneapolis with
baby Susan in her arms. Davie had tried to warn her: "It's
a little warm there, Betty, dress cool," he'd said.

Looking balefully at the dozen or so ramshackle buildings and miles of sagebrush swaying gently in the hot wind,
she'd asked him, "Where's the town?"

"This is only the backdrop, honey," he promised her.

When the Flamingo opened its doors the day after Christmas, 1946, patrons found themselves wallowing in Florida-
inspired glamor. They were greeted by pink flamingos on
the manicured lawn and at night the "carpet joint," as Siegel
called it, lit up the desert sky with its huge pink neon sign.
As he'd predicted, the gamblers poured in—but so did
gangsters from every major city looking to skim off a piece
of the action. Expenses were high, profits were slow and
the backers, the all-powerful East Coast Mob syndicate,
became impatient for payback.

By the following year, Siegel—a megalomaniac who
had a history of enraging his Mafia overlords, and who had
already bought a few years of extra life with his Las Vegas
brainchild—had become a major thorn in the syndicate's
side. After one tantrum too many, he was gunned down at
the Beverly Hills home of his girlfriend, a Mafia moll
named Virginia Hill. The shot that killed him blew out one
of his eyeballs. It flew across the floor, rolling under the
furniture and was later retrieved by Florabel Muir, an eagle-
eyed reporter with the New York *Daily News*. His assassin
has never been found. With Bugsy out of the way, Berman,
Gus Greenbaum, William "Ice Pick" Alderman and Moe
Sedway took over the now lucrative Flamingo. Davie was
the new boss.

Cocooned from the nature of her father's unsavory business, Susan grew up a little princess. The Bermans lived in a quaint, brown-and-white Tudor-style home at 721 South Sixth Street, which Gladys chose because the white picket fence that surrounded it reminded her of St. Paul. It was one of the few homes at the time that had efficient air-conditioning, installed by the same company that cooled down her father's hotels. To little Susan, her family seemed quite ordinary; she was a Brownie, she had dancing classes at Nancy William's Dance Studio in the afternoons and her pretty dark-haired mother was a volunteer at her school, Fifth Street Elementary. The only sign that the Bermans weren't regular folks was their windows, which were high enough off the ground to thwart any attempt to gun down the house's inhabitants from a passing car.

During the stifling heat that enveloped the city every May through September, little Susan lived in a bathing suit and flowered swimming cap at the Flamingo pool, splashing happily with the kids of Davie's partners. Only the children dipped; her father was never seen without his pinstriped suit no matter what the temperature was outside, and her mother lounged poolside with the other wives. Susan captured the atmosphere in "The Heat," a piece she wrote for *Las Vegas Life* magazine:

There they were, glorious in their one-piece
Catalina swimsuits, their hair protected from the
punishing sun by cotton scarves, the toes and
fingernails painted with Revlon's Jack
O'Diamonds red nail polish at Gigi's nail salon
at the Flamingo.
    They didn't even remove their cork-soled
wedges, just crossed their impossibly slim ex-
dancer legs on a chaise lounge and played gin
and canasta under navy umbrellas. The ash on
their Chesterfield cigarettes got so long it had to
ask for permission to drop off. We ate only club
sandwiches served on big silver trays by

waitresses in short white shorts. Our mothers
drank ice tea with a slice of orange and lemon
on a toothpick in it.

Susan had a room just for her toys and thought Lib-
erace and Elvis sang at every kid's birthday parties just as
they did at hers. Davie Berman might be the boss of the
Flamingo and its sister hotel, the Riviera, but every evening
he'd drop what he was doing to rush home in time to tuck
her in, read her a story, then hurry back to count the casinos' takings. When she was four he had her pose in jeans,
cowboy boots and a Western shirt for a portrait he hung
above the reception desk in the lobby of the Flamingo. He
taught her to play his favorite song, "The Sunny Side of
the Street," on the piano. Every year, wearing a red sash
emblazoned with "Flamingo Hotel" across her chest, she
rode on the hotel float in the Helldorado parade.

The Flamingo was her second home. She'd order to-
mato soup with crackers and chocolate ice cream from
room service and sign the check "Susie Berman" in her
childish scrawl. Chorus girls became her friends, she
learned arithmetic from a slot machine and knew what to
do if, God forbid, she was kidnapped. She described the
drill: "I was to run, scream, yell, use whatever to get away,"
she said.

When she was eight, she put the instructions that had
been dinned into her to use, when a man snatched her as
she walked to school and stuffed her into the back of a car.
As the man drove off, Susan remembered her father's
words. She lashed out, hitting her abductor in the head and
screaming at the top of her voice. She was rescued and
returned to her hysterical mother by a couple of quick-
thinking cops who heard the commotion.

Later she realized that the surprise "vacations" she'd
loved so much at the Beverly Wilshire Hotel coincided with
breakouts in gang warfare in Vegas or the nerve-wracking
times when the Feds turned up the heat on Davie. To her
it meant an exciting middle-of-the-night plane trip and

lunches with her father at the star-studded Ivy restaurant in Hollywood. Normality was never locking your door—who would dare break into a Mob boss's home? An army of "uncles," Mafia thugs with rap sheets as long as their arms, provided round-the-clock, live-in protection and willing playmates. By the age of 4, under Davie's expert tuition, she could play a mean hand of gin rummy with the goons who protected her, always mindful that the bright and enchanting child was the apple of the boss's eye. She got to win a lot.

"My father fabricated a childhood for me that seemed completely normal," Susan said. "He disguised his real career as carefully as he managed it—with no false moves. He told friends that I must never know the secrets of his past because the knowledge might destroy me. He was determined that the sins of the father would not be visited upon the child."

But although Susan was oblivious to the danger, living with it on a daily basis began to derail Gladys as she tried to reconcile her life of luxury with her fear of being murdered. There were times when her terror so paralyzed her that she spent weeks in bed. Susan remembered her mom explaining that she had headaches. She also recalled her mother flying into a panic if her father was even a few minutes late in coming home. Frequently throughout Susan's childhood Gladys would disappear altogether, spending weeks in mental institutions. These breakdowns usually occurred after the violent demise of yet another "uncle."

Susan was convinced that her mother's problems began with the kidnapping incident. Gladys's worst nightmare was that her daughter could become a pawn in the war between rival Mob outfits. She cried for weeks after Susan was safely returned by the police and there was nothing Davie could say to mollify her. Inevitably, some of her mother's foreboding rubbed off on the impressionable child. And this, coupled with the traumatic events that were to turn her childhood upside down, led to her developing her own laundry list of fears and phobias that were to haunt her for the rest of her life.

His wife's illness upset Davie so badly that his concern and desperation, unheard of in the average gangster, was monitored by the Feds and showed up in his FBI file. He'd coax her out of bed long enough to sing "Frankie and Johnny," and tried to will her better. "Come on, Gladys, honey, you can beat this," he would urge. He did everything he could to cure her, refused to farm Susie out to relatives who offered to raise her, while sending Gladys to the best psychiatrists money could buy. He took her for shock therapy, the most advanced treatment of the time, then installed her for months in the Beverly Wilshire to recover from its devastating effects.

Susie lived for the good times, when Gladys would make her a pink tutu, take her to the ritziest stores and come home with bags full of dresses for both of them, or when they'd sit together poring over photographs from her dancing days. When she'd grown up and learned the cause of her mother's fragility, Susan blamed it on "a world swank with sin. She knew we were living on the enchanted edge of a dark reality."

Just like Bobby Durst's had done seven years before, Susan's world came crashing down with repercussions that were to haunt her for the rest of her life. Davie died of a heart attack after routine surgery to remove rectal polyps at age 53 on Father's Day, 1957 at Rose De Lima Hospital in Henderson, Nevada. It was as if her home had been hit by lightning; within hours of his death, her bruiser "playmates" cleaned out the house and pocketed or gave away the contents, including all of Susan's toys.

Davie's lavish funeral drew as many thousands of people as a Frank Sinatra opening night at the casino. At the sight of her father laid out in an open casket, the hysterical 12-year-old threw herself on top of him, just as 7-year-old Bobby Durst had done when his mother was buried. One of Davie's well-meaning but loose-lipped goons had nearly spilled the beans at the funeral when he kissed her to comfort her and blurted out, "Susie, your dad was one of the greatest gangsters who ever lived. You can hold your head up high." But the dazed child didn't take it in and the truth of what he'd said didn't hit home until she was in her twenties.

Davie's death was a blow the stricken Gladys couldn't absorb. Without the devoted Davie to protect her, and with her mind destroyed with fear, stress and depression, she was carted off to a mental hospital. At 12, Susan found herself packed off to Idaho to be looked after by her dad's feckless younger brother, Uncle Chickie. With her went one trunk which had been hurriedly packed for her by Davie's most trusted friend, Lou Raskin; it would take her many years before she could bring herself to open it. Her dog, Blackie, had already been sent on ahead.

The handsome Chickie adored Susan. For the next seven years, he devoted himself to her happiness. A rake and a gambler who had closets full of expensive suits and Sulka silk dressing robes, he treated her like an equal, showing her the ways of the world and reminding her what a prince her father had been. Nothing but the best was good enough for Davie's little princess, and he made sure she had "class" and plenty of cash. He ordered her clothes from Saks and searched out the best schools and camps. First he sent her to St. Helen's Hall in Portland, Oregon, choosing it not only because Susie seemed to like it, but because it was far away from Las Vegas.

The following year Gladys felt strong enough to have her daughter back to live with her in Los Angeles. Susan found herself boarding at the exclusive Chadwick School in the Palos Verdes Estates. There she mingled with the sons and daughters of Hollywood: Liza Minnelli was a ponytailed, elfin creature in the year below; Rock Brynner (son of Yul) was crazy about Liza, and Dean Martin's daughters Gail and Claudia shared her dorm. Bette Davis's daughter B. D. Merrill was a classmate and *Rolling Stone* founder Jann Wenner became editor of *The Sardine*, the school newspaper.

She hated Chadwick. The school catered to the edu-
cational needs of Hollywood brats. Students were allowed
out of studying to watch their celebrity parents appear on
TV, for instance. And in an effort to give their privileged
charges a character-building dose of grim reality, the staff
had devised a system known as K.P. which involved everyone helping in the cafeteria and the kitchens once a week.
Susan, who had been raised on room service and had gone
through her early years saying, "Charge it to Davie Berman," was horrified. She stayed holed up reading in her
room, avoiding her fellow students whom she complained
were too blonde and too tanned, earning herself the nick-
name "Bermouse."

But it was there that she discovered a real passion for
writing, a talent that sustained her through her bleakest
times and latterly helped explain to others, but mostly to
herself, the circumstances of her bizarre childhood.

She went home every other weekend to Gladys who
was spiraling ever deeper into the depths of despair. In February, 1958, with a scary tone of finality, her mother told
her she was being shipped back to Chickie in Idaho. A
couple of weeks later, Gladys died, a broken spirit at 39.
Her death was officially ruled a suicide caused by an overdose of barbiturates. At the funeral, as he tightly gripped
the 13-year-old by the hand, Chickie assured her, "I won't
ever leave you, Susie. Don't worry about that, you're Uncle
Chickie's girl." But Susan did worry, and with good reason.
The people she loved kept dying and her fear became more
acute. The following year, Lou Raskin killed himself.

Uncle Chickie sent her back to St. Helen's Hall, the
school where she'd thrived. In the summer there were
camps; one year he arranged for her to go to the exclusive
Monticeto-Sequoia Camp for Girls in Monticeto, California, where President Nixon sent his daughters, Tricia and
Julie. Susan remembered Julie as being game for anything
and Tricia as a timorous creature who was constantly accompanied by her Secret Service detail.

She graduated from the Oregon school with honors and, at Chickie's suggestion, before starting classes at U.C.L.A., where she'd been accepted for the fall semester, she joined a United Synagogue Youth Pilgrimage Tour of Israel. When she came back, starry-eyed with a boyfriend in tow, Chickie gave the hapless lad the third degree in his suite at the Plaza Hotel in New York and let it be known, not too subtly, that Susie was destined for better.

She was a 19-year-old freshman when Chickie called with devastating news. An addicted gambler, he had been bailed out of frequent sticky situations by his brother, but now he was in a mess and no one could save him. He'd been convicted of stock market fraud and was being hauled off to jail for six years the next morning; he'd called because he didn't want her reading it in the newspapers.

"Take care of yourself," he told her, "and if anyone says anything bad about your father, don't even dignify it by a thought."

But she did hear something bad. Her college roommate was always strangely quiet when Susan talked about her parents. Then one day a friend of the roomie's told her about a book he'd read that described Davie Berman as a gangster who could kill a man with one hand tied behind his back. Keeping as calm as she could, Susan asked for the name of the book, then rushed to Martindale's Book Store in Santa Monica to buy a copy for herself. *The Green Felt Jungle* not only confirmed what her roommate's pal had said, it also claimed that Davie had done time in the notorious Sing Sing penitentiary in Ossining, New York. She was appalled. Why had nobody told her her father had been in jail? Because, she answered herself, it wasn't true. Her aunt, her cousins, Chickie, her father's friends—didn't they all say Davie was the greatest? He was a businessman, he owned hotels, she rationalized, and sometimes business gets a little rough. She dug no further.

Chickie wrote to her from prison, first from Lewisburg, Pennsylvania, then from Texas and later from Terminal Island in San Pedro. At least that was near enough to visit.

Susan started making monthly trips, making sure to splash his favorite Chanel No. 5 behind her ears. The perfume reminded him, he'd told her, of the world outside.

With Chickie banged up, Susan turned to the family of her dad's sister Lilian for support. Lilian's daughter Raleigh was married to an Italian accountant named Earl Padveen and they and their two kids, Denise and Thomas, lived in Pacific Palisades.

"Susan spent all her school vacations with us," says Deni. "She was 13 years older than me, and I just adored her. She was such a character. When I was a little girl I always thought of her as my Auntie Mame, a Bohemian, a hippie with a heart of gold. She stayed with us during vacations from U.C.L.A., until she left for graduate school at Berkeley where she made a life on campus for herself with new friends."

It was at J-school classes at Berkeley that Susan began to hone her writing skills. With her roomie, Sandy West, she moved into a beautiful little Spanish Mediterranean-style building with wrought-iron trim on Euclid Street on the north side of Berkeley, near the university. She and Sandy hung out with friends on the verandah.

Susan and Sandy had arrived at Berkeley just at the time the school was turning into a hotbed of activism and were quickly sucked into the antiestablishment fever that was sweeping the nation's campuses. It seemed like there were demonstrations daily against the U.S. involvement in Vietnam, in support of the feminist movement, demanding the legalization of dope—there were almost as many causes as there were students, and the place was drowning in drugs.

"It was during the antiwar, bra-burning protests of the seventies, and we marched against everything," says Sandy, who now works community liaison with the Oakland Police Department.

Several of their friends were involved with the Students for a Democratic Society, one of the radical groups spawned in Chicago in 1962 to push for civil rights and later, to end America's involvement in Vietnam.

"That brought its own sense of danger," recalls Sandy, "and sometimes we thought Susan's phone was tapped. During that time I moved to Oakland, and one night there was so much tear gas [on campus] that Susan came over and stayed the night."

Sandy had moved out when Susan fell in love with law student Alan Neckritz. Her romance with the excitement of Berkeley and with Alan, now a San Francisco lawyer, lasted nearly five years. Her friendship with Bobby Durst, begun at U.C.L.A., lasted to the end of her life.

Bobby looked like any other child of the sixties with long untidy hair, scruffy clothes and a joint hanging out of his mouth. He was living in one cheap dive after another, doing prodigious amounts of dope and, like so many kids of the era, was on a search for the spiritual enlightenment he wasn't finding in drugs. He dabbled in Primal Scream Therapy with famed psychotherapist, Dr. Arthur Janov. Through Janov he bumped into Beatle John Lennon, who, like Bobby, had some childhood issues: he'd been abandoned by his father at three, fostered out two years later to an aunt and lost his mother for good at 18 when she was mowed down by a drunken off-duty cop.

Janov held that all human beings needed to be fed and nurtured as babies and small children to maintain a neurosis-free psyche. Denial of these basic needs can make a person shut down the capacity to feel anything, and that can result in destructive behavior and neurosis. Primal Scream Therapy encouraged patients to relive traumatic incidents of childhood in a dark, womb-like padded room and release any suppressed tensions by screaming.

Next Bobby became fascinated with the Beatles' pet guru, a diminutive, perennially grinning Indian swami who called himself the Maharishi Mahesh Yogi and preached Transcendental Meditation to not only the Fab Four and their wives and girlfriends, but to the Rolling Stones, assorted Beach Boys, Mia Farrow and her sister Prudence and an estimated 5 million chanting followers around the world.

It was in Los Angeles that Bobby began his lifelong love affair with marijuana. He was never again without his comforting stash—he had a bag of weed on him the day he was arrested for the murder of Morris Black—but no one can ever recall his buddy Susan so much as taking a puff. Her father had told her that dope was for losers and his words stuck with her.

Their tragedy-filled childhoods, their powerful fathers, their grief for the beautiful mothers who both were destroyed by depression and left them so young and bereft, gave them an understanding of each other that they never really achieved again with the new people who came into their lives.

By the end of the sixties, Susan and her "brother" went their separate ways. In 1969 Bobby gave up pretending that he was studying for a doctorate at U.C.L.A. and returned East to his family in New York. Susan stayed on the West Coast where, in 1971, she got a job as a reporter with the San Francisco *Examiner.* Quickly she carved out a reputation for her ability to coax reluctant subjects, who'd turned down other journalists on the paper, into giving her exclusive interviews. Her first coup was cornering union boss Jimmy Hoffa and making him agree to a sit-down chat. She'd managed to hover nearby as he held court with his supporters at the Fairmont Hotel by dressing in a black skirt and white blouse and blending in with the wait staff. She found herself in his suite menaced by very unfriendly goons—hardly unfamiliar territory for the daughter of a Mob boss—when they twigged that she wasn't there to serve drinks. She was just about to be thrown out on her ear when she asked Hoffa if he'd known her dad, Davie Berman? From Las Vegas? She got her interview and her first major byline. She also wrote for the *Westinghouse Evening Show* on radio station KPIX. But her first real taste of fame came with an article she penned for Francis Ford Coppola's *City* magazine entitled, "Why Women Can't Get Laid in San Francisco." The sexy piece signaled her arrival as a writer.

CHAPTER 4

KATHIE

WHILE Bobby was experimenting with dope and savoring the craziness of the sixties, little Kathleen McCormack was growing up in suburban Long Island, New York. The fifth and last child of Ann Catherine and James McCormack, she'd come into the world on June 15, 1952, while 9-year-old Bobby was wrestling with his mother's death. The circumstances into which they were born could scarcely have been more different.

Bobby's birth had been as joyous for his parents as was Kathleen's to hers, but as the oldest son of a real estate baron and heir to a fortune, his tiny frame carried the high hopes and expectations of his hugely ambitious father; her mom and dad just prayed she'd be healthy and happy.

Kathie, as she was called by the family from the start, was a golden child, the much-loved baby of the rambunctious Irish-Catholic McCormacks who were short of cash, but long on love. When they married, James and Ann set up home in their old neighborhood of Bedford-Stuyvesant, where their first child, Carol, and three years later, James (Jim), were born. With another baby, Ginny, on the way, and needing more space, they moved to a row house in East New York right under elevated tracks. The little house shook when the trains rolled over their heads.

"It's amazing how quickly you got used to it," says Jim McCormack. "We had just moved from Bed-Stuy, the tough section of Brooklyn my mom and dad came out of. The Madison Street house was in a working-class neighborhood that was a bit rough around the edges. Everyone had a city job, but a couple of blocks away, the gangs were just beginning to get a hold.

"I remember walking under the Fulton Street el with my dad, climbing up two flights of stairs to the Chinese restaurant for takeout. My dad would wear his leather army jacket—he'd been in the U.S.A. Air Corps—and it was beginning to wear thin by that time."

James, a Bell Telephone employee, worked hard to give his children all the things he and his wife had missed out on as kids—a home of their own with a back yard so that they didn't have to play in the street and dodge the traffic every time they wanted to kick a ball. By 1947 Ann was pregnant with Mary and they were on the move again, this time to 13-21 202 Street between Murdoch and 113th Avenue in Hollis, Queens, where five years later, Kathie joined the family.

"I was 7 when Kathie was born, Carol was 10, Ginny was 6 and Mary, 5. After mom brought her home, she was sitting on the front stoop, the sun was shining and she put Kathie in my arms. That was my first memory of holding a baby," says Jim.

By the time Kathie was 10, the McCormacks uprooted again, forever swapping city streets for the neatly tended suburb of New Hyde Park, Long Island. During Christmas week of 1962, they moved into 83 Aberdeen Road, a pretty four-bedroom, Cape Cod–style brick home with white trim and black-painted shutters. The house seemed enormous to the children—it had two bedrooms upstairs, two downstairs, a living room and a family room which opened on to the dining area. It stood on a third of an acre with a small lawn in front and a yard at the back just big enough to accommodate five growing kids. Kathie's 88-year-old mom still lives in the meticulously kept-up home, surrounded by memories of her happy, boisterous brood.

If there was never much money, the McCormack kids were blissfully unaware of the fact. Their father kept a decent roof over their heads, their mother made sure they were well-fed and cared for, and they were all educated at local schools; for Kathie that meant the elementary school on Hillside Avenue, then a transfer to Notre Dame Grammar School where she stayed until the eighth grade.

"She was full of life," says her brother, who now runs a custom logo merchandising business, and lives with his wife and three daughters in Sparta, New Jersey. "She was the youngest and we all looked out for her."

By the time Kathie was in junior high school, Jim, like thousands of young men across the country, found that his career plans were put on the back burner by the government, who'd upped the "consultant" role of the military in Asia and had launched a full-scale war. "Before I even had my diploma from St. John's University, I got my 'Welcome to the U.S. Army' from Uncle Sam and orders to ship out to Vietnam," he says.

Jim's scheduled departure for the battlefields of Asia in 1967 was to coincide with a blow that sent his family reeling. James McCormack died of cancer. He was just 57. And just as similar childhood tragedies had scarred Bobby Durst and Susan Berman before her, Kathie was left with a sense of loss that she carried with her for the rest of her life.

"We knew he was dying for months before, and we older kids kind of dealt with that. But Kathie, she was just 14 at the time, she felt a lot of pain. You can't prepare a child for that, and she was just a child. It made her grow up a lot faster. I can still remember her sitting on the couch crying," says Jim. "It was her dad, and Kathie was devastated. This was not supposed to be happening. When I close my eyes it's as if it was yesterday.

"He died on a Friday night. By this time I had completed basic training in Georgia and was just about to leave for Vietnam duty. My troop was being sent first to Arizona, where we were going to face a simulation of the conditions we could expect in 'Nam, but because of the situation with my dad the Red Cross pulled me out of the formation and sent me home. I got to New York on the Monday night and saw him, then flew back to Georgia next day. The unit had already left. They had me stay overnight till Wednesday, then my father's condition deteriorated and I flew back home again on the Thursday. He died on the Friday. The terrible thing is," he says, "my father was misdiagnosed— he could still be alive now."

Without their father's paycheck, the kids rallied round to help Ann pay the bills. "We all had to work growing up and all of us had part-time jobs," says Jim. His mother and sisters encouraged him to apply for stateside duty. Though barely out of his teens himself he was now the sole surviving man in the family; his mom was a homemaker, Carol and Ginny were already married and out of the house. He felt responsible for his mom, and Kathie and Mary. "We pulled ourselves up by the bootstraps," he says. "My mom got a job with the telephone company where my dad had worked. My sisters Carol and Ginny and even Mary worked there for a short time too."

By the time she reached New Hyde Park Memorial High School, the baby of the family had blossomed into a lovely young woman with a mop of honey-blonde hair and an infectious sense of fun. "She was confident and poised and she was smart," says Jim. "She got great marks in school and she knew she looked good." She was athletic, joined the Ski Club, became the editor of the *Chariot*, the school paper, and made the Honor Society. She told her teachers and school friends that she was thinking of becoming a teacher.

Like her older siblings, she went to work. She'd found herself a part-time job as a model doing runway shows for local stores like Lord & Taylor in nearby Garden City and J. C. Penney in Lake Success. She was even written up in the local paper. "They took a photograph when she was modeling and she brought the newspaper in to school to show us," says former classmate Janice Martines.

Since she didn't have a driver's license, or a car, Jim became her designated chauffeur. "I drove her to work and waited for her outside in the parking lot," he says. "We all had to work. I worked three jobs while I was going through

St. John's. We were the average middle-class American family. We had our arguments and disagreements, of course, but we'd always hug and make up. We strove for what was moral and ethical and were taught not to do anything to offend other people. Our mom always made us say 'Please' and 'Thank you' and 'Bless you.' She had this saying that still makes me laugh today: 'Good manners are free and a bar of soap is cheap.'

"Vacations were at Grandma's cabin. It had an outhouse and a lake—we bathed in the lake. We couldn't afford to go to a resort. Kathie and I taught each other how to water-ski there," he says.

Six months after graduating from school, Kathie concluded that the local job market was not very exciting. She'd have more opportunities and a lot more fun, she decided, if she lived in the city. After poring through the want ads, she got a job as a dental hygienist in midtown Manhattan. Now she had to find somewhere to live. She went apartment hunting and settled on a small but ideal rental on East 52nd Street. The building was owned and operated by the Durst Organization.

Although Bobby Durst had returned from California in 1969, he was no closer to granting his father's wish that he stop messing around with wacky religions and dubious therapies and get down to the business of earning his keep. Instead, he was resolved to maintain the hippie life for which he'd developed more than a taste at school. After giving the matter some serious thought, he suddenly informed Seymour that he was going to move to Vermont and open a health food store.

His father was horrified. This was not the future he had planned for his son and heir. He had no intention of letting the third generation of Dursts spend his days dishing up granola and sunflower seeds to a bunch of barefooted, dope-smoking, long-haired layabouts who had, as sixties guru Timothy Leary famously intoned, "turned on, tuned in, and dropped out."

But he knew ordering Bobby back behind a desk would

be futile—it would only exacerbate his growing antipathy to any kind of authority. Besides, he was aware that his son no longer looked an eager young businessman. Like every other kid in the sixties, he'd grown his hair, dressed night and day as if he were on his way to a party and experimented with drugs. Only with Bobby it was more than a test drive: he'd bought into the whole marijuana culture.

But he also quickly recognized that, given the times, running an alternative business, however impractical, was a small rebellion. Seymour banked on the hope that after a couple of years mingling with the flower people in some awful commune-type setup, Bobby would get bored with the sticks and be ready to come back to the city.

And so, although he was opposed to the whole idea, he agreed to bankroll Bobby's dream of being a shopkeeper—with one stipulation: he could follow this crazy idea of being a hippie grocer with Seymour's blessing, if he did not cut himself off completely from the company that paid his way through a very comfortable life. Instead, father and son reached a compromise. Since he was going through this rebellious phase, Seymour decided Bobby would best be suited to handling tenants' complaints in the residential property owned by the Durst Organization. When a renter carped about a problem in his or her apartment, Bobby would drive down from Vermont and check it out, report back to the company and see to it that any necessary repairs were scheduled. He'd be in charge of tenant relations, Seymour told him. And that way, he told himself, at least he could keep an eye on his son.

Twenty-eight-year old Bobby reluctantly agreed, and promptly left for Vermont. He opened his store, All Good Things, near the college town of Middlebury, where he figured, there would be a ready market of like-minded lentil-loving students who wouldn't be caught dead in an A & P. He made the trips south as infrequently as he possibly could; placating elderly widows complaining about the air-conditioning or leaky toilets wasn't his idea of fun. When he was in Manhattan at his father's bidding, he refused to wear the conservative suits and tasseled loafers expected of other Durst employees, and he tooled around town in a beat-up Volkswagen Beetle—the chariot of choice for flower children.

Julie Baumgold describes her childhood pal as the kind of man who was happy living with old cars and clothes. His former brother-in-law says less charitably that he was "very protective about what he has in his pocket."

In January 1971 Bobby got notice that a new tenant wanted him to take care of some minor problems she'd discovered in her one-bedroom apartment. The call had come from Kathleen McCormack. She'd just moved in and there were a couple of things needing attention.

"She had found a job as a dental assistant and she moved into this place on the East Side," says Jim. "I was always coming into the city to help her fix up the place, change locks and generally help her get organized. But she was determined to show us that she was independent. There were some things she thought were the landlord's responsibility so she phoned the building management office."

The call landed on Bobby's desk. When he saw her, he decided that the complaint came from the loveliest girl he'd ever seen. After months of catering to hippie women with unkempt hair, their bodies encased in layers of shapeless woolens as protection against the Vermont winter, Kathie McCormack was a delight. At 120 pounds and 5'6", she had a model-girl figure, blonde hair tumbling over her shoulders and the most dazzling smile. Bobby fell in love on the spot.

"It was mutual," says Kathie's brother, "spontaneous attraction. She didn't know anything about him, except that he represented the landlord." By the time he'd promised to send a handyman over to fix her apartment, she'd agreed to have dinner with him. But if Bobby was smitten with the pretty young dental hygienist, she was no less swept off her feet by him. Nine years older and much worldlier, he had just enough shyness and vulnerability along with a quirky sense of humor to make him irresistible to her. They both had lost adored parents as children and although Kathie was barely out of her teens, she sensed he was needy. After a couple of dates, Bobby persuaded Kathie to dump her job with the dentist and move north to Vermont and live with him. Everyone who knew them could see they were blissfully happy with the simple life they'd chosen.

"We didn't know Bobby well in the early days," says Jim. "They were just two young lovers starting a life together. He was just someone Kathie was in love with and he loved her."

Now that his son had settled down into a serious relationship, his father was even more determined to rein him in. Seymour persuaded him to put All Good Things on the market and it was sold in December 1971. Bobby and Kathie moved into the comfortable and spacious new Durst home in Katonah, some sixty miles north of the city. With his kids all grown, Seymour had swapped the gloomy Scarsdale mansion for a brownstone townhouse in midtown. He had bought the Katonah house as a weekend retreat for the whole family. It boasted lavish grounds complete with tennis courts and a swimming pool, and they shared it with Bobby's younger brother Douglas and his wife Susannah.

The house itself was dramatically different from the home Bobby had grown up in. With flat roofs and floor-to-ceiling windows, the modern sixties-style house stood at the top of a hill on Salem Road, off Route 35, on nearly ten acres of rolling countryside. With all that space, they could crank up the stereo to full volume and make as much noise as they liked without upsetting the neighbors. After leaving the highway, the road up to it was unpaved gravel, a nice rustic touch which ought to deter uninvited guests, Seymour had thought, and the house itself sat at the top of a long winding drive. In the winter, when the trees were bare, the picture windows afforded sweeping views all the way down to Route 687. Today it's still the country home of Douglas Durst.

The huge living room Kathie and Bobby shared with Douglas and Susannah opened onto a deck which held the built-in swimming pool. Off to the right of the main house was an outbuilding where the equipment for the tennis courts was stored. "The house was big enough to make the arrangement workable," remembers Jim. "Kathie did whatever she did in the house all day and Bob was supposed to commute into Manhattan to rejoin the family business."

Although Kathie told her family that everything was just swell with the Durst boys when they all shared the family estate, it emerged later that the situation was often very uncomfortable. She confided to one of her classmates at the Western Connecticut State University School of Nursing, Eleanor Schwank, that the two brothers fought, bickered and constantly needled each other.

"She told me that Bobby and Douglas never got along, that there was lots of rivalry between them. When they all shared the house at Katonah, Doug kind of took over," says Eleanor. "Kathie used to joke about how he ended up with the family house. She said the rivalry had been going on for a long time and that Doug had no love for his older brother."

The reward for toeing the family line was a one-bedroom penthouse apartment in one of the Durst Organization's priciest residential properties at 37 Riverside Drive at 77th Street overlooking Riverside Park. With panoramic views of the Hudson River and the New Jersey shoreline, it was valued then at $500,000 but would fetch well over $1 million in today's market. Not only were Bobby and Kathie delighted to be back in the city, it was the first real home of their own.

Building employees remember them as a fun young couple. The outgoing Kathie always stopped for a chat and to borrow a cigarette. Bobby was more reserved, but always polite. He'd smile and say "Hi" as he went in and out, but he didn't talk to them and ask about their families the way the vivacious Kathie did. They liked to party, the staff recalls, and she liked to drink.

Bobby's deep pockets made life in the Big Apple exciting for the girl from Long Island. There was plenty of money for clubs, discos and drugs and mingling with the beautiful people who ruled Manhattan's nightlife in the seventies. Everyone from Henry Kissinger to Mick and especially Bianca Jagger hung out at places like Studio 54 and Xenon, where the ultraviolet lights lit up pretty much anything white with a surreal glow and could pick out who'd had their teeth capped and who still retained their God-given molars.

Bobby and his pals had no trouble waltzing past the velvet ropes; the clubs were located in Durst-owned buildings and the lackeys who patrolled the doors tripped over each other to usher Bobby and his party past the waiting mob over howls of protest. The wannabes waiting in line had put a lot of effort into looking as good as the celebrities who sailed past them unchallenged, and they couldn't understand how this little guy, who looked like he rented his disco duds from an extra in *Saturday Night Fever*, rated all this attention.

Although Bobby was no Tony Manero on the dance floor, he lapped up the frenetic atmosphere, swaying to the pounding music under the disconcerting strobe lights, which were known to trigger epileptic seizures. He also had no trouble skipping over the other rope that walled off the private lounge upstairs where revellers, with the appetite and the cash, could snort enough cocaine to make their noses explode.

When the fun of the disco wore off and Kathie's feet ached from dancing, they'd head uptown to Elaine's, the Upper East Side late-night hangout for celebrities which was presided over by its legendary steely-eyed owner, Elaine Kaufman. She had an uncanny antenna for ferreting out tattletale scribes who she unmercifully showed the door.

During the seventies booze and drugs flowed like water and, like most of their friends and acquaintances, the young Dursts experimented freely with both. In the early years of the relationship, Bobby was much more enthusiastic about consuming illicit substances than was Kathie. Red wine was her choice of relaxant.

Thanks to Seymour's connections they also partied with New York's richest and most powerful. The girl who only a couple of years before had been modeling polyester pantsuits for J. C. Penney, found herself nibbling on over-priced entrees at New York's most expensive watering holes across the room from Jackie Onassis. Bobby seemed to know everyone and, although her brother and everyone else who knew her insist that her feet remained firmly planted on the ground, brushing shoulders with A-list celebrities and politicians had to be an intoxicating rush for a girl who'd recently earned her living staring at people's tonsils. And since Seymour doled out generous contributions to the political parties as a cost of doing business, she also found herself at fund-raisers with the state's leading politicians.

"They were rich, they moved in high circles," says Kathie's friend, Dr. Marion Watlington. And then there were the trips. Kathie, who'd never been out of the country before, found herself whisked to Hong Kong and other ex-otic locations.

They were always on the move in those early years, says Jim. "They were given to will-o'-the-wisp vacations. He had the means and she had the wanderlust in her. If he said, 'Hey, let's take a trip to Florida,' then they'd drive to Florida. She kept a diary of these trips—in it she describes twenty or thirty visits to New England, staying in every kind of accommodation from bed and breakfasts to five-star hotels and everything in between. They also made fre-quent treks down to the Carolinas."

But while Bobby and Kathie seemed perfectly happy with each other, Seymour was growing more exasperated with what he considered Bobby's aimless and hedonistic existence, especially now that the two of them were talking about a wedding. With a wife to support, Bobby needed a proper job, Seymour told him. Even though his bank ac-count was bulging, being idle and squandering money to have a good time was unthinkable, tantamount to sin, especially if you were a Durst.

Bobby and Kathie exchanged vows on April 12th, 1973, Bob's 30th birthday.

"The wedding was unbelievably small," says Jim. "I was living in Chicago at the time, so I didn't go. In the end it was only Bob and Kathie, my mom, and Bob's father, Seymour, who were there. They were married in a civil ceremony by a judge in Bedford Hills, New York followed by a luncheon in Greenwich. None of us, Kathie's sisters nor I, or Bob's brothers and sister, or any of their friends, were invited."

Jim admits to having been uneasy at the idea of his baby sister getting married almost in secret. The way the McCormacks had been raised, family weddings were cause for celebration, with everyone invited to join in the fun. They involved weeks if not months of planning and Kathie's big brother thought she deserved better than a hole-in-the-wall affair. He also felt he should have been standing in for his father and giving her away.

"I was surprised at how low-key it all was," he says. "But it was a time when authority was being challenged and tradition was thrown out the window, and I put it down to that. But now, with hindsight, I see it was Bob being typically Bob. None of the rules applied to him. He made his own rules on a day-to-day basis. And Kathie was so much younger—she was just swept off her feet and went along with everything he wanted. He could be very charming. There weren't even any photographs taken. Kathie never had a picture of her wedding day."

What Jim McCormack didn't know then was that his sister had agreed to a prenuptial arrangement with Bobby which would have given her a pitifully small amount of money if the marriage broke up. Her new husband had also made it clear to her that there were to be no children. He didn't want them, he said, he didn't like them and didn't want to be responsible for them.

He'll change, thought Kathie. To be married and not to have kids? It was unfathomable to her, but she put it to the back of her mind. Love would conquer that hurdle, she was sure of it, and time was on her side. He'd feel differently in ten years, and anyway, if Bobby loved her, and she knew he did, then he'd come around.

Finally, in October 1973, Bobby went to work for his father.

CHAPTER 5

MARRIED LIFE

WHEN the first flush of marital bliss wore off, or at least settled into something more routine, Kathie began to find out that being with Bobby also meant sharing him with an inner circle of his closest friends, all of them a decade older than her, and all with amazing stamina for partying until dawn. For some of them it came with the territory—their media jobs required their regular attendance at the watering holes where the stars hung out. Others, like Bobby, just loved the nightlife.

In his posse were *Saturday Night Live* regular Laraine Newman; Julie Baumgold, who worked for *New York* magazine; Stephen M. Silverman, now the editor of PEOPLE.com.Daily; Bobby's buddy from U.C.L.A. Susan Berman, who had moved to New York in 1975 and started free-lancing for *Us* magazine; and whoever any of them were dating at the time.

Kathie, despite her youth, was wise enough not to question the attraction Susan held for her husband. Her brother, however, admits that he took an instant dislike to her: "I met her twice in the mid-seventies," he says. "Once was at a bar on the West Side of Manhattan, the other time was at the Katonah house. She was very self-absorbed, kept telling me 'I'm a writer' in a way that made it obvious she expected me to be impressed."

But Bobby was delighted to have 28-year-old Susan nearby—she had kept in constant touch with the man she called "my brother" when she was working in San Francisco and he'd encouraged her wholeheartedly to make the leap to New York when she told him she thought she'd taken her career as far as she could in the Bay City.

Susan breezed into town determined to become the next magazine superstar. She had the good sense to realize that her reputation for snagging the big interview in San Francisco meant nothing to the hard-bitten local press drones, but she was an irresistible force and she knew it. New York would soon come to heel.

Since her work for *Us* introduced her to the music industry and gave her access to the people who ran it, she didn't take long to move up. She started pulling assignments from the more happening *New York* via Julie Baumgold, whom she'd met through Bobby. At the time the weekly magazine was the hippest game in town; it bared the secrets of the movers and shakers in the city and was a must-read for everyone who wanted to know where to go, what to eat and where to shop. Within weeks of her arrival, Susan had a black belt in all three.

They were heady times in Manhattan if you were rich or famous or beautiful. Anyone who was young and good-looking, especially if they could flash credentials, got into the best joints. Storming the baize-covered doors with Susan was Silverman, who was then working the celebrity beat for the *New York Post*.

"They were fun times," he says. "We got into everything, every club, party—we knew everybody who was worth knowing." Susan looked the part, she dressed expensively, patrolling the posh stores on Fifth Avenue, especially Saks, where her mom had shopped for both of them and Chickie found her a midnight blue backless prom dress more suited to a 30-year-old movie star than a 16-year-old high school junior. She bought designer clothes by the cartload, dipping into the trust fund that Davie had left her.

"She was probably the most extravagant and generous person I've ever known in my whole life," says writer Hillary Johnson, who met her in 1975 when she was working at the fashion bible *Women's Wear Daily*. "I'd been an undergraduate at Berkeley's J-School and Susan had been one of their outstanding talents. The teaching staff had us read articles written by her when she was a graduate student. She had left by then and was working as a reporter at the San Francisco *Examiner* where she was pretty, witty and brilliant.

"When I met her I was just enchanted. I thought she was the smartest, funniest person I'd ever known. I admired her immensely and to my delight, we became good friends and stayed that way for twenty-six years until she died.

"She would never let anyone pay for anything. I remember one day she called me up and said, 'I want to get away, I want to go to Key West. Will you come with me?' I said, 'I'd love to, but I don't have the money to take a vacation in Key West.' She said, 'That's okay, I'll pay.' She bought my ticket, paid for my room in a lovely resort hotel—the whole trip was on her. And that was typical of Susan."

Among the men in her life were Austrian sculptor Oscar (Ossie) Bronner and Danny Goldberg, currently the Chief Executive Officer of Artemis Records, the label he founded in 1999 and the home of The Baha Men ("Who Let the Dogs Out?"). He's also been CEO of Atlantic Records, Warner Brothers and Mercury Records, and is credited with discovering Jewel, the Stone Temple Pilots and numerous other top-ten acts.

"I'd started a public relations company, [Susan] was at *Us* magazine and I was pitching her a rock band—I was representing Electric Light Orchestra at the time and we became friends, 1977 would be my guess, and we stayed friends until her death," Goldberg says. "She was very, very smart, but she was haunted by her childhood, her father's background." It was Danny who later, when she was cruelly confronted with Davie's Mob connections, encouraged her to dig up all the facts about Davie's "business." And when the reality, all the deaths and the memories, threatened to swamp her, he'd given her the strength to keep going.

"[Danny] was a nice guy," says Stephen M. Silverman. "Susan always dated nice guys and then they left. I think she burned them out with her over-the-top personality. She went at a hundred miles per hour. It was like she had a nuclear plant in her stomach. She was exhilarating and exhausting to be with."

But as intelligent and entertaining as she was, Susan was bedeviled by her irrational fears, which at first amused, then exasperated many of her friends. Her upbringing, the kidnapping drills and her subconscious awareness of her mother's constant terror, had left their mark. She was afraid of just about everything—bridges, elevators, heights, open windows, certain numbers and a whole list of foodstuffs she believed would make her ill.

"I know she hated bridges. I think she was worried that she would be tempted to kill herself, throw herself off—her mother had killed herself, and I think Susan was fearful she would lose her reason. I don't know if that was why, but I remember she did say that once to me," says Danny Goldberg.

According to Stephen, wherever Susie went, Bobby was sure to follow. "Durst was always around, tagging along to all these parties, openings and clubs we went to," he recalls. "He had a weird attitude though, sort of patronizing and puzzled at the same time. Although he didn't act like he was rich, he didn't throw his money around, he couldn't understand why Susan and I would be working for so little. He just didn't get it, couldn't see that we didn't care about that, we just found our jobs exciting."

"She loved the nightlife," says Rhoda Weyr, who became Susan's literary agent. Weyr was married with four children and provided the orphaned Susan with a family base in Manhattan. "I was an anomaly in many ways for her in New York. She hung out with people who were extremely social and went to clubs. I remember she mentioned the Knitting Factory and I thought it was something to do with fabric. I was just so not in that world. She did a lot of going out and Robert Durst was in that crowd, I know they were very friendly, that she relied on him, went to him for advice.

"I could never see why she was friendly with Durst. All I saw was that he was related to this God-awful real estate bozo, and I'd say to her, 'Why, why?' And she'd tell me, 'Oh, he's really nice and he's very good to me and he's a lot of fun'—the same reasons you'd be friendly with anyone. I was just being a snob, I suppose."

Susan also introduced Bobby to Danny, but the real estate heir made little impression on the would-be rock titan. "I met Durst once at one of Susan's book parties. I shook his hand and said 'Hello,' but that's about it," he says.

If Susan was up for it, Bobby would have gone to the opening of an envelope. Kathie tagged along too, but although with her family and friends she was extroverted and lively, she blended into the wallpaper when she was in the company of Bobby's more worldly pals.

"To tell the truth, I barely remember Kathie," says Stephen. "She was just . . . there. I don't remember her saying anything at all, but that was hardly surprising around Susan. She had to be the center of attraction, the life and soul of the party. She gossiped wickedly about everyone and she had a nasty streak which she turned on everyone, even friends, with often devastating effects." But if being around Susan and her dizzying pace of life made Bobby happy, then Kathie was content.

Deni Marcus remembers meeting the Dursts on her frequent trips to New York to visit her older cousin. "Susie would always make sure we had a dinner or a lunch with them," she says. Even on her first encounter with the couple, she, like Rhoda Weyr, was puzzled as to what Kathie saw in her husband; Deni couldn't figure out the attraction. She was underwhelmed by the unprepossessing Bobby. It wasn't his drop-dead gorgeous looks that had snared the lovely Kathie, that's for sure, she remembers thinking. At 5'7", 140 pounds, with unremarkable brown hair and eyes, he hardly struck an imposing figure, and his personality seemed just as bland, she decided. He also seemed so much older and more cynical than his sweet young wife.

"Bobby seemed very detached. He wasn't forthcoming at all and he struck me as a very private, eccentric kind of guy. I just thought, my gosh, she's such a young, be-boppy person, effervescent and outgoing. I was just 18 years old at the time and I was sitting there thinking, Why would a young, peppy girl do this, marry this man? I just didn't see it. He seemed very conservative and kind of stodgy and she seemed like such an energetic and fun-loving girl. She was nine years younger than him, just a few years older than me. I was just a little college coed at the time and I would never have gone out with a man like that. But what did I do when I got married at 22? I went out and married some-one who was eleven years older than me, and I got di-vorced, so who am I to talk? You just don't know.

"The nice thing about Kathie was, although she was very young, I don't think she was impressed by his wealth and all that stuff that went with it either. She was very down to earth," says Deni. "I think she just wanted to be loved. She was definitely in love with him. The first time I met them I was thinking, wow, this has got to be a love match, because I couldn't see what else it could be. And, oh God, he was crazy about her. Even after they'd been married a couple of years he was still fawning all over her."

If they had any misgivings about the match, Kathie's family kept them to themselves. They were determined to give Bobby the benefit of any doubts. If Kathie loved him, they'd keep welcoming him with open arms. And for the first few years at least, it looked like things were going to work out fine. "Kathie did wonderful things for Bob, I thought," says Jim. "She hosted affairs and brought him out of his shell. She expanded his horizons as, admittedly, he did for her. He introduced her to a world she'd never been exposed to, and it was very seductive, I'm sure. She was swept off her feet emotionally and economically and all that other stuff too.

"And at first, I liked Bob, even though he was so pri-vate you never really got to know him," he says. "He had some other strange traits, but he was my sister Kathie's husband, you just had to be accepting of the relationship and hope for the best. He was just part of the package. I thought in time he would have come to see what our family had, but maybe there was something in the individual that couldn't or wouldn't change. We didn't have much [in the way of possessions], but we had a lot of love and we went to work every single day."

Yet while Kathie's family was determined that any differences they had with her husband were not going to keep them away from her, to each other, her brother and three sisters admitted the truth: Bobby could be downright unpleasant.

Every year, the whole McCormack tribe hunkered down at New Hyde Park for Christmas dinner at their mother's home. It was always a double celebration because Christmas Day was also Ann's birthday. Kathie and her husband were at most of these gatherings but according to Jim, Bobby seemed like a fish out of water. Being Jewish, it was hardly surprising that he wasn't in a Christian holiday mood, but it wasn't so much the religious aspect of the season that fazed him, as the cheerful, mocking banter that went on around the table. Big happy families were something he didn't seem to understand and he had no idea how to behave.

"He didn't exactly make an effort to join in," remembers Jim. "He'd never actively start a conversation, but he would respond if talked to. At first we all took it as shyness but eventually we agreed privately he was just rude. And the rudeness extended to the point where it embarrassed Kathie. He constantly belched at the dinner table—he'd let out a real serious belch and never say, 'Pardon me,' or any of that stuff. He didn't feel he had to. The rules didn't apply to him and the world was his sandbox."

Sometimes, the price of keeping Bobby happy was too high. It cost his sister the baby she longed for, says her brother. "Kathie wanted to give him a family and when she got pregnant in 1974 she was so thrilled and proud. But Bob forced her to have an abortion."

Her friends say they thought then that the insecure Bobby was afraid that if Kathie became a mother, he would be relegated to second place in her affections. He was not going to share her love with a child, even his own, ever. Period. Now they wonder if he'd had troubling doubts about his sanity. His mother had suffered so badly from depression it had driven her to taking her own life. Maybe he'd had an inkling that he'd inherited a rogue gene and worried about passing it on to children of his own. Some reports say he told his friends that the child wasn't his.

It wasn't until years later, when he was reading the diary of her marriage which Kathie was putting together for her divorce attorney, that Jim found that there was an implied, if not actually written, understanding in their prenuptial agreement that they wouldn't have children. But like any woman aching to have a baby, when she accidentally got pregnant she hoped with all her heart that Bobby would share her joy. It might have been the saving of them both, says Jim.

"I firmly believe that they would still be married today had he gone along with the baby. His energies and resources could have gone to his children. I think he would have been a doting dad and [it would] have given him the chance to correct the things that were wrong with his own childhood. Kathie would not have been redirected to become her own self-sufficient woman. She would have [been a] dependent wife, the dependent mother of his children, which he would have liked. He would have had the best of all things." As usual, the self-absorbed Bobby got his way and, heartbroken, Kathie terminated her pregnancy. "You don't have any choice," he'd told her.

With no prospect of becoming a mother, Kathie needed to fill the void in her life. She decided to go back to school and in the fall of 1975, began nursing classes at Western Connecticut State University at Danbury. By then, the couple had acquired their own weekend house, a charming and substantial 1,200-square-foot stone cottage overlooking Truesdale Lake in the tiny upstate New York town of South

Salem. Since it was fifteen miles and a short car trip from the school, Kathie stayed there during the week while Bobby, who was working at the midtown offices of the Durst Organization, lived at the penthouse in the city. Although she was determined to study hard and graduate with honors, the days apart were difficult for Kathie. In the evenings, she'd sit with her textbooks spread out on the dining table barely able to concentrate on her work because she was waiting for Bob to call. The weekends couldn't come fast enough. Friday afternoons she'd head back to the city, or Bobby would drive up to the cottage.

Next door were William and Ruth Mayer who welcomed the arrival of a young couple their own age on the block. Quickly they became friendly. "Kathie was lovely, always with a ready smile," says Bill. "When she was out gardening we would stop and say 'Hi' and chat for a while, and when they had a party at their house they invited us. If we had a neighborhood party, we invited them. We invited them when there was no party.

"We liked them both. She was more gregarious and outgoing, but he was nice and unassuming, Supposedly he was this rich guy, but he didn't show a nickel. To us, he was just the guy next door. We weren't nosy or in their business or anything like that, but we saw them a lot when they were out in the yard, gardening or swimming or whatever, especially in the summer."

Ruth Mayer says that the Dursts rented the house at 62 Hoyt Street before buying it in 1976. "My daughter Sharon was just one-and-a-half when they moved in," says Ruth. "Kathie was already in nursing school at Danbury by then. I used to wheel the baby down to see her. I was much friendlier with Kathie than Bob. She was fun, very sweet and you could talk about stuff with her."

They also had no idea that she was married to a millionaire; they didn't find that out until Kathie disappeared. She'd started to redecorate the place herself, hauling out the bathroom and retiling it in a striking hunter green. She also covered the kitchen counters with a cheerful flower-pattern tile with a lemon yellow background, perfect for a quaint country cottage.

"They lived in the front area of the house," says Ruth. "The downstairs wasn't finished when Kathie and Bob were here. There was a secret room under the stairs they talked about, but the basement wasn't finished—it was stone flooring down there. But they did put in a dining room. The house was very dark when they bought it, the wood had gotten dark over the years, and they lightened the whole place up and made it much nicer.

"For people who had so much money—they were very casual. We didn't know until way later they were worth millions. I had no idea who the Durst family were. For all their money, they never put any into this house [next door]. They never had contractors in to work on it. Kathie did it herself. The renovations didn't happen until they sold it. And they never talked about doing it up—this was just their country house. She fixed up that bathroom, and the kitchen, the dining room and that little bedroom, and that was it."

While Kathie pottered around with her trowel and grout, Bobby fancied himself as a sailor. "He had a sailboat he'd take out occasionally," says food distributor Bill, who bought the little red craft from Durst when he sold the cottage in 1990. "He never gave it a name, and once it was either stolen or it washed away and ended up someplace else on the lake. When he retrieved it, he spray-painted it with his phone number on it. It was ugly, like graffiti all over the boat. When he sold it to me I had to remove it. It wasn't easy. It took a while to figure out how to get it off." When he wasn't sailing he was jogging along the narrow two-lane road that wound around the lake. A fitness nut, Bobby started each day with a regimen of push-ups, sit-ups and lunges that would have worn out a U.S. Marine.

Over cups of coffee and bottles of wine, Kathie would discuss her hopes and ambitions with Ruth, who is a psychologist. "After she graduated from nursing school we talked about what she wanted to do, and she said she wanted to be a doctor. I thought that was incredible," she says. "The next thing, she applied to medical school and got in and I saw her even less. It made the time she was here really precious—we would hang out. They mostly came up together, but I didn't have a heck of a lot to do with Bobby. We would talk about my daughter, working, the neighborhood, the neighbors, all kinds of good stuff."

It was while she was at the Danbury campus that Kathie met the women who were to remain among her closest friends for the rest of her life, her mentor at the nursing school, Dr. Marion Watlington, fellow student Gilberte Najamy, and classmate Eleanor Schwank.

"Kathie was 25 when I met her," says Eleanor. "She was a warm, wonderful, loving person with a great sense of humor. We spent three-and-a-half years working together on research projects and in class. We did the clinical part of our course at Westchester Medical Center at Valhalla and we shared the commute from the campus at Danbury. We spent hours in the car going back and [forth], I'd talk about my two kids, and she'd tell me about Bobby and the family. We'd go for lunch, she'd come over to my place and I'd visit her at the house in South Salem."

During these car trips, the two women talked about the school and about many of its practices which seemed to them antiquated and discriminatory. All colleges and universities at the time were having to deal with vocal student bodies that were no longer content to accept business as usual. Nursing school, Kathie and her friend agreed, was long overdue for a kick into the Twentieth Century. It was sexist, authoritarian and completely out of touch.

One of the most loathed rules imposed at the Western Connecticut school forced the female nursing students to wear caps while male students were allowed to go bare-headed. Eleanor, who had already campaigned successfully against the closing of the university library to nursing students except for a few limited hours each week, complained to the dean of the school about the hated caps. "It's blatant sexual discrimination," she'd protested to deaf ears.

Kathie wasn't about to let the matter drop, she was

ready to take on the administration again. What they needed was a cogent argument that not only were the caps demeaning, they were a threat to patient safety, she reasoned. "She decided to prove that the caps were not only discriminatory, they were unhygienic, and she used this as the basis for her mandatory project," says Eleanor. "She was sure that they picked up pathogenic organisms [germs] from brushing against things, which were then transported from bed to bed and patient to patient as the nurses made their rounds.

"She collected a bunch of the caps, tested them and found they did contain bacteria. 'We should get rid of these, Eleanor,' she said. She brought her concerns up to several professors who told her she was bucking tradition and, anyway, it was difficult for them as faculty to unfreeze the rules. They said that any changes had to be instigated by the students and approved by school officials. It was obvious their campaign was going nowhere.

" 'What should we do?' she asked me.

" 'Take it to the top,' I told her.

" 'Who's the top?' she wanted to know.

" 'The President of the United States,' I said.

"Kathie was like, 'Oh! Okay. How do we do that?'

" 'Write him a letter,' I said.

" 'Then I think it should be on Durst Organization letterhead paper,' she replied.

" 'Fine,' I thought, having no idea that it meant any more than it's better to have a business heading than not, but not knowing it meant any more than it was Bobby's family firm. I had no idea that this was a big deal. But shortly after, we got a reply from President Jimmy Carter, who told us he was passing our letter on to the Secretary at the Health and Emergency Workers Department to investigate the school. The dean of the school was dumbfounded. When we told her, she sunk her head in her hands and moaned, 'Do you know what you have done?' We knew that while an investigation was going on, the school would get no federal funds. The caps went."

The episode opened Eleanor's eyes. Like most of Kathie's friends, she'd had no idea of the power and influence wielded by Bobby's family. According to her brother, Kathie usually wore jeans and flannel shirts, and did most of the cooking and housework until she went back to school, when they hired a housekeeper for the cottage, a local woman named Janet Fink.

"Bob certainly could afford household help, but sometimes he complained about paying for it," remembers Jim. "He would never buy new cars. Kathie's been described as driving a red Mercedes, well, it was a used car. She had access to it, but it wasn't hers, it was owned by Bob. They also had that beat-up old Volkswagen which was the car he wanted her to use for the drive to and from school. But Kathie just accepted all that."

Eleanor, who now lives with her family in Matagordo, Texas, also recalls that the young Dursts lived well below their means. "The South Salem house was fairly modest, but it was beautifully decorated and had a pretty stone fireplace. It was perfect for a couple—with a dog," she says. "They didn't live an elaborate lifestyle, but that didn't seem to bother Kathie, even though I knew that there was money in Bob's family. I never heard her complain, 'My husband has all this money and I can't spend it.' And she wasn't the type of girl who said, 'Let's go shopping.' She always looked nice, wore nice clothes, but she didn't have drawers full of them."

Kathie tried to involve Bob in her new life, introducing him to the friends she had made on campus and dragging him out on dinner dates with them. But he made it abundantly clear that he preferred his buddies in New York. "He wasn't really a socializer," says Eleanor.

Marion Watlington, who moved to Bermuda in 1991, and became the island's leading oncologist, had done some of her training in Canada, and had a year to fill in before she could apply to a medical school in the States, when she took the teaching post at the Danbury campus. When Kathie Durst walked into her class, she was drawn to her immediately.

"She was extremely bright and grasped the material being taught with tremendous ease," she says. "One day we got talking and I told her I was going on to medical school, that I wanted to be a doctor. It was as if I could see the wheels turning, I could see it in her face. She was asking herself, 'Why can't I do that?' I promised I would share everything I learned with her from the application process on. I became a kind of role model for her."

The friendship continued even after Marion was accepted by the University of Connecticut in 1976. They no longer met on a daily basis, but they still spoke frequently on the phone. Once they arranged to meet and have dinner with their husbands.

"It was not a successful night," she says. "Bob looked like he didn't want to be there and just came along, for heaven knows what reason. He didn't even try to be sociable. My then-husband and I really didn't like him. Kathie was so delightful and he was, well, grumpy. We saw her often, but we didn't see him again until the graduation party she threw at her house in South Salem in 1978 when she got her nursing degree. She and Bobby dismissed it as 'our little country place,' but I thought it was huge and just fabulous, decorated with exquisite taste," says Marion. Bobby's friend Susan managed to overcome at least half-a-dozen of her phobias to make the two-hour journey out of the city to attend Kathie's party.

That fall Kathie was accepted by the prestigious Albert Einstein College of Medicine in the Bronx. She took to it like a duck to water. Pretty soon she knew what she wanted to do, open a pediatric clinic in a poor area of the city and take care of children with little access to a doctor.

"It wasn't like the rich girl went to medical school," says her brother. "In her last year of nursing school she was exposed to clinical work, and she looked at the medical staff, the doctors, and thought, 'Hey, I could do that.' That's how she was."

But while Kathie wanted to heal the world, Jim began to wonder if she could fix what was going horribly wrong in her own life after an incident that still haunts him.

"It was Christmas, 1980," he remembers. "We were all out at Hyde Park at mom's house for Christmas dinner. It was evening and we were all sitting around, enjoying a few drinks after the meal. Kathie was sitting at one end of the couch near the fireplace and I was at the other end. Bobby was restless. He kept saying to Kathie that they should get going. But Kathie didn't move. She was enjoying being with all her family and was in no hurry to leave. Bobby went outside, to warm up the car, but knowing him, no doubt he smoked a joint too. When he came back in, he was carrying her coat which had been thrown on the stairs like the others, and barked at her, 'Let's go.'

"Kathie said, 'Aw, come on, Bobby, can't we stay for a little longer?' He just lost it. He lunged at her, pulled her up off the couch by her hair, dragged her across the room and they were gone.

"It happened so fast, none of us could believe what we had just seen. My grandmother looked at my mom, we all just sat there dumbstruck. Kathie, who was always the dutiful wife, didn't resist. I think if she had, I would have torn his face off. Looking back, I wish I had.

"She should have reached out to her family, but it was an era when a lot of things were swept under the rug, and a lot of wealthy girls felt they were failures if they failed to please their husbands."

As she threw herself into her new life at Albert Einstein, Jim could see a change in his sister. She was still as much fun to be around, but she had a new maturity, a sense of purpose he hadn't seen before. Whatever was going on between her and Bobby at home, it wasn't keeping her from achieving her goal.

In late 1981 she was in her last year as a medical student doing her pre-internship at the Westchester County Medical Center when he asked her, "What do you do there?"

" 'I work in the emergency room,' she said. I thought of all the things she'd see, people with stab wounds, who'd been shot, people coming off the highway banged up in auto crashes and I asked her, 'Why? How do you handle that?' The answer she gave me was really profound," he says.

" 'The essence of being a doctor is to give care, immediate care and comfort to those who really need it, and that's what the E.R. is all about,' she said. She knew that lots of doctors chose to work on Park Avenue and that their patients are wealthy matrons who come in once a week for social support more than anything else, and they become extremely rich in the process. She wasn't interested in that. She wanted to cure people."

CHAPTER 6

SUSAN FACES THE TRUTH

WHILE Kathie was dealing with a husband who was becoming increasingly resentful of her growing confidence, and Bobby was watching his naive and trusting young wife blossom into an independent-minded woman, their friend Susan Berman was finding out that she was as interesting to her new colleagues as were the clever articles she penned on New York's celebrities.

After a slew of barely disguised insinuations had been sent her way, one of her coworkers at *New York* magazine finally confronted her: Was she, everyone wanted to know, related to the mobster Davie Berman?

Until then, Susan had refused to admit that her adored father could have had a dark side, that he could have been capable of killing. She had grown up thinking he was the Mayor of Las Vegas; the official ambassador for gambling. That's why the people around him were so deferential and quick to anticipate his every whim. That's why everyone had wanted to shake his hand and why the tough-looking men who worked for him had treated her mom like a queen and her like a princess.

At his funeral, an event which traumatized her every time she thought about it, the eulogy was fulsome in praise of her dad. "It's a sad day for all of Las Vegas," the rabbi had said. "There will never be anyone like him. Davie Berman had a vision. He saw a boomtown where others had just seen desert. He was Mr. Las Vegas." Susan had drunk in every word. It wasn't until she was grown-up that she realized that "we are not expecting trouble" was not the normal greeting mourners exchange with each over a coffin, especially when their shifty glances underscore that they are expecting just that.

Yet paradoxically, she had never quite believed that her mother had taken her own life. She was convinced that Gladys had been murdered by the Mob because she wouldn't turn over the substantial fortune Davie had stashed away, even though she wore blinkers when it came to the vexing question of how he'd amassed his wealth. On the few occasions she'd given the matter serious thought, she'd rationalized a scenario she could live with: her father was a hotel owner in a town filled with gamblers, and the huge sums of cash generated by enterprises like the Flamingo and the Riviera casinos were a magnet for organized crime. Of course Davie had known Mob characters, he'd had to protect his businesses from greedy gangsters who tried to muscle in on his profits; that's why he'd stowed away money in Los Angeles for Gladys and Susan. But it didn't make him one of them. She had spent her young years in such blissful ignorance that she was unwilling, as an adult, to deal with the overwhelming evidence that her father had provided her with life's luxuries through extortion and violence.

Davie had been so successful at creating an idyllic existence for his only beloved child, that it was easy after his death to listen to Chickie when he impressed on her over and over, "If anyone bad-mouths your father, don't believe a word of it." Whenever she'd caught a whiff of an ugly rumor she had asked him, "Everyone loved my dad, right?" And Chickie would assure her, "Of course they did. He was the best, a stand-up guy." Hadn't Chickie's huge gambling debts been paid off time and time again by his exasperated older brother? And, in return, he'd filled his niece's head with tales of her dad's cleverness, his character and generosity.

He'd been a good Jew who'd built the first *schul* in Las Vegas, kept all the Jewish holidays, could speak Yiddish and had matzohs flown in from New York for Passover. Hadn't he always given to Jewish charities and raised money for Irgun, the freedom fighters of Israel during that country's battle for nationhood, personally arranging for a planeload of weapons to be sent? If he was, as she was beginning to suspect, no better than a common hood, a Jewish Al Capone, why wasn't she told? Uncle Chickie, Aunt Lilian, or even Raleigh must have known. The truth was that they'd loved Davie too, and chose not to delve too deeply into where he got the wherewithal for his generosity to them. And nobody wanted to be the one who broke her heart.

Yet Deni, Raleigh's daughter and Lilian's granddaughter, says that they didn't have to shield Susan. "She always really knew," she maintains. "I think the reporter in her made it necessary to go back and find out all the details, but from the time I was very young she would say, 'My dad was a gangster.' She definitely talked about it. She was proud to be Davie Berman's daughter. He was the gangster with a heart."

But talking about her father to her younger cousin within the safe confines of the Padveens' home was one thing, admitting what he was to strangers was something else altogether. By 1977, with her nosy colleague's question ringing in her ears, she could hide her head in the sand no longer. For years she'd pointedly not dealt with the allegations that her father had been a Mob boss, ignoring the smart-aleck remarks from other students at the Chadwick School and the sudden silences that fell around her whenever the subject of organized crime came up.

When she'd read in a copy of a Chadwick classmate's *Los Angeles Times* that her parents' friends Gus and Bess Greenbaum had been killed and decapitated "gangland style" because Gus was a member of the Mafia, in her naïvete she had asked, "What's that?"

And later, when she read the book with which her college roommate's pal had taunted her, she hadn't exactly rushed to share her discovery with everyone, "Hey, guess what I've found out."

But while she had deliberately avoided dealing with

her unpleasant family secret for most of her adult life, it had festered, like a cancer, in the darkest recesses of her subconscious. In 1983, before she moved to New York, she'd sunk into a deep depression. For weeks she couldn't get out of bed. At age 28, she didn't want to go on living, she admitted later. And although, after a couple of months of black despair, she managed to pull herself together, the knowledge of how much she'd wanted to die lingered on for a year and left her forever afraid of her own suicidal tendencies. During the grim months of recovery, when she had to force herself to crawl out from underneath the sheets to keep her daily appointment with her shrink, she said she had to repress the constant urge to throw herself off San Francisco's Golden Gate Bridge. Her father's criminal past had been thrown in her face by a cocky scribe who'd persuaded her to meet him at Sardi's restaurant in the theater district off Broadway with the promise that he could introduce her to people who'd known her parents. Instead, the author shoved a wad of FBI files containing evidence about Davie's Mob activities in her face.

There it was, finally, in black and white—the irrefutable proof. The writer boasted about how he'd obtained the documents through Interpol and an Israeli contact. "Did you know your father was a killer?" he asked her. "What do you think of him now?" Swallowing her revulsion for this crowing creature who was grinning at her confusion, and fighting back the urge to smack him, Susan didn't answer. She jumped to her feet, threw the money for her juice on the table and ran out into the street gulping down a lungful of fumes from the midtown traffic. It smelled cleaner to her than the poisonous air she'd been breathing in the restaurant.

Shortly after, she had gone back to Los Angeles to visit Chickie, whose diabetes and other ailments were sapping his frail body of what little strength it had left. The last few years had been difficult for him. His stretch in prison had left him sickly, and without Davie to cover his losses at the gaming tables that had once provided him with a lavish living, he'd fallen on hard times, living in a series of low-rent dives, too embarrassed to let his former associates see him in his straightened circumstances, too proud to ask for help. He had suffered a heart attack in 1976 and was hospitalized in Las Vegas with congestive heart failure. After a couple of more episodes she'd persuaded him to check into Cedars Sinai Hospital in Los Angeles but the doctors there told him his condition was terminal. She then secured him a berth in a comfortable Beverly Hills retirement home, where he splashed on his French cologne and wore his Sulka robes in defiance of his death sentence. The one person he always welcomed with open arms was Susan.

"He was a character," says Deni, "eccentric and eclectic and very compassionate, an indulgent, self-centered guy, and so lovable. And he was good to Susan, he became the only parent she had. Chickie was limited by his own stuff, but as much as he could love anybody, he loved Susie. She paid for everything towards the end of his life, all his custodial care."

As she sat beside him, inwardly weeping over this emaciated shell of the dashing uncle she loved, his bent body wrapped in a pitifully frayed silk robe, he began to ramble on about the old days, and as he talked, for the first time ever, he let slip some things that contradicted the varnished version of her father he'd dinned into her for years.

"That officer that arrested your dad said he was the toughest Jew who ever lived," he told her.

"Why was he arrested?" she asked.

"For kidnapping. He kidnapped a bootlegger, they all did it. And he got shot in the leg," said Chickie.

In September 1978, she got a call telling her that Chickie was back at Cedars Sinai. Hang on for another day, she pleaded. "No baby," he told her. "I have to do this alone." By the time she arrived in Los Angeles, he was dead.

With her uncle's revelations ringing in her ears, and after the ambush she'd unwittingly walked into at Sardi's, she knew the time had come to face down her father's demons once and for all. She'd trace his steps from his impoverished beginnings on the farmlands of North Dakota to his grave and write a book about what she found.

Armed with the power of the Freedom of Information Act, she applied to the FBI headquarters in Washington for permission to view any files on David Berman. They were not available, she was told, but in a wave of sympathy for the ashen-faced young woman for whom the visit was clearly an ordeal, the clerk promised to see what she could do. For nearly a year, while the papers were being processed, sensitive information deleted and certain names and places blacked out, they talked frequently on the phone. Galling though it was to have a stranger pawing through documents that contained her beloved father's secret past, Susan would struggle to maintain her composure as the helpful civil servant matter-of-factly read out a litany of her father's felonies. When the vetting procedure was completed, box after box containing FBI files documenting Davie's indisputable part in bank robberies, gambling scams, kidnappings and gangland killings arrived in the mail.

"She came to me with the idea for *Easy Street* at the time I was working with the William Morris Agency," says Rhoda Weyr, who was then the only female literary agent in the company. "I first clapped eyes on her when she called to ask for a meeting. She came in my office. She looked like a waif, but she was somebody who just won you over. She started talking and half an hour later she finished her sentence. She talked about her father and her life and she felt this tremendous urge to write about it. She said she was a friend of Julie Baumgold and had done some stuff for *New York* magazine. I said, 'Okay, it sounds good, write something.' I repped her for articles she wrote for *Ladies' Home Journal*, *Cosmopolitan*, *The New Yorker* and *Parents*.

"She became a friend. Susan was such an obviously lost soul. I had her at my home, my children were quite young then, and they found her absolutely fascinating. She was wonderful with children. She always cared about them, never forgot their names—and since I had four daughters, that was quite a feat.

"She wrote a wonderful proposal, but it was all over the map. This was before computers and I literally sat on my living room floor with her and cut and pasted it together in different form. But it was all her, she just didn't know how to present it."

In August 1979 she landed a contract from Dial Publishing for $50,000, which was a huge sum at the time. With the money, she bought a little studio apartment at 34 Beekman Place in a gracious brick building with stone facing, white-painted trim, black wrought-iron fencing and window boxes filled with red and pink geraniums. It was one of the best and safest neighborhoods in the city, surrounded by foreign embassies, consulates and million-dollar townhouses.

Its only drawback was that the apartment was on the first floor and that made Susan, who was already plagued by a whole catalog of irrational fears, very nervous. She discovered that the studio next door was vacant and bullied Stephen M. Silverman into leasing it. "You have to," she told him. "I can't stay there by myself." As soon as she moved in she complained that her new digs may have a swanky address, but they only had a shower. Stephen's place next door at number 32 was no bigger, but his came with a bathtub.

That Stephen had the good fortune to score the studio with the tub was incidental to Susan, who exercised the same proprietorial rights to his home as she did to her own. "She just regarded my apartment as hers too," he says. "She'd walk in whenever she wanted, completely unannounced, any time of the day or night. It didn't matter what I was doing or who I was entertaining." And she often barged in having walked the few yards that separated their front doors in her flowing, Japanese kimono. "She looked like something out of *Madame Butterfly*," he remembers.

"When she first came to me with the idea for *Easy Street*, she had all the research to do, but the law changed

and her father's files had just become available," says
Rhoda. "I remember the day the boxes arrived, there were
stacks of them. She'd bought the apartment on Beekman
Place on the strength of the contract and I remember going
over there and there was nothing in the place but Susan
and boxes—furniture, she didn't have. Every once in a
while she'd call me with something she'd just found out
and it would either devastate her or thrill her."

As she plowed through the mountain of incriminating
documents, she was appalled. The Feds not only knew
everything about her father's crimes, but they had been
watching her family every single day of her childhood.
Government surveillance agents had noted every time she
and her mother left the house or took a trip, even what time
they ate dinner. There were pages commenting on Davie's
love for Gladys and his despair over her psychiatric problems. The spies knew how despondent he was when she
was carted off for treatment, his happiness during the periods when she was well. She also found out the details of
his seven-year incarceration in Sing Sing prison; despite
being interrogated for weeks on end, he had refused to rat
on his partners. For his silence, and his willingness to take
the rap alone, he won the admiration of the public and of
inmates alike. On his release he was rewarded for his dis-
cretion by Mob boss Frank Costello, who ceded him the
"rights' to run all the gambling in Minneapolis.

Armed with a list of names and places, Susan virtually
walked in her father's footsteps, from his birthplace in Ash-
ley, North Dakota, where his penniless Russian immigrant
parents had settled, to Sioux City, where he'd started work
as a newsboy at 12 and four years later was running a
successful bootlegging and gambling operation. She followed him through New York to the jail at Ossining, out
West to California, and finally to the Nevada hospital where
he'd died. Now she was sure he'd been murdered too.

It was gut-wrenching, stomach-churning work. The father who had created her magical childhood, took care of
his extended family and cared devotedly for her sick

mother, had been a Mob boss. There was no longer any doubt. For three years she tracked down former accomplices, talked to law enforcement officers and devoured the thousands of pages of police files filled with robberies, kidnapping, bank heists and murders. Yet she also discovered that he was a war hero—he had taken a bullet at Anzio for his country, for God's sake, with the 12th Manitoba Dragoons after being turned down as too old and a felon into the bargain, by the U.S. Army in 1941. Gladys joined the WACS.

She learned how her gentle mother, broken from years of fear and stress, had somehow summoned the strength to defy months of Mob pressure to part with the fortune Davie had left for her, afraid there would be no money to send Susan to college. There were times when, sick to her stomach, she didn't want to go on. The father she had put on a pedestal for all these years, keeping his mugshot in her wallet and "whipping it out the way the rest of us showed baby pictures," as her friend Dinitia Smith told *New York* magazine, was unarguably a brutish thug. He'd run the Flamingo, the Riviera, the Las Vegas Club, the El Dorado and the other Las Vegas operations for the Syndicate, the Chicago-based Mob bosses who'd fronted the $3 million start-up capital back in 1946.

Danny Goldberg says that although Susan came to terms with and eventually wrote extensively about her roots, she kept a lot to herself. It was just too hurtful to share. "She had a complicated mentality, and probably had a lot of things in her life that I wouldn't know about. There's no question that she knew the people her father knew. She grew up around those people. A lot of them died—some of them of just old age, that's the generation they were. But she was 12 when her father died and at 12 years of age you have a pretty clear sense of who your parents' friends are, and you remember them when you get older. But I don't think they were part of her day-to-day life," he says.

At one point during her research she told him, "Danny, I have to stop. It's so sad. They all died."

"Yes, but you didn't," he replied, "and that's why you must go on."

She went back to Las Vegas and the home where she'd grown up—it's now a landmarked building along with the other few Tudor houses in the city—and entertained the new owners with tales of Jimmy Durante sleeping in their guest bedroom. She went back to the Flamingo, which had been transformed into a Hilton Hotel, and to the Riviera, where many of the staff remembered her and greeted her like a long-lost daughter. One old survivor of the gang warfare said her dad had been enormously likable: "Davie Berman? He was the nicest killer you'd ever hope to meet."

It was in Las Vegas that she heard a version of Gladys's death that differed from the official determination of suicide that was on the death certificate she'd retrieved from the FBI files. Not long after her mother cut short their life together in Los Angeles and sent her back to Chickie in Idaho, she was cornered in her bedroom by two goons who forced barbiturates down her throat. Only then did Susan realize why her mother's tender goodbye had seemed to her, even as a 13-year-old, horribly final. There was scant comfort in recognizing that the brave Gladys, knowing that her tormentors had run out of patience, had sent her out of harm's way.

Faced with the undeniable truth, that her father had been a gangster and she was a daughter of the Mob, was at once shocking and exhilarating. She tried to square the loving and indulgent parent she knew, the man who had held Passover seders at his casinos, with the fact that he'd been a ruthless killer. The only way she could make sense of it all was to do what she'd done since she was a child: write it down. It turned into a labor of love and confession, and took another two years to complete.

When delving into her past became too painful, she turned to another project, a book about the trip she took to Israel the year before she started college. She called it

Driver, Give a Soldier a Lift, the title being inspired by a slogan posted everywhere in Israel, where hitchhiking soldiers used their thumbs to get around the country.

"The book never did anything, but it did have one claim to fame," says Stephen M. Silverman. "It turned up in the Woody Allen movie *Interiors*, one of his first serious movies, art-directed within an inch of its life and very stark, very minimalistic. But there's a bedroom scene that shows a book with a light pastel blue cover laying on the nightstand, and it's Susan's. God knows where it came from, but Susan thought it was an omen that better things were going to come."

She was full of optimism that the biography would be cathartic; it would help her close a chapter of her life and launch a career as a best-selling author. When it was finished, she had produced an honest, hugely entertaining account of her father's double life, her mother's troubling illness and death, and her own fragmented childhood. It was a memoir suffused with love and unhappiness, great devotion and above all, it was a testimony to her parents' achievement in creating a wonderfully caring home amid the violence and corruption that paid the rent. *Easy Street* was published in 1981 to instant acclaim.

"It was a terrific book," raves Owen Laster, who is now the executive vice president of the William Morris Agency. "There was a tremendous amount of film interest in it."

Danny and Hollywood producer Lynda Obst (*Flashdance* and *Sleepless in Seattle*), who was then the editor of *The New York Times Magazine*, cohosted a party to launch the book on November 11, 1981, at Sammy's Romanian, the landmark restaurant on New York's Lower East Side. Susan's pals Bobby and Kathie Durst were amongst the guests.

The evening was a huge success, remembers Stephen. "It was like a giant bar mitzvah," he says. "The restaurant itself has pitchers of chicken fat on the tables in lieu of butter. Here was really a room filled with really highly assimilated Jews. No one wore their religious or ethnic background on their sleeve. Their parents would have plotzed if they had seen them dancing the hora.

"Suddenly all these children, who had been sent to very good schools by their parents to learn to behave like non-Jews, were acting very ethnic. And a good time was had by all. The place was packed. We were all seated at tables, so it was quite orderly. Classy it wasn't, but it was well organized and Susan was the belle of the ball."

For Susan the evening was a social and a personal triumph. It was like coming out of the closet. Her father was who he was. She could talk about him openly, without reservation and with love. And now, everyone understood why. "I felt my father belonged more to Mob mythology than he did to me," she later wrote. "Now both of my parents are mine. I have reclaimed them." To show everyone, but especially herself, that she had come to terms with his past, she put her father's F.B.I. wanted poster in a frame and hung it on her living room wall.

She was giddy with success until Dial Press started to arrange a publicity campaign. The idea of having to travel aroused dormant fears. Her phobias were unbelievable, says Rhoda. "The first I knew about them was when she called me one day and said she really thought she should see a psychiatrist. I said I would recommend mine. She listened politely and said that would be absolutely fabulous, but: 'Well, here's the thing,' she burst out, 'I can't go above the ground floor.'

" 'You're in luck,' I told her, 'he operates out of a ground-floor office. But what the fuck are you talking about?' Because my office at William Morris was on the 31st floor and my home was on the 15th floor with a view of Central Park all the way to the Triboro Bridge. There was no way to avoid that you were up high in the sky in it, and the same was true for my office. And then she said, 'Well, if you notice, I never go near the windows in your apartment.' It wasn't something I had noticed and I forgot all about it until she called to say that the publisher wanted to send her on a promotional book tour. . . .

" 'Well, you understand I don't fly or go over bridges,' she said.

" 'How did you get to New York?' I asked.

" 'I never realized it was an island,' said Susan. 'When I landed and found out I was going to have to go over a bridge to get to Manhattan I was really scared, so I had them take me through the tunnel.'

" 'I think you had better talk to your editor,' I told her. What they actually did was hire someone to fly with her and drive with her. They were afraid she would kill herself."

To the public, Susan was captivating, but the publisher's assistant in charge of the travel arrangements nearly had a nervous breakdown. Added to her fear of planes and bridges, Susan refused to stay in hotel rooms above the fifth floor or in rooms with unlucky numbers. And when she went into a restaurant she'd repeat the performance she'd put on one night when Rhoda took her out for dinner just before she left for the tour. "All of a sudden she starts grilling this poor waitress about what was in each dish. She said to me she'd die if she ate eggs. I didn't know she had an allergy to eggs. She never mentioned it to me before, and she'd eaten at my house dozens of times."

Easy Street was bought by Universal Studios for $350,000.

CHAPTER 7
KATHIE VANISHES

Bob and Kathie drove up to the Truesdale Lake cottage on the Saturday afternoon of January 30 even though it was another bone-chillingly cold weekend in what had already been a harsh winter. The lake was frozen over and a biting wind snapped through the trees.

Despite the weather, they wanted to get out of the city. They had some serious issues to iron out and they needed to be alone to do it. Kathie was just a few months away from graduation, and it had been a struggle. Bobby had griped every inch of the way: She was never home, she put in hours that were way too long, he hated her friends. The closer she got to her goal of becoming a doctor, the worse his grumbling got. He'd begun complaining about how much her degree was costing, and he had cut off her credit cards and stopped paying her tuition, which she was scraping together by taking loans from several of her friends.

In the summer of 1980 she'd found a bolt hole on the other side of Manhattan. Life with Bobby had become unbearable. For years he'd been verbally abusive, belittling her in front of other people and chipping away at her self-confidence. He'd always had affairs, but now he was throwing them in her face. Despite her own hurt she made allowances for his damaged childhood and his destructive behavior and defended him even when bruises began appearing on her arms and face. But the abuse had been getting worse. Instead of dishing out a tongue-lashing when she annoyed him, he'd begun to emphasize his displeasure with his fists.

She'd rented an apartment in the Croyden Hotel, a

Durst-owned building on East 86th Street, and after each explosion, she'd stay there until it was safe to go home. Recently, she hadn't been home much. They'd talked of splitting up for good, but fought bitterly over how they'd divide their assets. Bobby's argument was, "Everything is mine, you have nothing," and she'd hired an attorney at the prestigious law firm of Milbank, Tweed, Hadley & McCloy to help her hammer out a settlement. When negotiations went nowhere—Bobby refused to part with even a fraction of his millions—the attorney had told her to document everything, especially any incidents of abuse.

But since Christmas, Bobby had been conciliatory, turning on a semblance of charm and begging her to give them another chance. So when he'd suggested, "Let's get away," just like in the old days, "we'll go up to the cottage and sort the whole thing out," she'd agreed—if only because dealing with Bobby trying to be nice was infinitely preferable to coping with his evil twin.

Throughout the day there had been flurries of snow, and as they got out of the car and hurried to the front door, sleety rain numbed their faces. Bob brought some logs up from the basement and lit a blaze in the stone fireplace while Kathie rummaged around in the refrigerator. They spent the evening in front of a fire that bathed the pretty living room in a warm orange glow. It should have been a storybook romantic setting for a couple trying to get their fractured marriage back on track.

Kathie surfaced on the Sunday morning and decided to brave the bitter cold to get some fresh air. Over layers of shirts and sweaters, she pulled on her down coat, wrapped a scarf around her neck and turned the collar of the coat up to give her neck an extra layer of heat. She stuffed her hands into mittens and looked around for something to put on her head. Dammit, she thought, I left my hat in Manhattan.

Next door, Ruth Mayer was in her kitchen when she heard the doorbell and then Kathie's voice: "It's me, Ruth, can I borrow your hat? I forgot to bring mine with me and

I want to go for a walk," she asked. Ruth remembers thinking her friend was insane to want to go out on such a "freezing, horrible day." Kathie didn't say whether she was going to walk on her own or if Bob was going with her. She pulled the hat over her blonde locks and yelled, "See you later," as she disappeared up the drive.

Ruth had been surprised when Kathie said Bob was at the cottage, considering how bad things were between them. The previous summer, she had confided that the marriage was in trouble. "She told me that he hit her, and that was when she told me his mother had committed suicide and that he had a lot of problems. It wasn't the kind of thing we usually talked about," says Ruth.

"I didn't see her for a while. Then when they came back up, they were obviously having problems. They were doing separate things—she was going to parties in one direction, he would go off in the other. She told me that fall that he was having an affair with Prudence Farrow, and she was upset about it. We called her and her sister "Mia and Pria," She told me that Prudence would call her up and tell her, 'Give him up. It's over, let Bobby go.'

Bobby had been rapt by Prudence's tales of meditating with the Beatles. And he was thrilled to be dating the woman who had been the inspiration for his idol John Lennon's song "Dear Prudence." He'd told Kathie all about it.

The song had been written in the late sixties when the Beatles and their wives and girlfriends traveled to Rishikesh, India, to sit at the feet of the charismatic mystic Maharishi Mahesh Yogi hoping for enlightenment or, at least, some pearls of wisdom. Prudence had tagged along with her famous sister.

She described the trip to the *Guardian* newspaper: "Mia found out that the Beatles were arriving in New Delhi so she had our driver reroute through the airport. She went running off and I was swept away by the crowd and the next thing I knew I saw her and the Beatles climb into their car and off they went without me.

"At Rishikesh I stood out because I was absolutely hysterically fanatical that I had to get my meditation in. I was meditating all day long, all night long, eventually. The song was mainly written by John. George was genuinely there for spiritual reasons. George and I talked more because we had more in common. John would listen and I remember noticing that there was a kind of wistfulness, and so that's why it's such a kind song. I felt very touched that they had written such a nice song."

Bobby was blown away. Prudence, for a time, looked like a kindred spirit; like him, she was searching for higher ground. He had struggled throughout his childhood to establish first place in the pecking order with his brother Douglas; she had been overawed by Mia and compared herself unfavorably to her: "She was extraordinarily successful and I felt I was at the other end of the scale—a complete and utter loser," she said.

That was something Bobby knew all about. How on earth could an uncomplicated Catholic girl from Queens compete? thought Kathie. John Lennon would never have written a song about her.

Ruth says that, at this point, the marriage seemed doomed:

"I thought they were going their separate ways. I knew she wasn't living at the Riverside Drive apartment, that she had another place and was very much surprised to hear that they were still very much together. He was giving her no money at all and he didn't want to give her anything to go away. He said he'd give her $100,000 and she wanted $250,000. Even that was ridiculous. I couldn't believe it when I found out later how much money he had."

As her friend disappeared out of sight, Ruth began fretting again about the conversation they'd had the previous Saturday when Kathie had driven up alone. It had disturbed both her and Bill at the time and worried her all week. After she'd seen the car pull into the driveway, she had called over to say that she and Bill were going out for dinner with another couple, but to come over for cocktails.

When Kathie arrived, she was in bad shape. She was in trouble, she blurted out. Bobby was being so pigheaded about money that she'd thought of a way of shaming him out of his stinginess. She had managed to get hold of some potentially embarrassing Durst financial records and she planned to mail them to someone powerful, even more powerful than Seymour.

"Who, for heaven's sake?" the Mayers had asked alarmed. "What the hell are you doing? Do you know what you are getting into and who you are going up against?"

What neither of them knew that night was that Kathie had already sent her explosive package to a U.S. senator.

She'd met the man at several political fund-raisers, and she'd been sure he would help her, have a quiet word in Bobby's ear perhaps. At worst, she'd figured, he'd do nothing. But she'd totally miscalculated; the senator sent the documents back to her father-in-law. Seymour had been furious and railed at Bobby, telling him: "You have got to take care of this."

"Kathie, she was terrified, absolutely terrified about what she had done, says Ruth. "And yet she was like, 'Well I'm entitled to this. I'm not letting him get away with giving me nothing.' "

As the evening wore on, Kathie didn't want to go home. The Mayers were convinced she'd been threatened.

"When our friends appeared, I asked, 'Do you mind if Kathie comes with us?' and they said 'Of course not,' " remembers Ruth. "The five us went out to dinner and the whole evening was spent talking about what she'd done. She was so afraid of what was going to happen, she knew she had crossed some line. Our friend warned her that taking on the Durst Organization would be like 'going after an elephant with a peashooter.' "

Ruth sensed that Kathy knew she was out of her depth. All of a sudden the realization of just how much clout her father-in-law had was sinking in. Kathie was drinking too much by then, says Ruth. "She was under huge amounts of pressure—her marriage was ugly, she was coming up for her finals and she was frightened about the situation with the Dursts.

"She told us, 'If anything happens to me, suspect foul play.' "

That night Ruth and Bill had persuaded her that she'd drunk way too much and made her promise that she wouldn't try to drive back to the city. To make sure she didn't, Ruth took her car keys.

All of Kathie's friends were becoming increasingly alarmed by the violent episodes with Bobby and the frequency with which they were occurring. In November, Kathie had bashed her knee climbing out of the window of her penthouse fourteen stories above the street. They'd been having dinner when a fight erupted over Prudence Farrow. It was supposed to be all over between them, but a couple of days before, Prudence had called Kathie again, telling her to clear off and leave Bobby to her. Bobby started throwing punches, several of which had connected with her face, and she'd backed up until she was at the window. To escape his blows, she'd scrambled out and edged along the terrace to the apartment next door and hammered on the window. The alarmed neighbor let her in and made her stay until after midnight when she thought Bobby would have calmed down.

Then the first week of January, she landed in Jacobi Hospital at 3:00 A.M. with bruises to her face and neck after another argument over money. She'd called Eleanor Schwank in tears and Eleanor urged her, "Kathie, you've got to get yourself to the emergency room. You have to have a record of this." Yet despite the urging of the hospital and her friends, she refused to press charges.

On the last day she was seen alive, January 31, 1982, Gilberte Najamy, who after college had started a catering business in Danbury, Connecticut, had invited a bunch of friends to a party at her Newtown house and was in the middle of her preparations when Kathie phoned. She sounded awful. She was at the cottage, she said, spending a supposedly reconciliatory weekend with Bobby, only it was turning nasty. "I have to get out of the house," she said. "Can I come over?"

"Sure," Gilberte told her.

When Kathie arrived an hour later, at around 1:00 P.M., Gilberte was shocked by her appearance. Usually Kathie was well-dressed. As Eleanor said, "She was always nicely turned out. The things she wore were always nice. If she had on a sweater it was always a very nice sweater." But on this filthy day, Kathie hadn't been worried about how she looked. She had thrown on a pair of sweats and had barely run a comb through her hair. Gilberte didn't have to ask; Kathie immediately launched into how bad things were at home. "It's awful, Bobby's insane," she said, shaking her head.

That afternoon he called several times and from across the room, Gilberte could hear him ranting at the other end of the phone. As his voice grew shriller, she got a sinking feeling in the pit of her stomach. Kathie should dump him, she thought for the umpteenth time.

Although Kathie didn't know all of Gilberte's guests, it didn't stop her from pouring out her misery. Fired by several glasses of red wine, she told them that the relationship was in shreds. They argued about everything, but mostly about money. Bobby was so controlling, he wouldn't give her a decent settlement to start a new life without him, even though she figured she'd earned it after nearly ten years of marriage. She didn't want much, just enough to start up in practice as a pediatrician. Her frustration kept tumbling out; she couldn't wait to graduate medical school and be able to support herself. She said she didn't know how much longer she could withstand the escalating violence that accompanied their fights. He hit and punched her, she said, and told them about the night she'd gone to the emergency room for treatment.

Then she launched into an incident the previous year that had sent one of her friends to the hospital. She'd been partying with a bunch of pals at Xenon on February 1,

1981, and afterwards they'd gone back to her East 86th Street apartment. Nobody was in a hurry to leave, and it was the early hours of the morning when, suddenly, the door burst open and there was Bobby, spoiling for a fight. He got it into his head that Peter Schwartz, a photographer who owned a camera shop in Stratford, Connecticut, had designs on Kathie. Peter was sitting on a cushion on the floor talking to another of Kathie's friends, Kathy Traystman. Bobby flew across the room and booted him in the face, breaking his cheekbone below the eye. "He went berserk," she told them, "he kept kicking Peter until we hauled him off." Schwartz went to the emergency room and filed charges a few days later.

Kathie and Gilberte agreed that the incident would reveal the truth about Bobby's hair-trigger temper and his irrational eruptions. She should use it to force Bobby to come to reasonable terms, and it would help back up her own charges of having been beaten. Bobby had pled guilty to lesser charges of disorderly conduct on July 26, and received a conditional discharge, but there was a civil suit pending against him for damages.

"I'll call Peter right now," said Kathie, "and find out what's happening with that." When she got the photographer on the phone, he told her that he'd settled with Bobby and was dropping the civil case. Kathie was furious. "He's getting away with it again," she shouted.

Her indignation fell on sympathetic ears. Bobby was a cruel, tightfisted bastard, the party guests agreed. Throughout the afternoon Bobby called several more times. Each time Kathie hung up, she was madder than before. This has got to stop, Gilberte's friends told her. She should stand up for her rights, demand her fair share of the marital spoils. Fight back, they urged her.

Around 7:00 P.M. Kathie called home. From her responses they could tell that Bobby was still fuming that she'd taken off without him. They heard her say, "Okay, okay, calm down. Stop calling here, I'll come home." She hung up and turned to Gilberte. "I have to go home. He's really upset," she said.

Grabbing her coat, Kathie reminded Gilberte that they were to have dinner in the city the following night, along with Kathie's cousin, Chuck Saaf, to finalize the plans for her grandmother's 90th birthday the following Saturday, February 6. It was to be a big family party with her mom, her brother and his wife, her sisters and their husbands, all their kids, aunts, uncles and cousins. Kathie had been looking forward to it for weeks and was anxious that everything go without a hitch. Gilberte was organizing the food.

As snowflakes swirled around them the two women hugged on the porch. Then as Kathie walked to the car, she hesitated for a second, turned to her friend and said: "Gilberte, If anything happens to me, you will check it out. I'm afraid what Bobby will do."

Stunned, Gilberte stood rooted to the spot as she feverishly digested what her friend had just said. She felt chills on the back of her neck as she watched Kathie climb in behind the wheel of the red Mercedes and set off for the forty-five-minute drive back to the South Salem house. Closing the door, she shuddered as she thought of the hostile reception Kathie would face when she got home. But she could never have foreseen what fate had in store for her friend.

Bill and Ruth Mayer were also out for the evening. "We came home later that Sunday night and as we passed Bob and Kathie's, we saw there was nobody home," says Ruth. "There were no lights in the house and no cars in the driveway. We thought that they had left already and driven back to the city. I remember thinking, 'Oh dear, it's freezing cold and I won't get that hat back for another week.'"

The living room in the Mayers' custom-built home has a floor-to-ceiling window that looks out over Truesdale Lake. In the depths of winter, when the trees and bushes are bare, it also provides a clear view of the Dursts' cottage. The house was still in total darkness when they turned in for the night.

The next day, Gilberte set off to meet Kathie and her cousin at the Lion's Head, a now-defunct bar which used to be a watering hole for writers in Greenwich Village, to discuss the last-minute details for Kathie's grandma's birthday bash. They knew that she was on clinical duty that Monday at the Albert Einstein Medical Center, so when she was late Gilberte and Chuck reckoned that she must have gotten held up at the hospital. They waited for nearly two hours. Why didn't she call? they asked each other. This was so unlike her. If anything, Kathie was a phone freak, she spent hours calling her friends.

Gilberte got up to use the pay phone. She called the Riverside Drive penthouse and Kathie's East 86th Street bolt hole. There was no answer at either apartment. She called the South Salem house, but there was nobody home there either. As the evening wore on, she began to worry. When she got back to Connecticut, Gilberte immediately lifted the phone. She called the penthouse number again and an answering machine clicked on. "Where's Kathie?" she demanded to know. She went to bed that night feeling very uneasy.

The next morning she phoned again, but still got no answer. She called again the next day, and the next. She called Kathie's family, and told them about the Monday night meeting. "Kathie would never just not show up," her brother said. "She would have called." Gilberte got in touch with all Kathie's other friends. Nobody had heard from her since the weekend. Then she called the police. "I think my friend has been murdered," she said.

Meanwhile back in South Salem, the Mayers had no inkling of anything abnormal. They didn't usually talk to Kathie during the week when she had classes. On Monday evening, Ruth was looking out the window when she saw something that startled her. There was a chink of light she'd never seen before coming from the basement in the Durst house. "It was a strange bluish light," she recalls. "I thought it was weird." She looked for it the next night, but it was gone.

On Thursday, February 4, Bobby Durst turned up on their doorstep. "I heard the bell and went to the front door. When I opened it, there was Bob.

" 'Have you seen Kathie?' he asked.

"My heart stopped, I thought, 'Oh God. . . .'

" 'She's disappeared,' he said. He looked awful and he wouldn't come in. 'Have you seen her?' he repeated. 'I don't know where she is.'

"I instantly thought he had done something to her. I never, ever thought that she just disappeared. Kathie would have never taken off and not contacted her family. He said he was searching hospitals for her, searching psychiatric hospitals in case she had amnesia, all sorts of baloney like that." Ruth's brain was ticking furiously. "I thought, Did she just run because she was afraid for her life?"

That same evening, four days after Gilberte had last seen Kathie, Bob finally returned her calls. "Where is she?" Gilberte demanded.

"I don't know. I put her on the train to New York," he told her.

The train? That didn't sound right to Gilberte. Kathie never took the train. She always drove the Mercedes back to New York. The weekend place was less than a couple of hours away from her apartment in the city. Did she take the train because of the snow? She asked him what Kathie was wearing. Jeans he told her, her boots, a shirt, the sweater with the cable pattern on it and her coat.

On Friday, February 5, Gilberte could take it no longer. She called the New York state police. "There's been a murder," she told the officer on duty. "This man has murdered his wife, you need to talk to him now." The desk cop listened to her tale, then told her that Gilberte couldn't officially file a missing persons report because she wasn't a relative. But he would, he told her, note her complaint. Gilberte seethed all night.

Hoping to uncover something—anything—that would make the police sit up and take notice, Gilberte called Eleanor Schwank and told her she planned to snoop around the Durst estate in Katonah. "I'll come with you," said Eleanor. They didn't find anything suspicious.

The next day, with a sister in tow, Gilberte drove to South Salem, marched onto the property, heaved a rock through one of the downstairs windows of the cottage and called the police from inside.

"I just broke in," she told them. "Now will you come?" They didn't.

She began to rake around. In the bedroom, amongst Kathie's clothes, she found her brown suede boots and a traditional cream-colored Irish cable-knit sweater. In the kitchen, her unopened mail had been dumped in the trash. She went into the dining room and opened the closet. Inside was an ominous stack of black plastic bags which she later said so freaked her out that she ran out the door. Outside the house, she lifted the lid of a garbage can and saw a dozen or so of Kathie's expensive medical textbooks.

That same morning, Bobby casually strode into the 20th Precinct on Manhattan's West 82nd Street and reported his wife missing. Under his arm was a two-year-old issue of *Time* magazine. On the cover was the headline "The Five Most Powerful Men in New York," and below was a picture of Seymour Durst. The message was given and received.

Veteran N.Y.P.D. detectives Michael Struk, Robert Gibbons and Thomas O'Brady were put on the case. Between them they had worked on hundreds of homicides. Gibbons was the head of the team and Struk was already something of a star, who'd attracted his own fair share of newspaper coverage by nailing the killer of a pretty young violinist at the Metropolitan Opera. His wife had gone missing in New York, Durst assured them. He had spoken to her on the phone on the Sunday night after she arrived back at their Riverside Drive penthouse.

She had been out for most of the day, he told them, then she'd driven back from Connecticut to South Salem where they'd shared a dinner of hamburgers and she had downed a bottle of red wine. They had quarreled, he admitted, and Kathie had decided to take the train back into the city that night rather than stay over. She had a neurology clinic early the following morning and didn't want to risk getting stuck in traffic.

Before leaving, she had changed into a blouse, a sweater and blue jeans, he said, and over them she had on a down coat. She was also wearing brown suede boots, her favorite diamond earrings and she had two gold chains around her neck.

He said he had driven her in the red Mercedes to the railroad station at Katonah and she had caught the 9:17 P.M. train to New York where he had spoken to her between 11:00 P.M. and 11:30 P.M. He could pinpoint the time of the call because Kathie had told him she was lying on their bed watching the late night news. After dropping her off, he'd returned to South Salem stopping off at the Mayers' for drinks. He stayed at the cottage overnight—Kathie and he had planned to spend the week there—and gone back to the city on Monday afternoon.

Struk and Gibbons dutifully wrote down everything he said. They were deferential—after all, he was the son of Seymour Durst; any misstep on their part and they could kiss their careers goodbye long before their police pensions would kick in.

They started their inquiries by questioning the staff in the Durst-owned building on Riverside Drive where an elevator operator, Eddie Lopez, said he saw Mrs. Durst go into the apartment around 11:00 P.M. on January 31. He also claimed he'd seen her open her door in her nightgown and let a well-dressed swarthy individual into the apartment. He'd hung around long enough to make sure Kathie knew the man. The next morning, February 1, the super said he saw her walk up West 76th Street at around 11:00 A.M. Another employee thought that Mrs. Durst had come into the building between 6:00 P.M. and 8:00 P.M. on Monday evening.

Bobby told the police that he had returned to the city on Monday about 4:00 P.M. and stopped by the penthouse to pick up some business papers before going to his office at the Durst Organization headquarters on 6th Avenue. There was no sign of Kathie, but he didn't think that unusual, since she was either at classes or working at the hospital during the day.

The police also went to the Albert Einstein College of Medicine where the dean, Albert Kuperman, told them that Mrs. Durst had called in sick on Monday morning complaining of an upset stomach.

At first, especially since there seemed to be some corroborating evidence, the cops were inclined to believe Bobby's version of events. Although he'd been composed enough to make sure they knew all about his family's influence, his friends assured them he was "anguished." He'd admitted that the marriage had gone sour, but maintained that Kathie and he had reconciled and everything was fine. A week after she vanished, he announced that he was offering a $100,000 reward to anyone who could come up with information that would lead to his wife's whereabouts.

"At the time, one or two people thought they had seen her," said Michael Struk, who is now retired from the N.Y.P.D. and works as a consultant with the NBC police drama series *Law and Order*. They received over thirty phone tips; they followed up on all of them, but none checked out. Intensive interviews with her family, friends, classmates and neighbors revealed no clues as to why this clever and vibrant young woman, only four months away from graduating as a doctor, would just run off.

According to a Durst family spokesman, Bobby remained sedated and in seclusion at the Riverside Drive penthouse. He said, through the company flack, that he'd hired a private investigator, Jerry Martin, to help in the search for his wife. "He is completely distraught and is clinging to hope and praying that Kathie is alive," said the mouthpiece. "He loves her very much and is terribly worried."

While Bobby was playing the concerned husband, Kathie's distraught family was consumed with fear and grief.

"We're all praying," her tearful sister Mary Hughes told the newspapers. "We just want my sister back safe and sound and happy again," said Jim.

To Struk and Gibbons, some very troubling aspects were surfacing. First of all, Kathie's friends weren't buying into Bobby's "anguish." They were bombarding the cops with phone calls and visits demanding that they take a closer look at him.

"I think I was the most vocal," says Eleanor. "I told them that Bobby had killed Kathie and there were no ifs, ands or buts about it. Where others were more careful or treading water at that time, I never had any doubt that he played a part in her death. I had pleaded with her to leave him and come live with me, even though I knew that it wasn't really practical, since I was married with small children.

"I'd been very alarmed because she had told me that Bobby was taking Primal Scream Therapy, and he growled. I never heard him do it, but Kathie would say to me when she was on the phone, 'He's doing it now, can you hear him? He's growling now.' That made me very afraid for her safety. And then when she told me that she'd obtained some financial papers that could make trouble for the Durst Organization, I was even more scared for her."

Other friends like Gilberte, Kathy Traystman and Dr. Marion Watlington also told the investigators that in the weeks before she went missing, Kathie was convinced her life was in danger.

"I called the New York police," says Dr. Watlington. "I told them that Kathie was afraid, that she had told me she thought she was being followed and she was scared to be alone. She told me, and all her friends, that she was afraid that Bobby might do something to her. I told them about our last conversation, a few days before she went missing. 'If anything ever happens to me, don't let the bastard get away with it,' she said. When I heard she'd vanished, I knew instinctively he had done her in.

"The cop I spoke to sounded bored by the whole thing. He said: 'That's interesting, we'll get back to you. You are just one of the many who have phoned.' I was told, 'We'll be in touch,' but they never contacted me again."

Bobby had threatened Kathie, insisted her friends. She was afraid of him. Everyone knew he had a vile temper—hadn't he viciously kicked Peter Schwartz in the face and broken his cheekbone? They all knew that he was mentally and physically abusive towards his wife and that the violence had recently upped a notch. There was documented proof of that, they said. Just three weeks before she disappeared, on January 5, she had gone to Jacobi Hospital in the Bronx to seek treatment for bruises on her face and neck, inflicted, she had said, by her husband Robert Durst, during a domestic spat that had turned nasty. Check with the hospital if you don't believe us, said the pals.

With the chorus of Bobby's detractors becoming deafening, Struk and Gibbons began to take a closer look at his story. He was a cool customer, they thought. Why would any husband take nearly a week to report his wife missing unless he had something to hide? His excuse, that they'd sometimes gone a couple of days without talking, still didn't explain why she'd just get up and vanish without saying anything. And Mary Hughes swore Kathie called Bobby every single day, even when they'd lived apart. "As far as I know, she had no medical problems and no personal problems other than the day-to-day things that affect everyone," admitted Struk.

The cops then took a different tack. Where was the evidence that she had ever boarded the train at Katonah? After all, they hadn't been able to back up the claims by the Durst employees at the Riverside Drive building that they had seen her on the night of January 31 and again the next day. Detective Struk had circulated a police sketch of the man who had allegedly visited her late Sunday night; he'd been described as white, about 35 years old, with dark hair, an olive complexion and a mustache, of medium build and average height. The drawing had elicited not one call.

The red Mercedes was reportedly in its usual parking spot on Monday. If Bobby didn't get back into the city until 4:00 P.M., as he'd claimed, how did the car get there before he did?

They knew, because she'd rammed it in their faces that Gilberte Najamy had taken the same 9:17 P.M. from Katonah to New York on the following Sunday, February 7, exactly a week after Kathie's supposed journey. The small train was just two carriages long, with one car for smokers. Kathie was rarely seen without a cigarette in her hand, so Gilberte started in the smoking car. She showed a picture of the pretty blonde to every passenger, most of whom told her they were regular riders on the Sunday night train. Gilberte told the cops that not one person recognized her.

The N.Y.P.D. then turned to the New York state troopers for help. "We are assisting the New York City police in every way possible," Robert Lowell, a senior investigator, confirmed.

Let's check his phone, said one bright state cop. If Durst had made a call to Kathie at the penthouse from the South Salem house late Sunday night as he'd claimed, it would show up in his phone records. The call had never been made.

Well, it wasn't exactly from the house, Durst backtracked when Struk and Gibbons asked him to explain the discrepancy. He'd taken the dog for a walk and stopped at a pay phone on the way. The two case-hardened New York cops were skeptical. It had been a bitterly cold and snowy night, and the nearest pay phone was three miles from the house, right around the other side of the lake. Who in their right mind would take their dog out for a hike in such terrible weather?

To muddy the water even further, Durst's own family had yet a different version of events. They said that Bobby had told them that he'd called Kathie from a phone in a restaurant in South Salem. He'd given Mary a similiar story.

More than a week after Kathie vanished, Struk and

Gibbons finally headed upstate. They went to talk to Bill and Ruth Mayer, to find out what they knew about Kathie and Bobby Durst and to check out Bobby's claim that he had stopped by their house after dropping Kathie at the railroad station.

"Never happened," Bill Mayer told them flatly. Even more intriguing was Ruth Mayer's account of the blue light coming from the basement of the Dursts' otherwise unlit house. The Mayers repeated what the two cops had heard from half-a-dozen witnesses, that Kathie had also warned them that if she went missing to "suspect foul play."

"We told them absolutely everything—the blue light, the rest of the house in complete darkness, what she told us, you know, 'If anything happens to me, suspect foul play,' the financial documents . . . everything. I had no idea that Bob had lied to them about coming to my house. They asked me if he had been here, I said no," says Ruth.

The Mayers also told the two city cops how they, and the other neighbors on Hoyt Street, had gone out with their dogs and spent hours sweeping the woods, searching for Kathie, in case she'd fallen or taken ill or had an accident. "I had a dog at the time who roamed free and would have found anything. If she'd been dumped in the woods, I know my dog would have found her, but he didn't," she says.

"They went away and we never heard from them again. Bill and I began to wonder, what's happening here?" says Ruth. "They never even went into Durst's house. If they had, they may have found something, but they didn't. They just went to the entranceway and never searched the place. Why not?"

None of Ruth's account found its way into the police report.

Even more puzzling was what workers in Bobby's office at the Durst Organization told police. They had gotten collect calls from the New Jersey coast that first week in February, before he reported his wife missing. He often made collect calls to his office phone, the cops were told. Phone records showed that the calls were made from a laundry pay phone and a call box in a motel in the seaside town of Ship Bottom but they never were able to establish what Bobby Durst did during those four days before he contacted the police.

CHAPTER 8

THE TRAIL GOES COLD

DESPITE the high profile of the Dursts and the lurid head-lines in the local newspapers trumpeting, "Millionaire's Wife Missing" and "Hubby Posts 100G Reward," the New York police remained clueless as to what had happened to Kathie weeks after she'd seemingly fallen off the planet. Bobby could offer no explanation as to why his lovely young wife had simply vanished. He insisted that he had loved her and was just as baffled as the authorities by her disappearance. Like all married couples, they'd had their falling-outs and there were times when they'd been es-tranged over the last year or so, he admitted, but they had been happily living together in the months before she van-ished. "Bobby didn't kill Kathie," his friend, advertising honcho Nick Chavin told *The New York Times*. "He loved her."

The carefully constructed public image of Bobby as a caring, bereft husband was a crock, says Jim McCormack. To his way of thinking, his brother-in-law was a cold-hearted snake who couldn't be bothered to pretend to Kath-ie's grieving mother, or her sisters, that he felt any empathy for their pain.

"He didn't even have the decency to call my mom. He called me," Jim says. "I didn't know she was missing for four days. He called me that Thursday, the day before he finally went to the police. If she had just walked out, wouldn't her family be the first place you'd start looking?

"Gilberte put a lot of pressure on Bob. 'Where's Kath-ie, what's going on?' she kept asking. During that week she also put a lot of pressure on police up in Westchester

County and Bob was forced to file the report.

"My wife, Sharon, had just given birth to our first child, Elizabeth, ten days before, and Kathie had sent flowers to the hospital with a note saying how much she was looking forward to seeing us and the baby at grandma's 90th birthday. The party went ahead, but it was a dismal affair with most of us in tears," he remembers.

A few days later Jim heard that Bobby was disposing of his sister's belongings. In fact he crammed so much of her stuff down the garbage chute at her apartment on East 86th Street that it jammed the system and got him in trouble with the super. Then, incredibly, they discovered that a few days after she'd vanished, on February 4, before he had even reported her disappearance to the police, Bobby had shown two prospective women tenants around Kathie's bolt hole. "He was trying to rent it right away to save the $900 a month rent," says Jim.

Determined to find something to nail Bobby, Gilberte made it her mission to conduct frequent searches of the garbage at the South Salem house. For six months, she drove to the cottage every week and sorted through the trash. She uncovered more of Kathie's clothes, her unopened mail and notes written by Bobby. The Westchester D.A.'s office has asked her not to disclose the contents of the notes, but she told now-defunct *Talk* magazine, "If you needed to get rid of a body and you were a control freak like Bobby, you might want to make a checklist."

She got in touch with Jim McCormack and told him what she'd found. "Gilberte called me and said that Bobby was throwing Kathie's things out of the house at South Salem. Mary and I drove up there and confronted him. 'What's going on?' we asked. 'She's probably left me,' he told us, 'left me for some other son of a bitch.' We never saw him again."

When Gilberte told her she was going to Durst's house to dig up evidence, Eleanor Schwank urged her to check the garbage disposal. "I had this strong feeling that he had gotten rid of the body, and even though I knew intellectually that a garbage disposal would never be able to handle human bones, I just had this strong sense that she had been chopped up," she says.

"As soon as I heard that she was missing, I knew that he had killed her. That's why I was so adamant in the newspapers at the time in directly accusing Bob of murder."

Despite Eleanor's clearly inflammatory claims, there was never a lawsuit or even a legal letter from the Durst lawyers threatening to sue her if she didn't stop shouting from the rooftops that he had killed his wife.

Then Bobby started slinging some mud of his own. Changing his tune, he began to accuse his wife of using cocaine and had his lawyer hand over to investigators some coke he claimed he had found in their apartment. His new story went along the lines that she had become unhappy with her life and probably just ran away. "I think Kathie's alive," he said.

"At first he told us that they had had a good marriage. Then he told me she had difficulty with alcohol, drug issues and relationships outside the marriage," said Detective Struk.

Jim says that Seymour, who had just joined America's billionaires on *Forbes* magazine's 400 richest list, told a reporter that Kathie was shacked up with a lover someplace. If that was true, she'd gone into hiding with the boyfriend with only the clothes on her back and never took another cent out of her bank account. In short, it was not a feasible scenario, but it was incredibly hurtful to the McCormacks.

Then Bobby said that Kathie hung out with drug dealers, and one of them must have abducted her. Next he maintained that she dressed too flashily. He'd warned her about it, he told Marsha Kranes of the *New York Post.* "I used to tell her she dressed too nicely," he said. "I told her she attracted too much attention. If someone was looking for someone who looked wealthy, it would be her. She wore the diamond earrings everywhere, even to the hospital in the Bronx—not the safest place in the whole world," he said. Yet from all other accounts, Kathie was never a flashy dresser, and on the night she disappeared she was wearing jeans and a down coat.

Twenty years later, what Kranes remembers most vividly about covering the story was Bobby Durst's surprising affability. "He was very talkative," she says. "He's one of the few people I've ever encountered whose wife was the victim of a crime like this that you could call up and chat with him casually. I mean, he was very accessible right after she disappeared. He returned calls. I talked to him within a few days. I'd left a message and was stunned when he returned my call. I was just surprised that he was so willing to talk. I suspected him at the very outset, and that's why I was amazed he was chatting away."

He told Kranes that he was sure that Kathie hadn't run away. "We've had the same problems that most married people have," he said. "We've had our arguments and disagreements, but nothing new or unusual. There have been times when she has gotten angry and has stayed over at a friend's house for the night." What he didn't tell her was that Kathie had taken the apartment on East 86th Street because the nights she'd wanted to stay away from home were stretching into months as the marriage deteriorated.

He next spoke to the paper's Charles Lachman. "I think Kathie's alive," he repeated. "She must have run away. Maybe she suffered some sort of breakdown," he added helpfully. "She was doing badly in medical school and she was doing badly in our life. She was unhappy. All I want to do is to know that she's someplace and all right. I'm not trying to drag her back." He then told the reporter about his affair with Prudence Farrow, but insisted that Kathie had known about it all along, and maintained that at the time she disappeared, the fling had cooled to a friendship. "The last thing Prudence wanted to do was see me [when Kathie disappeared]," he said.

Then Susan Berman chimed in. She had been Bob's unofficial mouthpiece since his wife went missing, fielding phone calls and talking to the press. Kathie had been having difficulties with school, she claimed, she wasn't really up to it. She also had problems with drink and drugs. Yet the medical school told the police that although she had missed a few classes, she was a student in good standing and was fully expected to graduate in May with the rest of her class. What's more, friends of the couple also knew that for Bobby to accuse his wife of being a junkie was a joke. He was the one who was heavily into drugs, and had been since his student days. When they were first married, Kathie didn't touch them; it was Bobby who had turned her on to them, and some of the friends attributed his increasingly aggressive behavior to drugs.

A few weeks after Kathie vanished, Bobby showed up once again at the Mayers' door. "He came back up here and invited us out to dinner. I didn't want to go—but part of me wanted to see if I could find out anything," admits Ruth. "We went to the only restaurant around, it was called Alexander's back then, over on Route 35. Later it burned down. It was the same place we had dinner with Kathie the week before she vanished. It turned out be to a very uncomfortable night. Bob was creepy. He was charming, but he was creepy."

The conversation at the dinner table, not unnaturally, revolved around Kathie. The Mayers listened in disbelief as Bobby trotted out theory after implausible theory about what had befallen her. "He didn't know what happened, she must have amnesia, he was checking out the hospitals, and I'm sitting there thinking, yeah, sure. It was very, very scary," says Ruth.

While Susan was rallying behind Bobby by backing his attempt to assassinate Kathie's character, her next-door neighbor Stephen M. Silverman had moved away from Beekman Place and their stifling friendship. "I had to get some distance," he says. "They were good, fun times, but I had no privacy." He found new digs on the 24th floor at 62nd Street on Central Park West overlooking the park. "I took it to get away from Susan, in part—the fact that it was on a high floor is what really kept her away, though she did come to my housewarming party after having insisted that I send some guests down to the lobby to "hold her" and escort her upstairs.

"One of Susan's phobias was elevators. She wouldn't live above the fifth floor anywhere, and she wouldn't ride in an elevator above the fifth floor unless she had company," he says. "So when I heard of this apartment on the twenty-fourth floor, I thought, Yes!" They remained good friends, but no longer on a twenty-four-hour basis. Stephen says he never called Susan when Kathie Durst's disappearance hit the headlines even though he'd often partied with the couple. "To tell the truth," he says, "I was scared to. I was afraid of Robert Durst. He was scary and intimidating to be around. You were always waiting for him to lose it."

By March 1982, after six weeks had passed without a shred of evidence having surfaced as to Kathie's whereabouts, her family reached out to her father-in-law. There had been no contact between them, not even a solitary phone call of condolence. They requested a meeting with Seymour, to beg for his help. With his enormous wealth and power, they hoped he could pull some strings, pick up the phone and have the mayor or another of his connected acquaintances force the police to step up their lethargic search. "We called ahead," says Jim, "and were told he'd meet us at his home in the East 40s off Second Avenue.

"My mom, my sister Mary and her husband, Tom Hughes, and I were met at the front door by an employee and ushered up to a second-floor room. I remember being awestruck by the place. There were books everywhere, and old maps of New York City, all sorts of historical material. It was obvious he was a serious collector.

"We were shown into this large room which had a long polished table. Seymour was sitting at one end, we all sat around the other. We asked him for information, hoping that maybe the police had told him things they'd not shared with us. But he was diffident, he came out with non-answers, he showed no sympathy to us. He just shrugged and said, 'I don't know,' to most of our questions. 'What can I do about it?' was his attitude. Then one of his other sons, Tom, who'd just arrived in town from Los Angeles, came in to the room wearing a long trench coat. 'This meeting is over,' he said." As they went back down the stairs, their hearts heavy, the McCormacks realized that the 69-year-old patriarch considered them no longer family, now that his daughter-in-law had vanished off the face of the earth. "That was the last time I saw anyone in the Durst family except for Bobby," says Jim.

By April 1982, Bobby had stopped talking to Detective Struk and his team. The investigation, it seemed to Jim McCormack, was all over the place, there was no sense of direction. The family kicked up a fuss when the N.Y.P.D. wanted to move the case over to the Missing Persons File, "where it would have died; those missing persons are never found," he says. It ended up there nevertheless.

Next, the police began scouring reports of unidentified bodies state by state. "We were told that there were remains found in Vermont, that there was a patient discovered in Massachusetts General Hospital that Bob was somehow connected to, another in Pennsylvania." One source claims that police raked through ashes in the basement of a Manhattan building after getting a tip that Kathie's body had been incinerated in the furnace. "There were a lot of sightings, near-sightings and leads. None of it panned out," says Jim.

Sergeant Thomas O'Brady, second in command of the 20th Precinct's Detective Squad confirmed that they'd received calls from Massachusetts to West Babylon, Long Island, and from several hotels and hospitals in the city. "We are checking every one," he said. Two dozen detectives and cops searched Long Island after getting tips, and they even brought in a psychic who had been useful in other cases. She told them that Kathie was on a boat in warm water and was sick to her stomach.

Struk and Gibbons assured the McCormacks that they

were doing everything they could, but in months the case
went cold. The N.Y.P.D. never really challenged the prem-
ise that Kathie had disappeared from Manhattan, the house
at South Salem was never searched, Truesdale Lake was
never dredged. The official view came from Michael Struk,
a veteran of some two hundred homicides. "There were
always a lot of unanswered questions, but we had to move
on, because I did not have the luxury of working one case,"
he said.

The authorities' inability or unwillingness to punch
damaging holes in Bobby's story tortured Kathie's grieving
family. To the McCormacks it looked like the only person
the cops were listening to was the very man they were sure
wasn't telling the truth. "The police took Bob's word for
everything" says Jim. "That she did make it back to New
York, that he did make the call from the telephone booth,
even though it was a cold, rainy night while he was walking
the dog. That dog, Igor, he couldn't have walked that far.
He'd never have made it; he was a short-legged Norwegian
elkhound, a fat little thing.

"Before Igor, they had a series of huskies. They owned
four or five of them which either died or simply ran off
after relatively short periods of time with Bob and Kathie,"
says Jim. He remembers being disturbed by the way Bob
treated the animals. "He was always teasing the dogs, pulling their ears, etc. That in itself may seem innocent to some,
but I perceived it more as a lack of affection normally associated with pet ownership. He did seem to be better with
Igor.

"They took his word for all this stuff. . . . as profes-
sionals, police officers are trained to question everything,"
he says. "Why didn't they go up to Westchester and retrace
everything he claimed happened starting at Gilberte's Connecticut house? In theory, she could have been a suspect,
and so could anyone else at her party. There's just no way
Kathie would have taken off and wouldn't let Gilberte
know, or her mother or somebody, where she was or that
she was okay or that she had to leave."

Kathie's mother was inconsolable. "My mom would sit in Kathie's old room and cry," says Jim. The family tried to keep interest in their case going, but by spring Bobby had totally stopped cooperating with the investigation and had moved out of the Riverside Drive penthouse to a new apartment in a Durst-owned building at 441 East 43rd Street. Although he'd never been named as a suspect, he'd hired top criminal defense attorney Nicholas Scoppetta to keep any would-be inquisitors at bay. Scoppetta went on to be the New York City Commissioner for Children's Services during the eight years of the Rudy Giuliani administration, and in December 2001 was named New York's Fire Commissioner by Mayor Michael Bloomberg.

His appearance troubled Jim. "He was of the top order, hired by well-heeled people suspected of crimes. He became Bob's spokesperson," he says. "Why would you lawyer up and hire a criminal defense attorney if you've gone to a police precinct five days after your wife went missing and you're concerned?"

With the months passing and the case at a virtual dead end, Kathie's family's lawyer tried to force Bobby onto the witness stand. In early 1983, he raised a civil action in Surrogate Court before Judge Marie Lambert, to have Kathie's mom named temporary conservator of her estate. In a civil case, a defendant can't hide behind an attorney and refuse to answer any questions put to him. If he does, he can be held in contempt. A similar strategy would later be used by the family of Nicole Brown Simpson to have O. J. Simpson declared fiscally liable for her murder.

During the hearing, which was held exactly a year and a day after she vanished, Kathie's sister Mary lashed out in an affidavit: "The questionable circumstances surrounding my sister's disappearance and her husband's behavior and reactions following this event strongly suggests that my sister may have been murdered and that Robert Durst is either directly responsible for her death or privy to information concerning her disappearance." He'd told too many conflicting stories about that night, she said.

Mary also swore that "Mr. Durst was often hostile and even violent toward Kathleen." She then described, in cold legal terms, the Christmas Day outburst that had so shocked the McCormacks: "At one point, Mr. Durst told my sister that he wanted to leave; she expressed a wish to stay; whereupon, he grabbed her by the hair and pulled so hard that a large chunk of her hair came out in his hand." She also accused him of disposing of Kathie's belongings without consulting even her mother, and swore that she had found the jewelry which Bobby had told police his wife was wearing the night she disappeared.

"My sister customarily wore a pair of diamond earrings, a watch, a wedding band and two gold chains. When she disappeared, her husband told the police, she had been wearing this jewelry. In March of 1982, I was looking through my sister's possessions, at her husband's request, and I found all the jewelry in a suede container in her drawer." Mary also charged that Bobby had refused to take a lie detector test.

The family was anxious for him to submit to the test because of the inconsistencies in his version of events, she said. Bobby had told the police he'd put his wife on the train and called her at the Riverside Drive penthouse at 11:15 P.M. Yet when she had asked him why he thought Kathleen had returned to the apartment, he had never mentioned the phone call, telling her instead that when he'd gone home on February 1, "he'd found cigarettes in the ashtray, an empty soda bottle and a general atmosphere which suggested that someone had been at the apartment."

He'd also told her that after dropping Kathie off at the station, he had gone out for dinner, then stopped at a pub called Tatters and called his wife from a phone booth in the bar. "He made no mention of the [drink with] the neighbors, the dog or his three-mile walk in the rain, which were central to the story he gave the police," she said in the affidavit. He also didn't mention that an official at the medical school had called him asking him where Kathie was, because she hadn't been at classes all week. Mary also said that Scoppetta had told her in an April 29, 1982, phone call, that his job was to insulate his client from police "harassment," and since he'd been retained he'd refused to allow the cops near Bobby. He refused to let Bobby take the lie detector test, saying "My advice would be that Mr. Durst has no obligation to submit to any sort of test of that kind."

Kathie's mother's affidavit said that she sued to prevent him from dissipating her daughter's estate after he refused to give a complete accounting of Kathie's property. She swore that the marriage was "beset by difficulties and violent quarrels," and claimed he'd even tried to cheat her out of the little money she had. "Kathleen told me that Mr. Durst had forged her signature on some stock transfer documents in an attempt to sell stocks which were held in her name. After Kathleen's disappearance, we were advised that Mr. Durst's attorneys, Paskus, Gordon and Hyman, had written to D.H. Blair Investors Corp. and instructed my daughter's stockbroker to direct any correspondence concerning her investments to their office. The representative at Blair refused to follow these instructions which, she said, were 'highly irregular.' " She added that his attorneys had quit over the matter.

The super and other people at the East 86th Street Durst-owned building where Kathie had her bolt hole, confirmed that Bobby had jammed the trash chute with items from her apartment that he was throwing out.

The court also heard that in May 1981 Kathie had retained attorney Dale Smolen Ragus to help her negotiate a financial settlement with Bobby. The lawyer's affidavit charged that Kathie had been treated by Dr. Leslie Hain at Jacobi Hospital on January 5 for bruising sustained after her husband punched her, and that Kathie feared for her "physical safety, indeed her life."

The judge also read a letter from Bobby to Karen Hogan at the Croyden Hotel. In it, he asked permission to lease Kathie's apartment to Durst employee Ilene Weiss and a friend of hers. He would continue paying the $952.18 a month rent, he said in the note, which was printed on Durst Organization notepaper. It was signed Robert A. Durst and was dated February 4, the day before he reported his wife missing.

But the hearing turned into a David and Goliath battle, only the McCormacks were on the losing side. "Bob didn't show up," says Jim. "Six of his lawyers turned up instead." The legal team produced affidavits of their own, including one from Susan Berman in which she claimed that Kathie had "severe emotional problems, abused alcohol and was hysterical about medical school."

Bobby's lead counsel, former Judge Millard Midonick called Mary's claims "vicious and scurrilous," and railed, "There's no murder involved here." At a subsequent hearing Bobby's lawyers then accused Mary of demanding a rent reduction and then of trying to extort $100,000 from him, first over the phone and then in person. It was an unsubstantiated claim that she instantly refuted. "I don't want or need his money," she told the court. She had a good job in advertising, her husband was a city fireman, they had an apartment in the city and a home in Long Island and anyway, at no time did she she talk to Bobby alone. She had a witness with her both times.

The case dragged on for over a year. To Judge Lambert it was plain that the animosity between Bobby and his in-laws was so deep-seated that neither side could be trusted to act impartially. On February 24, 1983 she handed over Kathie's estate to the temporary care of the Public Administrator of the County Court of New York. She also threw out the McCormacks' request that Bobby be deposed and with it, their last chance of forcing Bobby to testify under oath about his wife's disappearance evaporated. "We had our one lawyer and the thing went nowhere. We were all very disheartened and obviously depressed. And we didn't have deep enough pockets to fight him," says Jim. "We all had young families at the time and had to get on with our lives, had to earn that day's living."

What was truly astounding was Bobby's contention

that despite his millions, Kathie's estate was a modest $50,000. And in that sum he included the Mercedes that Jim McCormack maintains was his, her few pieces of jewelry, some shares in the phone company (what is now Verizon) and a bank account. He wanted expenses incurred in the effort to find her and the cost of any litigation was to come out of her estate. Bobby's argument was "Fight me on this or anything else to do with Kathie, and her estate will be depleted."

Not only had Bobby ignored the proceedings, the gaggle of lawyers that he hired to shield him was a mere indication of how he would dodge and run. On the advice of his attorney Bobby issued a terse statement: "I am not privy to any information concerning Kathie's disappearance which I have not disclosed to Kathie's family, to the police department and to those, who, at my own expense, I have engaged to investigate her disappearance. I never assaulted Kathie or caused her any physical harm."

Jim had all but given up when he received a strange call. The voice on the other end claimed to be a private eye from Nassau County in Long Island. He told Jim he was looking to collect the $100,000 reward for finding Kathie and thought he had a plan that might work. Would Jim meet with him?

With Mary, who lived with Tom in a Durst building on East 51st Street, he met the detective at a little restaurant on the Upper East Side. Over dinner, the gumshoe revealed his plan: He was going to abduct Robert Durst, lock him in a basement somewhere and pump him full of truth serum to force him to reveal what he knew.

"Mary and I looked at the guy in disbelief," says Jim. "I said to him 'Wait a minute, you want us to help you commit a crime to solve another crime? I'm sorry, but we are not going to do that.' And we left. That was the end of it, but later I heard that a similar offer had been made to someone else, completely independent of us. When I think back now, I'm sure we were being set up. Thank God we had the presence of mind to say no. We were emotionally distraught over Kathie, but still, you just can't do a thing like that."

Jim, cleaned out of money and trying to support his wife and new baby, was forced to cry uncle. He couldn't fight the mighty Dursts, and he was an emotional mess. He'd be driving on the highway and the tears would flow. Sometimes he could barely see out the windshield for the tears coursing down his face. He'd pull over to the hard shoulder and wait till the wracking sobs subsided. "I couldn't stop crying," he says. "I couldn't stop thinking of her, the stress she endured that made her have to get out of the house that last day. And then she had to go back to get her things for school, she had to get herself organized for the next morning. I wonder about her last hours."

Out of money and time, and disheartened with the Dursts' lack of concern and the lukewarm police response, the McCormacks simply had to get back to raising their families and hope that soon the investigation would turn up a clue, or a witness would come forward.

"I don't think there is a day in my life I haven't thought about Kathie. But gradually, it isn't as pressing," says Jim. "I think I always had the feeling that somehow, someday we would have an answer. We prayed for her in church every Sunday, always lit a candle for her."

After lying low for several months, by the beginning of 1984 Bobby was back behind his desk at the Durst Organization, making money and keeping his mouth shut. From the sale of just one building the family owned on East 55th, he pocketed his quarter share of the $30 million profits and promptly picked up some choice property in Dallas.

CHAPTER 9

LIFE WITHOUT KATHIE

ALSO keeping quiet except to vociferously defend "sweet Bobby" against any doubters, was Susan. Flush with the success of *Easy Street,* she sold her Beekman Place studio, bought a flashy convertible into which she packed her belongings and headed across the country to storm Hollywood. Selling the movie option on her book had prompted her to try her hand at screenwriting. She settled into a small, wood-shingled bungalow in Benedict Canyon.

She wanted to go back to her roots, to reinvent herself in Los Angeles where she had a lot of friends. She had also wanted to be near Uncle Chickie, whose high-roller lifestyle had fallen victim to poverty and old age.

It was a frightening brush with street crime that had been the deciding factor in Susan's leaving New York, says Sandy West. "She had been doing well until she got mugged. She was on her way home one night and was just about a block from her apartment when someone grabbed her bag and stole her money. It really terrified her—nothing like that had ever happened in L.A. It was right after that she decided to move."

But Susan found that the overnight success in Hollywood was more elusive than she had envisaged. "L.A. is a tough town—and Susan just wouldn't play the game," says Sandy. "I was working as a realtor at the time and came down to Los Angeles for a conference. I had been very impressed with one of the speakers, a publicist who gave this real rah-rah, 'Aren't I wonderful?' speech. I was telling Susan about it. 'Yeah, well,' she sighed, 'it is always possible in Hollywood to sleep your way to the top.' And there was no doubt in my mind that the comment was based on hard facts. She always had the inside scoop on everyone."

But although fame and fortune were proving more difficult than she'd expected, there was one consolation. She had fallen in love. A few weeks after arriving in Hollywood she bumped into a handsome young man in the script register line at the Writers Guild. She'd been flattered when he'd recognized her from her picture on the jacket of *Easy Street*. As they waited to copyright screenplays they had written, they swapped bios. He told her that he had grown up in Las Vegas. Even better, to Susan's ears, although he went by the improbable name of Mister Margulies, his given name was David. His father had been such a fan of Davie "The Jew" Berman, he told her, that he'd been named for him. To Susan that made him irresistible.

Within weeks, Mister moved into the Benedict Canyon house. If she had one reservation, it was that her 25-year-old lover confessed to having been a heroin addict. But he swore to her that his junkie days were over, he was clean.

In early 1984, she called Bobby. "I'm in love," she told him, "and I'm going to get married in June. I want you to be there, can you come?"

Over the next couple of months, Susan planned her dream wedding. She pored over menus, ordered flowers, booked a rabbi, picked out her dress and scoured her address book making sure that nobody was forgotten. Invitations went out first to Raleigh and Deni and her other surviving blood relations. Susan had always kept in touch with her mother's cousin, Lorelei Hjermstad, and after she died, with Lorelei's daughter Peggy, and with her cousins on Gladys's side of the family, Tom Patton, Sr., and Tom Patton, Jr.

"The wedding was exactly what she had fantasized about since she was a little girl," says Deni. "It was at the Bel Air Hotel, because that's where my parents were married—Davie Berman had picked up the tab—and my mother had this saying, 'When you fall in love with the man you want to marry, is he good enough to take to the

Young, beautiful, and dreaming of becoming a doctor: Kathie Durst celebrating her graduation from nursing school in 1978.
(*McCormack Family Photo*)

A fed up–looking Bobby Durst around the time his marriage with Kathie was foundering.
(*McCormack Family Photo*)

Kathie Durst, seen here in a 1975 photo (*New York Post/REXUSA*), grew up the baby of a big Irish-American family in this modest New Hyde Park, Long Island, home. (*Onnie McIntyre*)

Across the tracks . . . Bobby Durst's childhood was wealthier but a lot less happy. When he was seven, he saw his deranged mother plunge to her death from the roof of the family mansion in Scarsdale. (*Onnie McIntyre*)

Years later, Bobby and Kathie are pictured at her mother's home during the 1980 family Christmas gathering. After dinner Bobby wanted to leave; Kathie wasn't ready. Kathie's brother vividly recalled that's when Durst dragged her out the door by her hair. (*McCormack Family Photo*)

Bobby and Kathie's country "cottage" in South Salem, NY, where they were staying on the last day she was seen, January 31, 1982. Durst told police he dropped his wife off at the Katonah commuter rail station to catch the 9:17 P.M. train to the city. (*Onnie McIntyre*)

Did Kathie ever make it to the Riverside Drive penthouse apartment? (*Onnie McIntyre*)

Jim McCormack, Kathie's big brother, quickly became convinced that she never got out of South Salem alive. He says that her family soon came to doubt Bobby Durst's version of the events surrounding Kathie's disappearance.
(*New York Post /REXUSA*)

Mafia princess Susan Berman, Durst's college buddy—and some say confessor—stuck loyally by him. The only child and heiress to Las Vegas gangster Dave Berman's legacy, she was killed execution style in her Los Angeles home. Her body was discovered on Christmas Eve 2000, shortly after Westchester County, NY, authorities reopened Kathie's case.
(*Mary Ellen Mark*)

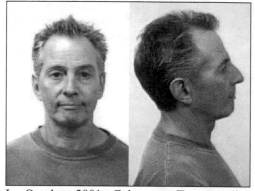

In October 2001, Galveston, Texas, police arrested what they thought was a down-on-his-luck drifter named Robert Durst and charged him with the murder and dismemberment of his eccentric neighbor, Morris Black. No one imagined he would make bail. But the "drifter" turned out to be the heir to a multimillion dollar New York real estate fortune. After posting bail, Durst skipped town.
(*Galveston Police Department*)

Bobby Durst claimed he killed 72-year-old Morris Black in self-defense. This November 19, 1997, mug shot of Black was taken after he'd been arrested for threatening to blow up a Charleston utility company over a disputed $50 bill. (*South Carolina Police Department*)

Morris Black's long-estranged brothers hired Houston private detective Bobbi Bacha to find out what happened to him . . . and to his head, which was still missing.
(*Bobbi Sue Bacha/Blue Moon Investigations*)

Bacha put her team of investigators to work in Galveston's harbor, along the stretch of beach where Morris Black's body parts had washed up in trash bags. They were looking for his head but the search came up empty.
(*Bobbi Sue Bacha/Blue Moon Investigations*)

Multimillionaire fugitive Robert Durst—after police captured him stealing a sandwich from a rural Pennsylvania convenience store. (*Colonial Regional Police Department*)

Kathie Durst's disappearance remains a mystery. She's seen here in the fall of 1975 with the couple's Norwegian Elk Hound, Igor, at the Durst family country home in Katonah. Bobby told police that he took Igor for a 3-mile walk the night Kathie vanished, then called her from a pay phone. The temperature that night was in the bone-chilling teens. (*McCormack Family Photo*)

Bel Air?' She chose everyone on the guest list: her best friends, the people who were closest to her, the people she had adopted as her family."

The wedding took place on the last Saturday in June. It was a late afternoon ceremony, followed by a sit-down dinner. "Susan was a beautiful bride, she wore a gorgeous white dress, she had flowers and a veil—the whole bit," says Deni. "I stood up for her, and her friend from college, Barbara Goff, was her matron of honor." Hollywood movie producer Bob Evans (*Chinatown, Marathon Man, Urban Cowboy* and *Wag the Dog*) gave the toast and called her "the most seductive woman I've ever met." Bobby Durst gave her away.

"It was a particularly fun day," Sandy remembers. "My daughter Alexandra is her godchild and Susan had called to apologize for not having her as a flower girl because under the chuppah, she wanted all Jewish people. I told her that was fine. Bede Roberts's little daughter was the flower girl and her son Sam was the ring bearer. It was a very Jewish wedding. We danced Jewish dances and sang traditional Jewish songs. And as all brides do, Susan glowed." She also picked up the bill.

Hillary Johnson flew out to Los Angeles to watch her friend tie the knot for the first time at 39. "It was very lavish and very beautiful," she remembers. "It was your classic, traditional, very expensive Bel Air wedding with a huge banquet, three hundred guests and people from every part of her life."

With the money that remained from the movie rights to *Easy Street*, and the proceeds from the sale of her apartment in New York, she bought a larger house in Brentwood, down the block from the townhouse where in 1995, Nicole Brown Simpson and her waiter friend Ron Goldman, would be stabbed to death.

But Susan's marital bliss was to be short-lived. "Mister was an extremely bright young man. But he was an extremely complicated person," says Hillary. "She used her considerable contacts in Hollywood to get him writing assignments and work on screenplays. I think he probably had a lot of talent, because Susan wouldn't have been attracted to him if he hadn't been extremely intelligent and talented. This was all part of the mix for her."

She had found out almost immediately after they'd swapped vows that Mister had lied to her. He was still a doper and most days was strung out on smack. Susan was fanatical about drugs—she would have nothing to do with them. After six harrowing months, the marriage was over.

Miserable and humiliated, she poured out her heart to "wonderful" Bobby, the one man in her life she could rely on. She turned to him again when, two years later, Mister took his last fix and died of a heroin overdose. Susan was distraught. Although they'd divorced, she'd harbored hopes that they could be reconciled if only he could kick his destructive habit. She convinced herself that somehow Mister's fate had gotten mixed up with her own. "Did he meet the doom meant for me?" she wrote. "Is there a curse on Vegas parents and children?"

Near demented with guilt and grief, she had another nervous breakdown. In a bizarre twist, she nearly ended her own life in the same way that Bernice Durst had taken hers: she clambered onto a Los Angeles roof and threatened to throw herself off. According to *New York* magazine, psychiatrist, Barbara Stabiner, was called and managed to coax her to safety by foreseeing a great future for her in the tarot cards.

While Susan was trying to cope with the death of her ex-husband, Kathie's friends kept up their campaign to keep her unsolved disappearance in the news, yet despite the accusations they made to any passing reporter that Bobby Durst had killed her, no one seemed to be listening.

"We tried hard to keep the case alive, but the Dursts are a very powerful family," says Eleanor. "I never had any doubts that Bobby was responsible and I was getting very frustrated. It speaks volumes for Kathie that she had so many friends who would not let this case die, who were speaking out for her and were willing to go to any lengths to resolve it. Gilberte spent a fortune on private investigators, but there was just no break, and we were limited in our financial assets while battling millions and millions of dollars."

Eleanor claims that Kathie's friends' phones may have been tapped. Listening devices back in the early eighties were not nearly as sophisticated as they are now—they tended to tip off the subject of the surveillance with the eerie echo and unexplained clicks. In Eleanor's case, there was so much activity on the line that she stopped discussing anything about the case except in person.

With no arrest in sight, Gilberte resolved to keep her own tabs on Bobby, to dog him for the rest of his life, if necessary, and to make sure he knew she was watching. Every time he moved to a new house, she'd phone him and hang up. She'd call on his neighbors and leave the message: "Tell Bobby that Gilberte was here." She became so obsessed with Kathie's disappearance that it would ruin her own life.

But Gilberte Najamy's vow to be a thorn in Bobby's side didn't seem to cramp his style. He had seemingly put his missing wife out of his mind and resumed his life. It was as if she had never existed. Despite his professed disdain for the real estate business and contrary to his father's earlier misgivings, he had inherited the Durst flair for making money after all. For the next decade his genes took over from his inclinations. He no longer hung around clubs and he dropped most of his partying pals. His new closet contained suits, although not the conservative Brooks Brothers three-piece versions worn by his colleagues, and he transformed himself into a major player, an accomplished wheeler-dealer who pulled off several major real estate coups in New York and Texas worth millions of dollars. He not only made money buying and selling existing properties, he drummed up new business all the time trying to outsmart his ambitious younger brother. The passing years had only increased their mutual loathing. The only vestige of the old Bobby that remained was his dope; he clung to it like a security blanket. And it never occurred to him that he, as the oldest and the heir, would not be the obvious choice to take over the company when his father retired.

In just two generations since Joseph Durst stepped off the boat at Ellis Island, the Durst Organization had acquired some of the choicest buildings in New York. By the 1940s, Joseph had been joined in the business by his three sons, Seymour, Roy and David, but it was Seymour who was the quickest learner. Soon Joseph left the bread-and-butter operations to his college-educated heir, who once said, "I've spent most of my life buying buildings and canceling leases and negotiating to get tenants out." Seymour was known as a man of his word, and for a reluctance to part with cash.

With the company's dominance of midtown secured by his father, Seymour turned his attention to the largely underdeveloped area west of Fifth Avenue. If Joseph had lived by the rule "Don't buy anything you can't walk to," his other motto could have been "Patience." Buy a vacant lot, a property that could be torn down, and wait: sooner or later it would turn a nice profit. In the meantime, the existing renters can still provide a reasonable return for the investment. Timing is everything, he intoned; you can always chuck the tenants out later.

When his father died in 1974, Seymour took over an empire that had accumulated ten acres of prime Manhattan commercial real estate throughout the previous decade; it already owned and operated sixty residential apartment buildings. He also ventured into the world of philanthropy. Appalled by the woeful public education system and mindful of the privileged upbringing his own four children enjoyed, he looked for a way to parlay some of his growing wealth into a program that would benefit the city's youth. In partnership with financier Irving Khan, he set up the

New York City Job and Career Center to provide job training and career advice to school dropouts.

In the early seventies Seymour began to get involved with the long-term redevelopment of 42nd Street and Times Square. It had been years since the intersection dubbed "the Crossroads of the World" was the pride of the city; its reputation as the mecca of drug dealing and vice had scared away everyone except perpetrators and the most reckless tourists. It had degenerated into a seedy clutch of peep shows, X-rated massage parlors, raunchy video stores, and live sex shows. Whores openly plied their trade, watched from doorways and parked cars by their evil-looking pimps.

Seymour embarked on a buying binge. Quietly he bought up every store and lot that became vacant, amassing some eighty-two properties on one block of 42nd Street alone. At the time, no other developer was interested in investing money in the dubious area, so he drew up short leases for existing tenants and built new stores to rent out, until the market would catch up with the area's potential.

Many of his tenants were the very pornographers that were bringing such disrepute to the strip. At one point, the then Mayor of New York, Abe Beame, accused him of making the flesh industry possible. Seymour shot back that his organization had already closed down over 100 pornography shops and it was the city's own bylaws that made storekeepers who peddled filth difficult to evict.

Throughout the eighties he was heavily involved with the proposed multibillion-dollar rehab. Other companies flocked to the drawing board eager to be part of the resurrection, but when Seymour got a look at the redevelopment plans, he was against them. For ten years, he fought the city and the zoning regulations every step of the way. But by the end of the decade, a more acceptable future had been drawn up for the area. The city put the merchants of sleaze on notice that it intended to take back Times Square and the streets surrounding it from the vice peddlers, and Seymour was in a prime position to sell, build and reap the vast profits.

Bobby, who had never quite seen himself as a realtor, found himself caught up in the sheer scale of his father's project, enjoying the increased visibility that came with the company's higher profile. With his wife no longer around, and as the heir to the Durst fortune, he'd become one of the most desirable "bachelors" in town, a catch in anyone's book.

He had a close but intensely loyal inner circle of friends that included realtor Douglas Oliver, advertising honcho Nick Chavin, his childhood friend Stewart Altman and his wife Emily, and Julie Baumgold, none of whom could believe he had anything to do with Kathie's disappearance. He was godfather to the Altmans' son and Emily once described him as "the most kindhearted person I've ever met."

Bobby always had plenty of girlfriends. According to *Vanity Fair* magazine, every year he and his buddy Oliver took off with their current girlfriends in tow for the ritzy Mediterranean resort of Saint-Tropez which had been put on the jet-setters' map by its most famous resident, sixties sex kitten Brigitte Bardot. While Bobby and Kathie were together, Oliver was married to Rachel Hirschfeld, daughter of the parking garage magnate Abe Hirschfeld who spent two years at the Sullivan Correctional Facility for offering $75,000 as a down payment to a hit man to whack his former business partner, Stanley Stahl. A few days after his father's July 26, 2002 release, Rachel was given police protection when her name surfaced on a new hit list that the 83-year-old tycoon had allegedly drawn up while still behind bars. Authorities suspect that he mailed a $109,000 check to suspected drug dealer Larry Davis, who was accused of shooting six New York police officers in 1986. Hirschfeld has denied the allegations. Rachel, who converted to Christianity from Judaism after her divorce from Oliver and is studying to be a lawyer, once sued her father claiming that he bilked her out of several million dollars in a real estate deal. One girlfriend who made the trip to France was a Manhattan real estate broker named Debrah

Lee Charatan, whom he had met in 1988 at a Christmas party in the Rainbow Room. She had just extricated herself from a failed marriage to a New York lawyer named Bradley Berger. Bobby was restless, unsettled and had as many addresses as he had women at his disposal. And the vengeful Gilberte noted every move.

He had hung on to the stone cottage on Truesdale Lake and visited it often in the years after Kathie's disappearance. Some years later he started to bring "Debbie" with him, and introduced her to the Mayers. She had a little boy named Ben. "My younger daughter is now 18, so Debbie's son must be 17," says Ruth Mayer. "She was here quite a few times and there wasn't a lot of kid stuff at his house, and with two kids we had lots, so we used to tell them, 'Come over and let Ben use the swing set.' Debbie was really sweet. But when she and her son came over I had to put a muzzle on my older daughter Sharon not to blurt something about Kathie.

"I assumed that they had gotten married and moved to the West Coast, because I never heard any more about him after the house was sold," she says. "I thought, well, Kathie has been missing for seven years, so I guess he can declare her missing and get married to this one. In my mind that's what happened."

But Bobby hadn't slunk off to the West Coast. He'd begun to enjoy his position as the prospective boss while his eccentric father obsessed over the country's growing financial problems. For years, Seymour had written letters to *The New York Times* about the nation's precarious finances, in particular, its rapidly accumulating debt. America's fiscal responsibilities were no different from any other business, he lectured; it had to balance its books.

To make sure that people understood that the country was running up huge bills on credit which could result in its destiny falling into the hands of ruthless international bankers, he invented the National Debt Clock, a 25' by 10' flashing sign that toted up the total debt second by second from data supplied by the U.S. Treasury, and calculated each family's individual share. The staggering numbers, he reckoned, would draw public fury over the scandal of the red ink on the nation's balance sheet and shame legislators into doing something about it. The device was erected in 1989 on the side of a building on West 42nd Street at the corner of Avenue of the Americas, just up the block from Times Square.

"My father's purpose in setting it up was to show the increase in debt and to get people aware of the size of the debt and how it was growing," explained Douglas Durst.

For the next eleven years, the flashing figures sent chills down the spines of New Yorkers as they rushed to their desks in midtown high-rises, barely able to comprehend the evidence that showed that the country was growing poorer at the rate of $13,000 per second. By the mid-nineties, the debt accelerated so quickly that the clock became a blur of lights. How much Seymour's one-man campaign contributed to the reversal in government policy is debatable, but after the Clinton administration announced that $100 billion in debt had been paid off, on September 7, 2000, the clock was put into semiretirement and covered with a red, white and blue drape. It was revived in the summer of 2002 during the stock market plunge.

In 1990, Bobby put the South Salem home up for sale and moved into luxurious new digs at 923 Fifth Avenue with Debrah Lee. She was smarting from the collapse of her first foray into the real estate business and had begun to revive her career, starting another company registered as Debrah Lee Charatan Realty. The daughter of a Brooklyn butcher, she was reportedly thrilled with the swank address, but Bob felt stifled by the arrangement and moved out nine months later. They never lived together again.

Debrah moved down the street to 860 Fifth Avenue and also acquired another enviable piece of real estate in Surf Side Lane, Bridgehampton, on Long Island's gold coast, the summer playground of moneyed New Yorkers. Bobby was a frequent visitor.

But though he seemed to have successfully buried the

ghost of Kathie—only her still-grieving family and friends even talked about the case anymore—he was becoming odd, unapproachable even, around his family, friends and colleagues. At work he grew noticeably moody and unpredictable. Although he attended Durst Organisation board meetings regularly, he'd sit sullenly staring into space and contributing nothing. Despite regular sessions with a therapist, it seemed the only emotion he displayed was rage.

Not surprisingly, these reports of Bobby's weird behavior filtered back to his father who had gone into semiretirement in 1992, but still kept a finger on the pulse of his company. On one hand, Seymour understood and sympathized with his oldest son: he had been through some tragic experiences, the suicide of his mother when he was a child, and then the disappearance of the wife he had sincerely loved, at least in the beginning. But the old man knew that, in business, especially at the rarefied level of top management, where millions, billions of dollars could depend on a handshake, getting along with people was essential. He himself had built a solid reputation for courtesy and reasonableness, even when he was planning to toss a recalcitrant tenant out on his ear.

As Seymour weighed up accounts from his clients and employees that Bobby would sit at business meetings for hours and never utter a syllable, in 1994, he issued a statement which surprised no one else in the Durst Organization, but stunned Bobby. He made Douglas President and CEO, and relegated his heir to the lesser position of Chairman of the Board; in effect, he'd be Doug's number two.

Bobby was blindsided. He'd been betrayed, knifed in the back by his own father, no doubt egged on by his ambitious and conniving younger brother! Upon receiving the news, he walked out of his office without a word.

The loss of face was unbearable for Bobby, but to his brother-in-law, he had it coming. "He didn't have much self-control, and his father, understanding that, didn't favor him with business responsibilities," says Jim McCormack. "He had a job with the company, a kind of 'Here, take your check and get out of here' job. Douglas was more cast in the mold of Seymour. One of my kid sisters described Douglas as 'evil.'

"You couldn't trust Bob. I found that out when I read Kathie's private letters after she disappeared. She wrote: 'From the time of our marriage . . . Bob told me that he had a doctorate degree in economics from U.C.L.A., Berkeley. While traveling across the country three months after coming back to New York City he said he really didn't have a degree, but not to tell anyone, especially his family.' He lived his own lie and had his own agendas.

"His personal character, or lack thereof, hinges on a studied practiced deception," says Jim. "The sad thing is, given the set of circumstances he was born into, he was living the life."

According to the *New York Post*, Bobby plotted a bizarre revenge. He would have a child with Debrah Lee, not because he was madly in love with her or because her biological clock was ticking or because he wanted to become a father: he devised the plan to spite his family and hit them where it hurt the most—their wallets.

The two had allegedly schemed to use a baby as a way of extracting more money from the Dursts. Forty years before, his father had set up a trust fund for Bobby which paid him an allowance of $3 million a year. But the trust would die along with him—unless he had a child. In that case, the family would be forced to keep paying out the $3 million for the duration of that child's life.

The couple drew up legal papers, but they couldn't agree about who would control the fund, claimed the *Post*. Bobby wanted his child to have at least 51% of its fortune, Debrah Lee demanded that she would have sole say-so. Then he thought up an alternative way to annoy his family—he'd adopt Debrah Lee. Both schemes were eventually abandoned, said the *Post*.

With access to plenty of money, an inherited knack for pulling off lucrative deals and harboring a grudge the size of Texas, Bobby began a nomadic existence, drifting between company-owned properties in Northern California, New York and Colorado.

He cut his family out of his life—the only sibling he kept in occasional touch with was his sister Wendy Durst Kreeger—and shunned his former friends. He'd phoned them, said he had issues to deal with and would be in touch later. Only he never called again. Even those who stood loyally by him, like his childhood friends from Scarsdale High School, the Altmans, were dropped without explanation. Much to the bafflement of Douglas Oliver, his ally in hedonism, Bobby never tried to contact him again; neither would he talk to Nick Chavin, who had insisted all along that Bobby would never have harmed Kathie.

In May 1995, after his father had a stroke and lay dying in New York Hospital, Bobby came back to town, but refused to visit the old man's bedside until his brothers and sister had physically left the building. The extent of the rift between Bobby and his siblings became obvious to everyone when he was a no-show at his father's funeral. At the time of his death, Seymour's fortune was pegged at $650 million. He also left an enormous treasure trove of New York memorabilia, the same collection that had awed Jim McCormack thirteen years before when he'd gone to him to beg for help in finding his sister.

Before he died, Seymour had extracted promises from the children who were still speaking to him that his prized possessions would not be stuck into storage and forgotten. There were 15,000 books, 20,000 postcards, 3,000 newspapers, 3,000 photographs, Broadway playbills, tickets, guidebooks and assorted treasures like a penny peep show machine in perfect working order, two cast-iron manhole covers from the West Side Highway and a life-size cardboard dancing girl. The collection had expanded from the library to take up almost the entire four floors of the East 61st Street brownstone that had been his home for the previous nine years.

"We knew he was serious about the collection when

the refrigerator disappeared from the kitchen and was replaced by a bookshelf," Wendy told *Forbes* magazine. For the next four years, she and Douglas catalogued every item.

"If it was relegated to boxes in the basement, it would have been appalling to Dad, and to me," she said. But it was such a huge, time-consuming undertaking that some days, she admits, she could have gladly walked away.

While Wendy and Douglas dutifully sorted through their father's beloved possessions and created an endowment to the City University's Graduate Center, Bobby had nothing to do with the legacy. He wasn't on hand on September 7, 2000, when the University dedicated the Seymour B. Durst Library, and the Old York Collection, the same day that the National Debt Clock was switched off.

Bobby was flitting around like a wealthy hobo staying for a few days, weeks, or even months at one or another of the lovely homes he had acquired across the country. In 1994 he'd bought an oceanside property in Trinidad, California, 300 miles north of San Francisco. Three years later he picked up a one-bedroom condo in Liberty Terrace, 377 Rector Place, in Battery Park City, a few blocks from the World Trade Center. The apartment was on the 14th floor with a breathtaking view over the New York harbor to the Statue of Liberty from the terrace. Seventy miles to the north he'd picked up a 60-year-old, three-bedroom, $650,000 ranch-style house with dramatic vistas and soaring ceilings at 9 Neds Mountain Road, in rural Ridgefield, Connecticut.

In April 1998 he leased a luxurious $3,875-a-month apartment in Dallas describing himself on the lease as a botanist for a California lumber company and divorced. In September 1999 he added another place to bunk down, forking over $2.8 million for a twelve-room penthouse condominium overlooking San Francisco Bay on the top floor of a seven-story building in the Bay City's tony Telegraph Hill section. Shortly after, he shelled out $1,800,000 for another three-story home in the same neighborhood.

But he couldn't abandon his former life altogether.

When he read the newspapers or tapped into the Internet it must have been galling for him to see how Douglas had become the toast of the real estate world. The Durst Organization was nearing the end of the multimillion-dollar redevelopment of Times Square and was about to unveil its major contribution, an impressive tinted glass and blonde stone headquarters for Conde Nast (publisher of *Vogue*) at 4 Times Square. At 48 stories and with 1.6 million square feet of floor space, the building was so advanced in its planning and construction that it was given the 2000 Energy Star Award for its innovative solutions to saving resources and reducing pollution.

The building is widely regarded as a feather in the cap for Bobby's young brother, whose interest in being an ecologically-conscious citizen extends to operating his own organic farm in upstate New York. His shepherding of the company since he took over the reins has raised the family fortune to over $1 billion; some estimates say it is already nudging the $2 billion mark. In Douglas's capable hands the powerful Durst Organization was on the march. And Bobby was not banging the drum.

CHAPTER 10

TIMOTHY MARTIN: THE KATHIE CASE REOPENS

BOBBY might have been free to continue his life as a millionaire drifter flitting between his gracious Connecticut estate, his surfside property in California and his aerie apartments in New York, San Francisco and Dallas. And Kathie's pretty face might have remained frozen in time on the New York Police Department's Missing Persons File if some upstate cops hadn't tumbled over Timothy Martin.

In the fall of 1999, police in Westchester County were on the lookout for a pervert who had exposed himself to women joggers and horseback riders on rural paths. They all gave the same description—he drove a pale blue car, waving them over to the vehicle as if he'd broken down or taken ill and needed assistance. When the women approached the car he began masturbating.

Local police soon tracked him down and made an arrest. He was convicted of "public lewdness," but before he was sentenced, he told them that he had some information about another case, an unsolved case, that they might be interested in. He knew, he said, what happened to Kathie Durst, and he would be prepared to divulge what he had heard in return for a lesser stretch in jail.

Mrs. Durst had been murdered by her husband at her South Salem home and her body had been buried by a tree on the property. He was privy to this, he added, because his sister-in-law, Janet Fink, had been the Dursts' housekeeper.

The case fell in the lap of Detective Joe Becerra of the Somers Police Department. He had heard of Kathie Durst but, at 36, he was still in high school when she'd gone missing and, as far as he knew, there had been no murders in South Salem. When he pulled the Durst file, he saw that the contents barely scratched the surface of what he knew by instinct was a career-making case. It had all the right ingredients—a beautiful young wife who had vanished on a brutal winter night, an uncooperative husband and charges made by friends of the woman that the marriage had been abusive. He made a couple of inquiries and learned that the rest of the files were with the New York Police Department, who'd had jurisdiction in the case. And just like Timothy Martin had claimed, it had gone unsolved.

Becerra asked for the files to be sent from Manhattan. When they arrived, he read through them with growing disbelief. There were some puzzling contradictions here, he thought, and some gaping holes. He'd only been a detective for six years, but it looked to him as if these guys had just been going through the motions. Had anyone really looked for this woman? Why was the South Salem property never searched, why did her husband, the textbook first suspect in the case of any missing wife, get such an easy ride? By the time he'd finished, he was convinced: something here was clearly out of whack.

"When Joe Becerra looked into it, he said, 'This case stinks,' " says Jim McCormack.

In early November he took the file to his boss, Westchester District Attorney Jeanine Pirro. Like Becerra, she was struck by the clashing statements, unanswered questions and what seemed on its face to be sloppy police work.

"My, my," she said. "Isn't this interesting? This woman was a vibrant young medical student. For her to disappear off the face of the earth doesn't make any sense."

Why don't you have a look around and see what you can find? she told Becerra. He took a police search team to the South Salem house and had them dig up an area around the tree where Martin had claimed Kathie's body had been buried. After a backbreaking day with shovels, and aided by a mechanical digger, they came up empty. Martin's information turned out to be wrong. But there was one thing on which Jeanine Pirro and Joe Becerra could agree with their informant: Kathie Durst was almost certainly dead, and it was not out of the realm of possibility that she'd been interred somewhere on the property.

With his boss's okay to kick the case into high gear, Becerra began tracking down and re-interviewing everyone in the files—except for Bobby Durst, whose lawyers hadn't let anyone talk to him since a few weeks after he reported his wife missing. He went to Manhattan and met with the elevator operators and other staffers at the Riverside Drive penthouse where the couple lived. He found the employee who'd reported seeing Kathie going into the building on the night she went missing, Eddie Lopez, later said he'd been mistaken and had since died. And the super who'd spotted her walking up West 76th Street admitted he'd never actually seen her face. He'd thought it was Kathie because the woman he'd seen was wearing a similar long beige down coat.

Becerra contacted Dean Kuperman of the Albert Einstein College of Medicine. He was the only one to stick to his original story. A woman who identified herself as Mrs. Durst had called and he still had no reason to think that he'd been duped by someone impersonating her. "It never occurred to me that it wasn't her," he told Becerra.

He talked to the N.Y.P.D.'s lead investigators in the case, Robert Gibbons and Michael Struk. They allowed that they'd been troubled by the discrepancies in Bobby Durst's account of what had happened that night.

Becerra also wanted to talk to Kathie's friend Gilberte Najamy, who had been very vocal in her suspicions about Bobby. She'd made so many calls to the cops that she'd become a pain in the neck. In the years since Kathie disappeared, Gilberte had moved away from Newtown, but Becerra tracked her down farther north in Hampden, Connecticut. He called her and got an answering machine, identified himself as an investigator with the state police, and left a message that he was looking into the suspected homicide of Kathie Durst. He asked her to call him back and tell him all she knew.

The call, coming out of the blue after so many years of frustrating attempts to get someone to take her seriously, took her breath away. She didn't know whether to laugh or cry. She'd been ignored for nearly twenty years. Skeptical, Gilberte called Becerra back. She would meet with him, she agreed, but only at his office in Somers. And she wasn't coming alone, she told him. She'd be bringing someone with her who could back up everything she said. The woman she brought, it turned out, had stories of her own to tell the young detective. Her name was Kathy Traystman, and she provided an eyewitness account about what happened to anyone who roused Bobby Durst's hair-trigger temper. He'd sent her friend Peter Schwartz to the emergency room with a broken face, she claimed, been charged with assault and then quietly settled with his victim out of court.

Becerra took note of everything the two women told him. Start with the timeline, Gilberte had urged, then you'll see that Bobby had to be lying. A few days later Becerra tested for himself Bobby's account of what had transpired that night, from the time Kathie hugged Gilberte goodbye and turned the red Mercedes out of her friend's driveway.

He started at Gilberte's old front door and drove the same route Kathie would have taken to the South Salem house, slowing down to navigate the winding and narrow lakeside roads. How treacherous they must have been in the icy sleet, he thought. He waited there long enough to account for what Bobby had claimed had happened next: they had shared a hamburger, a bottle of wine and an argument, before she changed her clothes, gathered her things together and got back into the Mercedes for the ride to the railroad station at Katonah.

"He told me, 'Jim, I did it on a clear day, in a police vehicle. I couldn't do it. I couldn't make the time.'" recalls Kathie's brother. "What Durst claimed couldn't have happened. Try making that drive on a cold and rainy night.

And on top of that, she'd downed a few glasses of wine at Gilberte's. She simply couldn't have done it in that time."

Becerra began to contact other friends of Kathie's who, just as they had done nearly two decades before, told their stories of the crumbling marriage, of Bob's jealousy and temper, of Kathie's fear and of her chilling plea that still made their stomachs churn after all these years: "If anything happens to me, don't let Bobby get away with it."

Becerra talked again to her family and discovered that, far from giving them all the information he could, as he had publicly claimed through his attorneys, Bobby had made just the one call, to Jim, on the Thursday night before he was finally forced—by Gilberte's relentless prodding and the call from the medical school—to walk into the 20th Precinct in Manhattan and report his wife missing.

Becerra also heard from Jim that Kathie had documented her increasingly violent treatment at the hands of Bobby. Her brother had suspected that she was abused, and had been floored by the shocking Christmas Day incident at his mother's home in Long Island. But he had no idea of the extent of the cruelty she had suffered until he read the report she had written for her attorney. In the aftermath of her disappearance, he learned that she had hired a divorce lawyer who told her that, if she was serious about forcing her miserly millionaire husband to the bargaining table, she should chronicle every instance of violence. She'd also written to her sisters describing her pain.

"I knew that Bobby could be charming—that's the side of him that Kathie fell for. But when I read what Kathie had endured I became aware of his dark side. He was his own domestic terrorist. In her own writing I saw a pattern of abuse. It started off with verbal abuse, psychological abuse, emotional abuse and it escalated into physical and economic abuse. He used his economic power as a means to control her. He abused my sister on many, many levels," says Jim bitterly.

He told Becerra that Kathie had retained lawyer Dale Smolen Ragus in 1981 to help her negotiate a way out of her marriage. Bobby and she could barely stand to be in the same room anymore, she had said. When they were together they'd do nothing but fight—over her career, her friends, but mostly about money.

As he went through the legal files, Becerra found Kathie's handwritten account of her relationship with Bobby along with the affidavit that the attorney had entered as sworn testimony during the 1983 court case when the desperate McCormacks had tried to force Bobby to come clean about her disappearance. Statements from her family, her friends and her lawyer all confirmed that she'd been convinced that his affair with Prudence Farrow would make her already foundering marriage crash and burn.

When he drove over to South Salem to talk to the Mayers, Ruth repeated what she'd told Struk and his sidekick in 1982, when they had turned up at her door on the Monday after Kathie vanished. Kathie had confided to her how upset she was over Bobby's infatuation and she'd told her that Prudence had called her on the phone and said: "Give up Bobby, he doesn't love you anymore. It's over, Bobby wants to be with me."

The friends Becerra talked to told him that Kathie was fed up with Bobby's moods, the ill-treatment and his cheapness. They were living way below their means, she'd complained. But she wasn't leaving without a fair settlement. The prenuptial arrangement she'd agreed to nine years before as a trusting teenager wouldn't provide nearly enough for her to realize her dream of setting up a pediatric clinic after she graduated medical school.

That was in the Mayers' original statement too, they said. Kathie had told the Mayers that she'd asked Bobby to give her $250,000, chump change to a man whose family was worth hundreds of millions of dollars. He'd laughed at her and said she wasn't getting a cent over $100,000. "She wasn't looking to take the bank and retire," says her brother, "she just wanted a little foundation money to start her medical practice. And she deserved it, after all, a marriage has to be worth something."

Becerra got the same story when he tracked down Eleanor Schwank in Texas. "He could have divorced her," she says. "He could have given her $10 million and parted. It was unspeakable, and Kathie was not going to give up. 'I will not come out of this marriage penniless,' she said. We'd tell her, 'Kathie, you don't need his money, just leave,' but she was committed to winning against the Dursts. I tried to convince her that it was a losing battle. If she had just pursued a divorce . . . but if you knew Kathie, she had to win big. It wasn't just about the money, it was about the victory, the principle of the thing."

Eleanor told Becerra how alarmed she'd become when Kathie had told her that she had pilfered bank statements and tax returns from Bobby's desk because she was collecting information about the Durst Organization's financial dealings. She'd given the documents to Gilberte and Kathy Traystman to keep them out of Bobby's clutches. Both women confirmed this to Becerra, then told him that within a year of her disappearance, their homes were robbed and the papers were amongst the missing items.

Although the property at New Salem had been sold twice since the Dursts had lived there, D.A. Pirro wanted the place searched. She'd been riveted by this case ever since Becerra had brought her the file. She'd built her career cracking down on domestic abuse, and this case was a beauty.

On June 15, 1999, she'd joined with Chief Judge Judith S. Kaye to announce the opening of New York's first combined felony–misdemeanor domestic violence court to handle all domestic abuse felonies in Westchester County. At the official launch she'd said: "Victims of domestic abuse face unique challenges while navigating the criminal justice system. This new court will ensure that judges are specially trained and procedures are in place to deliver justice in the manner that balances the needs of the victim with the rights of the accused."

Right here in front of her was a case where the N.Y.P.D. seemed to have bent over backward to protect the rights of everyone except Kathie Durst. Surely there was enough motive to at least turn up some serious heat on the husband, and yet the investigation had simply petered out. If this wasn't a case crying out for justice to be done, she thought, what was?

After reading the reports and hearing Joe Becerra's account of how he'd tested Bobby Durst's version of what happened that frigid Sunday in 1982, she became convinced that Kathie Durst had never caught that train to New York; she had never left South Salem. Then there was another puzzling entry. The cops in New York had noted that three days after his wife went missing, Durst had called his office collect from the Jersey Shore. Why on earth would he have been in a town on the windswept coast of the Atlantic Ocean, a place that was shuttered and nearly deserted in February? Was his real destination the nearby New Jersey marshes that never freeze over even in the harshest winter?

In the summer of 2000, Jim McCormack was contacted by Joe Becerra and asked if he would come to the district attorney's office in White Plains for a meeting. When he got there the elegant Pirro was sitting behind her desk. Jim shook hands with her and with the darkly handsome Becerra. To Jim's surprise there was an older man there too, and although he hadn't seen him in nineteen years, he recognized him at once. It was Michael Struk, the detective who had led the N.Y.P.D. probe into Kathie's disappearance all those years before. To Jim, Struk and his team had never come up with a convincing explanation of why his sister had never been found, and why the investigation had simply petered out.

"The D.A. told me she had called me in to talk to me about Kathie," says Jim. "She said some new information had come her way and she was reopening the case. Struk was retired, but they called him in. He was, and I hate to say this, embarrassingly vague. The guy is a professional, trained to remember the important stuff, he had a file that was half an inch thick with paper. But I was not comfortable with what I heard."

With the case officially back on the front burner, in the upcoming months Westchester detectives began re-interviewing anyone who had known the couple. Jeanine Pirro knew she was taking a chance and playing for high stakes. If she could uncover what happened to Kathie Durst and put her killer behind bars, that would be a tremendous boost to her already stellar career, yet she didn't underestimate the difficulties of unearthing evidence that had lain dormant for twenty years.

But she wasn't used to losing. Since taking over the district attorney's job in 1994, she had a conviction rate second to none, of 97.3%. If she reopened this case, then, by God, she'd bring in the killer.

Over the next year, investigators crawled over the South Salem house and the property surrounding it. The K9 squad arrived to help in the search. Police divers dredged a section of the lake. Cops and dogs swarmed over the house again and again; it was searched six times in all and a section of wood paneling was removed from the dining room for forensic tests. Jim McCormack says he was told to prepare to give a sample of his DNA. Westchester cops have never divulged the results of the tests, but it has been reported that human blood was found.

"We're not sure Kathie actually arrived in New York City. We certainly can't confirm she did," the D.A. explained. "The investigation is now expanding into whether or not she ever made it out of Westchester."

Becerra went back to talk to Ruth and Bill Mayer. He asked if they knew Janet Fink, the woman who Timothy Martin had claimed was the Dursts' housekeeper. "Of course I know Janet," Ruth told him. "She used to baby-sit for me." She also told him that Janet used to party with the couple.

The Mayers immediately discounted Martin's tip that Kathie was under a tree. "There's no way she could have been buried under a tree," said Ruth. "The ground was frozen solid—it was a cold, cold winter. He [Bobby] got her out somehow, or someone else got her out."

Then, she says, she repeated to Becerra what she'd told Struk years before, that Bobby Durst had lied when he said he'd spent the night at the cottage after taking Kathie to the train on January 31, 1982. "He wasn't here the night she went missing. He told the police he was here, but I know he wasn't. There were no lights on in that house and no cars in the driveway. Nobody was there. And the idea of taking the dog for a walk for three miles in a blizzard on an unlit pitch-black country road. . . ." she shakes her head in disgust. "His dog, Igor, wasn't a real sweet dog."

Becerra also tracked down the couple who had bought the cottage from Durst in 1990, David and Carmen Garceau. They told him that the place was a wreck when they moved in. They could hardly believe it had belonged to a millionaire. There were holes in the living room floor, and Durst had been sleeping on a mattress in the unfinished downstairs room, next to a trap-door entrance to the crawl space underneath the house.

The frequent searches have been traumatic for Gabrielle Colquitt, the present owner of 62 Hoyt Street. "Since the case reopened, her home has been overrun with state police and press," says Ruth. "The police have been here several times. They dragged the lake, for God's sake. What a waste of money that was. What did they think they were going to find in that lake? It was frozen over when Kathie disappeared; there were twelve inches of ice on it that winter. You could never have put a body in there, or buried it on frozen ground. And then they brought dogs. They searched every inch of that house and took stuff away for testing."

On Saturday, November 11, 2000, *The New York Times* broke the story that the police were once again on the trail of Kathie Durst. The case had been reopened, the Westchester house had been searched with dogs, and with new information available, New York state investigators were working with the N.Y.P.D. to solve the mystery of her disappearance. The article also said that the Durst employees who had put her at the Riverside Drive penthouse the night she disappeared were having second thoughts.

Suddenly, Bobby began to feel the heat. Jeanine Pirro didn't mince her words: "We are very optimistic that the case will be solved. There are plenty of people who thought that they had gotten away with crimes that we are now finding can be solved based on DNA evidence that might be left over. When we go back and look at these old cases, it's for the purpose of finding what kind of physical evidence remains and what witnesses can be re-interviewed," she said, adding ominously: "I am sure there are a lot of people out there on edge."

According to the *Times*, though Bobby had cut off ties to his family when Douglas took over the company, he had recently reconciled with his kin. He had his own real estate business. Although he was still not named as a suspect, his family felt compelled to defend him. "Robert Durst continues to maintain his innocence," said Douglas Durst's terse statement.

This wasn't what Bobby had bargained for. For years, while the case lay dormant, he'd managed to carve out a very nice life away from public and police scrutiny. The *Times* piece had ruined that. He knew, of course, that Jeanine Pirro was eyeing him as the number one suspect in the case of his missing wife. But he was convinced that she'd get her own comeuppance in November. She was running for a third term as D.A. and this time, he thought smugly, her snappy designer suits and perfect makeup weren't going to be enough to get her reelected. She was carrying some serious baggage of her own, and he had every confidence that the Westchester voters would show her the door.

He wasn't the only one to doubt her chances. In what had been an excruciatingly embarrassing scandal for the high-flying D.A., her husband Albert had been indicted on sixty-six counts of tax evasion. He was charged with hiding $1 million in income between 1988 and 1997, and falsely claiming all sorts of luxuries as business deductions, including his $130,000 Ferrari, as well as his wife's Mercedes and another one driven by his mother-in-law. The Feds claimed that Albert, a real estate lawyer who worked for high-profile clients like Donald Trump, had also written off as business deductions $40,000 electronic gates for the couple's $1.7 million mansion in Harrison, New York, furnishings for their West Palm Beach vacation home, luxury cruises, wines, toys for their children and countless other obviously personal expenditures.

Although their tax returns were signed jointly, Jeanine had managed to convince the authorities that she had had nothing to do with, indeed had no knowledge of, the alleged fraud. Albert and his accountant brother Anthony were the ones who were cooking the books, she said, while blasting the federal investigation as "invasive and hostile."

But she did suffer major collateral damage as details of the couple's lavish lifestyle were gleefully revealed in court. The Pirros, it was clear, had lived like royalty. They employed a sizable staff to take care of mundane duties like baby-sitting, running their house and hauling their potbellied pigs to the vet. After a very public trial, Albert was found guilty of tax evasion and on January 9, 2001, he swapped his suave Italian suits for prison duds as he started a twenty-nine-month sentence in a Florida jail. Anthony drew thirty-seven months.

Although Jeanine had escaped closer scrutiny, Bobby was banking on the voters' skepticism. Would people really believe that this powerful woman, with a mind like a steel trap and a messianic zeal for tossing felons behind bars, could have been ignorant about her family finances? How could an attorney, never mind Westchester's top lawyer, not have read the forms before she signed them? Come November, he was sure, she'd be history, and the Kathie case would disappear all over again. He was counting on it.

But the woman who had been one of *People* magazine's 50 Most Beautiful People in 1997, and whose iron fist was barely concealed in a velvet glove as she talked tough about crime on *Larry King Live* and *Nightline*, was made of sterner stuff. On election night she won a third term as Westchester's District Attorney. With Albert incarcerated in Florida, the celebrations were very subdued and, the morning after, she was back at her desk. One of the first orders of business was the Durst case.

Just before the holidays Pirro decided she had to talk to Susan Berman. She'd become fascinated with the woman who'd been billed as Bobby's best friend and longtime confidante. When Kathie disappeared, Susan had ferociously defended her "brother" Bobby and had enthusiastically gone along with his campaign to paint his missing wife as an unstable hysteric with drug problems who was not up to the challenge of medical school. Over the years, she'd stalwartly stuck to that position. Any suggestion that "wonderful Bobby" knew more than he was telling was "ridiculous." It was "so unfair" that he'd been targeted in this way. It was widely known that Susan would do anything for Bobby. Did that include providing him with an alibi? Pirro wondered.

Dean Albert Kuperman had said that the call he received the morning of February 1, 1982, was from Kathie Durst. She'd said she was sick, suffering from nausea and diarrhea, and wouldn't make it to class. Pirro believed him; what she didn't believe was that it was Kathie on the other end of the phone.

Stephen M. Silverman doesn't believe it was Kathie who made the call either. In fact, the unnecessary medical information is what triggered his suspicions that it was Susan on the line. "She was a hypochondriac and always talking in gruesome detail about her symptoms," he says. "She always told you way more than you wanted to know. Once I was waiting for her with another friend and she called to say she had to cancel. I remember turning to my friend and saying, 'Susan can't make it, she's got a spastic colon.' "

The idea that a professional woman would call the dean of her school to say she was sick was ludicrous, thought Pirro. In that she was inclined to agree with Dr. Marion

Watlington, who also scoffed at Kuperman's account. "That never rang true to me. By that time Kathie was in the wards—third- and fourth-year students work in the hospital wards—if she was going to tell someone she wouldn't be in, that's where she would have rung. She'd never have called the dean of the school," she says.

So if Kathie didn't make the call, who did? Pirro asked herself. There seemed to be one logical answer, the woman who'd do anything for Bobby Durst and the person Gilberte Najamy was convinced for years had provided Bobby with an alibi—Susan Berman. In December 2000, Pirro began to make arrangements to fly to Los Angeles with Joe Becerra.

CHAPTER II

SUSIE HITS HARD TIMES

WHILE Bobby was clocking up enough frequent flyer miles to buy a stake in a major airline, the passing years had been less kind to Susan Berman. She was never able to replicate the runaway success of *Easy Street*. The fat check she received from selling the film rights to her book had bought the spacious home in Brentwood, paid for her lavish wedding to Mister Margulies and, for a while, afforded her a comfortable lifestyle. But to her everlasting disappointment, no movie was ever made and the cash was running out. She'd also been through the mill emotionally, first losing her young husband to drugs and divorce, and, just when she thought she'd won him back, losing him again, this time forever, to an overdose.

In 1987, she hooked up with divorced Los Angeles money manager Paul Kaufman, whom she'd known years before when they were both students at the Chadwick School. For someone whose finances constantly teetered on the brink of ruination, this seemed an excellent choice to her friends. Even better, Paul was raising his two young children, Sareb, 12, and 10-year-old Mella. Susan unconditionally adored them, and the kids, especially Sareb, loved her right back.

It was no secret that she'd always longed for children of her own. At one point, with her love life looking pretty bleak and no likely candidates for fatherhood on the horizon, she'd even mulled over asking Bobby to father a baby with her, and had discussed the idea with friends. But Hillary Johnson dismisses the notion as no more than a fleeting fancy. "That was an idea she floated for about five minutes," she says. "It was a thought that occurred to her and she talked about it for, maybe, one twenty-four-hour period, but it wasn't something she seriously considered."

Yet there was little doubt that not having a family of her own was a great disappointment to Susan. Kids naturally gravitated to her. "She would have made a wonderful mom," says Deni Marcus. "My little boy Tommy, who's now six, was crazy for her. She always thought of herself as my older sister, and wanted to be called Auntie Susie. She spent all the holidays with us, and if Tommy and I were going out for lunch we'd call her and ask her to come along. She'd drop what she was doing and come right over. She never missed a chance to be with me and Tommy.

"I think one of the things she liked about Paul was that he came with Sareb and Mella," she says. "She very much wanted children, and she had a great rapport with them. Honest to God, I've never met anyone who related better to kids.

"She was typical of her generation of women who put tremendous energy into their careers, but had never really given up on the idea of having a family. Then they wake up at 40 and think, 'Oh my God, I have to do something about this,' " says Deni. "Susan was very loving with Paul's kids and, typically Susan, very generous to them. They were 10 and 12 when she got them, not an easy time for kids with puberty and all that involves coming up, and they were also going through all kinds of personal turmoil when she came into their lives. She was very loving and nurturing, and they all magnetized to each other.

"I think if you ask either of those kids to describe her, they'd say she was their mother and not their stepmother; even though she wasn't legally married to Paul, they adopted each other as mother and children."

For a while it seemed as if Susan's life was back on track. She was never happier than when she was playing mom. It was as if she'd been given a family to make up for the one that was so cruelly wrenched from her as a child. "She was very unusual, intelligent and very loving," says Deni. "The best thing about her was that she empowered everybody she came into contact with. She did have her own demons and wasn't capable of making herself happy necessarily, but she always gave everyone else the tools to make the most of their lives."

Sandy West also thought the bond between Susan, Sareb and Mella was extraordinary. "Susan considered herself an orphan and these kids were kind of orphans too," she explains. "Their mother didn't take much interest in them and Paul was a real jerk. He seemed like a nice guy at first, but he was a real jerk.

"She was really the only mother they ever had, dedicated and supportive, and it wasn't always easy because Mella was resistant, being the girl, I guess, but Sareb liked Susan right away."

And she provided surroundings in which they felt totally comfortable. "There was no 'good' furniture to wreck, it was a laid-back home where you kicked your shoes off," says Deni. "Her house was very Bohemian—she was a total hippie at heart, although she never took drugs, ever, and wouldn't touch alcohol at all. She was into herbal tea and soya cappuccino and all that good stuff. She loved things for their intrinsic value, she loved books, particularly classic books, art, photographs; she had very bare minimum things, she didn't live in grand style, she just had whatever she needed around her."

For the first two or three years, Susan was blissfully happy. Paul and the kids had moved into her big house in Brentwood. She continued her quest for recognition as a screenwriter while Paul made a living as an accountant and financial adviser. But like almost everyone else in Hollywood, he harbored dreams of seeing his name emblazoned in neon lights. It turned out to be a fantasy that was to spell disaster for their finances and their relationship.

Although Susan worked as hard as she'd always done at her writing, she knew she needed a hit if they were to continue living in the style to which they'd all become accustomed. The Brentwood home was expensive to maintain and the children were growing up—college and all the expenses that that would entail loomed ahead. Since none of the studios would bite at any of her movie proposals, maybe what she needed, she decided, was a Broadway smash. Make it on the Great White Way, she convinced herself, and Hollywood would come begging.

Susan and Paul started working together on a musical based on the nineteenth-century scandal which became known as the Dreyfus Affair. Her hero was Captain Alfred Dreyfus, then the only Jewish officer in the French Army. He was accused in 1894 of spying for Germany and convicted by a note fished out of a trash can by a servant. Prosecutors claimed that Dreyfus had penned the letter even though the handwriting bore scant resemblance to his. He was found guilty anyway and sentenced to life imprisonment on the infamous Devil's Island off the South American coast.

With Paul's encouragement, Susan threw herself into the script which, as it began to take shape, she was sure would be a sensation; a show that would have audiences standing in the aisles. She poured her remaining funds into it, using her house as collateral to help bankroll the project. She tried to drum up investors and couldn't understand it when the response was less than lukewarm. Prospective producers simply did not share her enthusiasm for the subject matter, which they failed to visualize as suitable material for a Broadway show.

She and Paul traveled to New York, where they held a reading of the play for their well-connected friends and potential backers. But the Dreyfus case, which had triggered anti-Semitic outbursts and near-riots that had put Parisian Jews in fear for their lives, failed to light a single candle in the imaginations of Broadway's moneyed investors. The play was "interesting," they told her, while sitting firmly on their wallets.

The hottest tickets in town at the time, she was pointedly reminded, were the stage version of *42nd Street, The*

Best Little Whorehouse in Texas and the perennial *Peter Pan*.

Disgusted by what she viewed as their cowardly lack of vision, Susan turned again to the most reliable man in her life, her millionaire buddy, Bobby Durst. But for once, Bobby balked. Although he loved her dearly and would help her out of any jam, he had much too much respect for his money to throw it into such an iffy proposition.

Truth to be told, says Stephen M. Silverman, in turning her down, Bobby merely exercised sound judgment. The show just wasn't any good. The last thing Bobby needed was to be associated with a Broadway flop. God, how his family would laugh. It was one thing to quietly give a financially strapped friend a helping hand, it was quite another to publicly pour money down the drain in a questionable artistic enterprise. Susan was stunned. Although she hadn't talked to him so much since Paul and the children had moved in with her, they were still close. Nobody, nobody, meant more to her. And he'd lent her money before—lots of money. How could he turn her down? Without financing, the musical was going nowhere. Without the musical, she was broke. The bank called in its loan, and she lost the beautiful home she loved.

She was forced to declare bankruptcy. The relationship with Paul didn't survive the blow and, amid bitter recriminations, they parted in 1992. The sole consolation from the whole humiliating debacle, and for Susan it was huge, was that the children still adored her. Although Sareb went to live with his father, he kept in close touch. Mella stayed with Susan.

With nowhere to live, no money coming in, and a 15-year-old girl to support, Susan was desperate. Once again there was a friend with a safety net in the shape of a one-bedroom condo on Sunset Boulevard in West Hollywood. It's a bit small, he told her, but it's currently empty. Why don't you move until you get back on your feet? It was cramped, but Susan was grateful for the offer. She gave Mella the bedroom and slept on the couch. "She lived like that for five years. She was incredibly poor," remembers Hillary.

Stymied by the film industry, and now spurned by Broadway, she turned her hand to writing mysteries to pay the bills; ironically, the most successful, *Spiderweb*, was about a man wrongly accused of murdering his wife.

"I think Susan's lack of real success was just the sad luck of bad timing," says Deni. "She was busy doing journalism at an age when people in the entertainment industry were writing for the movies. By the time she came around to a passion for that, her age and sex made it practically impossible. A woman over 40 writing for Hollywood? Forget it."

Susan turned again to the formula that had brought her fame and at least some fortune. The American public had an insatiable appetite for gangsters—and who better to feed that hunger than Susan Berman? Hadn't she lived the life of a Mob princess? Forget the Dreyfus Affair, it was *Easy Street* she should be turning into a musical, she decided. And she knew exactly who would help her do that: Broadway impresario Cy Coleman. She also knew who could open the door to him: her old New York neighbor and pal, Stephen M. Silverman.

"Susan remembered that back in 1978 when I was at the *Post*, I had interviewed him and done a nice profile on him which he had liked. Then in 1996 she called me. I had just gone back to work at *People* and she was desperate for money. *Easy Street* would make a great musical, she told me, and I had to get it to my friend Cy Coleman. She would not take no for an answer.

"Coleman wasn't my friend, I knew him enough to say hello to him at Elaine's, but that was all. I thought, What will I do? She'd said: 'I'll write the book, and you know what a great writer I am,' that was her standard rallying cry. Finally, I got his address and simply wrote him a cover letter and sent him the book. He never got back to me. Susan kept asking me in desperation, 'Have you heard from him?' But what could I do? I couldn't press the issue or make him be captivated by the material. Just less than a year later I bumped into him at Elaine's. He said, 'I owe you a response. I liked the book, but I'm just too busy.' "

With no musical rendition of *Easy Street* in the offing, Susan came up with another alternative. She would write a sequel to her memoir about her childhood as Davie Berman's kid. She set to work with renewed zeal. Dipping into a cache of memories available only to the offspring of mobsters, she produced "Lady Las Vegas," which was bought by the A&E channel, turned into a two-part TV special and brought in her first real influx of cash in years. It also earned her a nomination for a Writers Guild of America Award in 1996 which in turn led to an invitation to become a regular contributor to the Showtime comedy series *Sin City*.

With money in the bank at last, in 1997 Susan persuaded her former landlady, Dee Schiffer, to let her rent the small wooden-shingled, one-story house on Benedict Canyon Road where she'd first lived when she'd moved to Hollywood in the eighties.

Despite her success in bringing her colorful childhood to television, Susan persisted with her dream of movie fame. "The documentary on Las Vegas for A&E and the book she wrote to accompany it were utterly brilliant," says Hillary. "There had never been a documentary on Las Vegas before—hers was the first. When she talked on camera, you got a sense of how funny and smart she was. She did the whole thing. It was her idea, she wrote it and produced it. But she was trying to do something that every person in Los Angeles wants to do, write for the movies. She was so talented, but it didn't really count.

"She could get a meeting with just about anyone in Hollywood, and they'd be fascinated. She could hold an audience spellbound pitching stories, but I had the feeling that when she'd leave the room, these 28-year-old male executives at the film studios would look at each other and say, 'Wow, what a fabulous idea. Who will we get to write it?'

"She would drive her little car back to her little house

in Benedict Canyon and on the other side of the hill, these same executives would be matching up her ideas to twenty-something male writers. It was very frustrating. I didn't know how to help her."

What Hillary and Susan's other friends did was try to keep her afloat by sending her whatever money they could spare. She was not only struggling to support herself, she was paying for Sareb's classes at Santa Monica Junior College, and for Mella to go to school at the State University of Oregon.

According to Susan's friends, Mella and Sareb's mother hadn't been part of their lives from quite an early age and as they grew up, their father became less involved with them, too.

One of the pals who bailed her out was Danny Goldberg. "We kept in touch, and at the time I was spending my summers in Los Angeles, and Susan always came over and spent the day with my family. I lent her money a couple of times. It wasn't much to me, but it helped her out and I was happy to be able to do that for her," he says.

"Susan was a real feminist and supportive of all women," says Susan's friend Sandy West, "and she was adamant that Mella get a college education no matter what. Every penny she earned went towards Mella's tuition. It was very expensive and another reason Susan was poor. She made incredible sacrifices for these children to make sure that they got a decent start in life. They weren't her natural children, but she always referred to them as 'my daughter' and 'my son.'

"But I never heard her once complain about the sacrifices she was making to put the kids in school; she was so proud of how well they had turned out." And her influence on them was clear. Susan's fascination with the movies rubbed off on her son, who works in the industry and wants to be an actor, according to Sandy. "And Mella inherited Susan's need to take care of people and run their lives," she says. "After she graduated from Oregon State she went to work in a community-based program, tutoring children."

• • •

Once they were through school and carving out careers for themselves, Susan had made another attempt to jump-start her career. She was tired of the mystery stories she'd penned out of sheer necessity and was longing to return once more to her extraordinary roots for inspiration. She called Owen Laster at William Morris in New York. Twenty-years before, he'd given her advice on selling film rights to *Easy Street*. Now he was an executive vice president with the company. What he remembered about Susan Berman was that she had written a terrific book and that she was smart and pretty, with a bewitching smile.

"After Rhoda [Weyr] left William Morris I gave Susan some advice, but she went off my radar after that," he says. "I was involved in the publication of her first book and there was a fair amount of excitement about it. I liked her, she was very vibrant. I read the book and I thought she was talented. I hadn't seen her for a long, long time, then she got in touch with me a year before she died and submitted a proposal which I read. I wasn't too encouraging about it," he recalls. "But I told her if she had anything else, to get back to me."

Susan had also found herself a manager. She'd bumped into Nyle Brenner on the street when she was walking her dogs near the West Hollywood apartment she'd shared with her daughter. It was, by all accounts, a love–hate relationship, and it didn't hurt that he was a dead ringer for Mister. They were together for three years. She was his only writer client—he usually represented actors. She treated him alternately as a sounding board, a boyfriend, a gofer and a nursemaid, and they seemed to be codependent almost to the point of self-destruction. Whether or not they ever became lovers is in doubt but it was clear that Susan was infatuated with Nyle. He reportedly explained his side of the attraction: "She was like an addiction."

Whatever their personal arrangement, the partnership failed to pay off businesswise. It also took a toll on her

relationship with Mella, with whom she'd written an un-
published book called *Never a Mother, Never a Daughter*.
With her children gone, she lavished all her affection on
her three unruly dogs, Lulu, Romeo and Golda, and increasingly gave into her phobias; the residual lessons
learned growing up the daughter of a gangster were coming
home to roost with a vengeance and wore thin on Nyle,
who bore the brunt of helping her deal with them.

"I have uncontrollable anxiety attacks," she had admitted in *Easy Street*. "I am never secure and live with a
dread that apocalyptic events could happen at any moment."

Desperately needing another hit, her financial situation
again deteriorated. By summer 2000 she'd fallen months
behind with her rent and was feuding with her landlady.
They'd argued about everything from her barking dogs to
the rent arrears and Dee Schiffer made no bones about the
fact that she wanted to throw her out. Susan panicked when
her eyes began to trouble her and she could barely focus
on her computer screen. She was diagnosed with glaucoma
and Nyle arranged for her to have surgery.

And whatever was going on in Bobby's life, she complained to friends, it was clear that he was becoming more
reclusive, or trying to put more distance between them. She
was having difficulty tracking him down. At any rate he no
longer confided in her the way he used to, and Susan
blamed Debrah Lee Charatan for usurping her longtime role
as Bobby's best friend.

As luck would have it, as her debts mounted, her car
began to die. The old Chrysler she'd driven for years had
developed the disturbing habit of catching on fire; she told
friends she needed to replace it before the damn thing incinerated her. She found a used silver Isuzu Trooper to
replace it, but the owner wanted $7,000. Once again she
turned to Bobby and his deep pockets for help, but she
couldn't get through. None of the numbers she could usually reach him at were working. It seemed like he was making a determined effort not to be found. Out of other

options, she wrote him a letter and mailed it to the Durst
Organization headquarters in New York.

By August 2000 she was desperate. According to Deni,
she resorted to selling the jewelry that her besotted father
had showered on Gladys. "She sold some bracelets and
watches—actually there wasn't very much left," she says.
"She only had a couple of pieces of her mother's jewels
because when she passed away some of the other relatives
took the lion's share of it. She didn't even have her
mother's engagement ring and wedding ring. They were
buried with Gladys."

With the trust fund Davie left her depleted and her
mother's baubles gone, Susan had few mementos of her
parents. All she had was the trunk the faithful Lou Raskin
had hastily packed for her and sent to Chickie's before her
father's henchmen took the Las Vegas house apart. It had
taken her over forty years to open it. When she did finally
get up the courage to prise the lid off, she found four exquisite evening gowns, some of her baby clothes, china,
silver, some of her grandmother's treasures, books, her
mother's family Bible, hundreds of photographs of Susan,
her childish diaries, a pile of receipts and most poignant of
all, a tape of her, aged six, singing, with her mother and
father in the background giving encouragement. She'd
taken it to a recording studio to listen to it and as the voices
of her long-dead mother and father filled the room, she was
nearly undone by the flood of memories it released.

"She called me in October," says Stephen M. Silverman. "I was out and she left a message on my answering
machine. She sounded awful, it was heartbreaking. Her life
was in a total shambles and she was desperate for money.
She told me she was on Prozac but it wasn't working. I felt
terrible for her. Then she called back in November and
everything was fine. But that was so typical of Susan."

What had made everything fine was an envelope that
had landed in her mailbox with a North California post-
mark. Inside was a check for $25,000 and a loving note
from Bobby. "It's not a loan, it's a gift," he'd written. "You

can always call on me for help." She bought the car and began to tackle her mountain of debts. A few weeks later, another check, for another $25,000, arrived from Bobby. She paid off her landlady and arranged to move out in June.

In November, she called Owen Laster again. "A couple of months before she died she sent me two more proposals, and I remember thinking one had some potential. I told her if she reworked it, I'd be happy to take another look at it," he says.

On December 17 Sareb came over. He was about to leave for a vacation in Europe and, being Susan, chronically phobic and fearful of life's unwelcome surprises, she had a list of things he should avoid in foreign ports. He stayed nearby and they talked daily on the phone, but he wanted to see her before he left, especially since this would be the first Christmas he would spend without her. She'd talked excitedly about her latest projects, he said. "She was happy. She told me she had a couple of new possibilities."

Two days later she called her friend Kim Lankford, the flame-haired actress who played Ginger Ward on *Knots Landing*. Susan spoke to all her friends every day and in every call she discussed every aspect of her life. Her relationship with Nyle was always a favorite subject, her latest writing project was another. There was always a drama in her life. She could be on top of the world one minute, in the next she could be in the depths of despair.

In this call, she was particularly upbeat. She was spending Christmas Eve, as usual, with Deni and Tommy and she was going with her friend Susie Harmon to Susie's mother's home on Christmas Day. Kim usually saw Susan over the holidays, but this year, like Sareb, she was about to depart on vacation.

Life, she told Kim, was looking up. Thanks to Bobby, her bills were paid, and she had two book proposals and a TV script on the boil. One of the books would be about the high rollers in Vegas. She'd also been working on a miniseries with her friend, Hollywood director Jonas McCord. "The Vegas Diaries" was a look at the gambling strip through the eyes of Mob women. They were going to pitch it to ABC and NBC. She had good vibes about "Diaries," she said; it could be the hit she'd been looking for.

According to *New York* magazine, Susan next confided that she was working on something so big, there were going to be explosive repercussions when it was revealed.

"I have information that's going to blow the top off things," Susan said.

"What do you mean, what information?" asked Kim.

"I don't have it myself, but I know how to get it."

"Well, be careful, for God's sake," Kim told her.

Kim didn't press her further—she figured that Susan had come up with another theory about the death of Bugsy Siegel or her father, and her immediate reaction was "So what?"

Then Susan told her something that sends chills up Kim's spine every time she recalls the conversation.

"I've been talking to this psychic," she said. "She told me I was going to die a violent death and that there'd be a gun involved."

Kim didn't take this seriously, as Susan often consulted psychics. Shaking her head, she told Susan she would talk to her as soon as she returned to L.A. and hung up.

On December 22, Susan had dinner with her friend Rich Markey, producer of "For Goodness Sake" with Jason Alexander, Scott Bakula, Faith Ford and Bob Saget. She was in a great mood that night too, describing a new book she was planning, to follow where *Easy Street* and *Lady Las Vegas* stopped. This, she laughed, was to be truly autobiographical—it was to be called *Rich Girl Broke*.

They talked about Mella and Sareb and swapped stories of Las Vegas—Markey was about to visit family on the desert strip—before using their Writers Guild passes to see the movie *Best in Show*, the dog-show spoof starring Christopher Guest. Susan had thought it hilarious.

CHAPTER 12

SUSIE'S MURDER

ON Christmas Eve, 2000, Susan's neighbors called the Los Angeles police. Her dogs had been barking incessantly for hours on end and one of them was running loose on Benedict Canyon Road. Something had to be wrong, they said, because she never let her dogs out of the yard except when walking them on a leash. When a squad car from the West Los Angeles Police Department arrived around 12:30 P.M., it was greeted by three hysterically yapping wirehaired fox terriers. There was no sign of forced entry, the front door was unlocked, the back door was lying open and there were bloody paw prints everywhere.

They found Susan in the guest bedroom at the back of the house, sprawled on the wooden floor, with a bullet in her brain. A clump of her hair, matted in blood, was lying beside her. The bloodstained hank was still on the floor the next day when her friends visited the murder house. She had on pants and a T-shirt and she was stone cold. She must have been dead, the cops figured, for at least a day.

Behind hedges that had afforded some privacy, the detectives combed the house for clues while the forensic people did their gruesome work. They talked to neighbors. Nobody, it seems, had heard a thing, until the dogs started up. The police were closemouthed. Susan had been shot at close range by a slug from a .9-millimeter gun. There was no obvious motive and nothing had been stolen from the house, not that Susan had anything of value to steal. The shot was to the back of her head—her murderer hadn't wanted her to know what he was about to do. The killer had been thorough—he or she had left no fingerprints or anything else to give a clue to his or her identity. L.A.P.D. spokesman Eduardo Funes said, "It's a terrible homicide. We are looking into several clues."

Deni, who had last seen her cousin two weeks before, found out she was dead when a cop picked up the phone at Susan's home. "She was supposed to come to my house on Christmas Eve. We always spent Christmas Eve together. She was late for dinner and hadn't called, so I rang her to say, 'Where are you?' A policeman answered the phone and told me she had been shot."

She could hardly take in what she was hearing from the calm, authoritative voice at the other end of the line. Numb with shock she told the cop that she was Susan's cousin, but they were more like sisters, that she'd been named for Susan's father. On Christmas Day, she drove to the West Hollywood Precinct to meet with the detectives in charge of the investigation into Susan's murder. "They had me thumb through her Rolodex and point out the numbers of people who would know what was currently happening in her life," she says.

Susan had arranged to spend Christmas with her friend from her Chadwick School days, Susie Harmon. She had moved away to Prescott, Arizona, but she spent the holidays with her mother in Los Angeles and Susan had been invited over for Christmas dinner. She had been looking forward to it for weeks, especially since Nyle Brenner had agreed to go with her.

He called early in the morning to make final arrangements and was surprised when she didn't pick up. She's probably out walking the dogs, he thought. After several fruitless attempts to reach her, Nyle decided there was something wrong with her phone and drove to the house. When he got there, it was locked up, there was no sign of Susan or the dogs. What he did next isn't clear since he seems to have given differing accounts of his actions to different people, but one version that has been reported has him knocking on the neighbors' door. Haven't you heard?

they asked him, the woman that lived at 1527 was dead and the police had said she'd been murdered.

Nyle got back in his car and drove home. There he started burning up the phone lines, calling everyone he could think of who was close to Susan to break the dreadful news. He spoke to Mella in Oregon and to Sareb, who was still in Europe. Being Christmas, most people were spending the day with family or friends and came home late to find the lights blinking on their answering machines. When they clicked them on they heard Nyle's agitated voice deliver the shocking message: Susan was dead and had been slain "execution-style."

"I didn't go to the house, I couldn't," says Deni, "but friends of Susan's who did go over there told me there was nothing missing, in fact, the people who were there the next day said there were things still sitting undisturbed on her kitchen table as if she was just about to use them. It was almost eerie." The only indication of the horror that had taken place in the guest bedroom was the hank of her hair clotted with dried blood and the reddish-brown stain on the hardwood floor.

By the following day Susan's close network of friends hit the phones, buzzing with rumors and theories. Any suggestions that she'd been the victim of a Mob hit killed in revenge for exposing their secrets were quickly dismissed. They had stemmed mostly from what Nyle Brenner had told *Daily Variety*. "I don't know that there was anything she was working on that had any relevance to the current Mafia, although she had been talking to a lot of people in Las Vegas recently, people who had 'a past,' " he'd said.

That much was true, they agreed, because Susan was working on her *Easy Street* and *Lady Las Vegas* follow-up book, *Rich Girl Broke*, but it was still highly unlikely that any present-day gangsters would care, since everyone she wrote about had either been wiped out long ago or were in wheelchairs. And anyway, Susan's colorful revelations had hardly damaged any reputations; if anything, she'd coated their thuggish misdeeds with a glamor and style they'd have loved, so much so that Rich Markey was once prompted to wisecrack: "If I were a gangster, I'd have encouraged her to write more." Writer Dick Odessky, who lives in Las Vegas and wrote about the Mob in *Fly on the Wall*, and who had known Davie Berman, agreed. "All the people who her father knew are gone, and as far as the Mob is concerned, the Mob as we knew it has gone too."

Sareb didn't believe his mom's death was Mob-related either. "There was a theory going around that the Mob did it, but I don't think they would have anything to do with this," he said.

Some of her friends remembered that Susan had been wary of her landlady, Dee Schiffer. They'd fought for months over the rent, her dogs and Schiffer's unwelcome habit of popping in unannounced, but that situation had calmed down when Bobby sent Susan the money and she'd paid the woman what she owed, and then some.

It could not, everyone agreed, have been a stranger. The paranoid Susan would never have left her doors unlocked or admitted a stranger, she had to have known her killer. There had been no signs of a struggle, so it appeared that she had opened the door willingly, and she'd been so unsuspecting of her murderer that she'd turned her back on him (or her).

Nyle Brenner's behavior had tongues wagging too. For someone who had been with her day and night for three years, he seemed curiously conflicted, almost annoyed by her death, professing to be heartbroken at one moment and pointing out her faults the next.

Sareb, who according to *New York* magazine had had a premonition that something was terribly wrong when his mother hadn't phoned him on Christmas Eve and didn't return his calls to her, caught the first flight he could get out of Amsterdam. He was picked up at the airport by Nyle who, immediately regaled him with complaints about his "difficult" mother. This didn't sit well with Sareb, who was genuinely distraught over Susan's death. He knew she could be, as Stephen M. Silverman tactfully puts it, "a lot of work," and that she was viewed as somewhat eccentric and had all these crazy phobias, but she'd always been a loving mom to him.

"She was a gentle woman who lived life with great caution," Sareb told writer Peter Huck. "She loved a lot of people and had no enemies. If she didn't like you, she would not let you get close. Nobody had the opportunity to develop a grudge."

Saddened to the core, Deni began to make the heart-wrenching funeral arrangements. "It was wretched that she was murdered right before Christmas. Because of the holidays everything got stalled at the coroner's office and her body was in refrigeration for a few days," she says. "And unpopular as it was, the first day I could bury her was the next Sunday, New Year's Eve."

Deni went over to the funeral home and fixed Susan's hair. It had been her crowning glory, and she'd worn it in the same style since the sixties flowing down her back with bangs that covered her eyebrows, like Cher wore hers in her first incarnation. The medical examiner's office had chopped it off to examine the wound. "Deni was upset about that," says Sandy.

"The police had taken Susan's Rolodex, which made it hard for Deni to let people know about the funeral, but I had sent Susan a Christmas present which arrived, and it had my address and phone number on it, so she called me right away. She also had to pay for the funeral, because there was no money," Sandy West adds.

The service took place at 2:00 in the afternoon on the last day of 2000 at Hillside Memorial Park. Despite the awful timing, fifty of Susan's beloved friends and her few remaining relatives crowded into the chapel.

"We got a rabbi at very short notice. Sareb and I spoke, then she was transported to the cemetery where her parents are buried," says Deni. On January 2, she was interred in a mausoleum which holds the remains of Davie, Gladys and Uncle Chickie, at the Home of Peace Cemetery in Los Angeles. Some of her friends sang the song she'd learned to play for her dad, "The Sunny Side of the Street." According to *New York* magazine, she was dressed in a long black velvet dress that had belonged to Sareb and Mella's grandmother, and her friends put photographs of all her favorite people in the casket. Susan was placed in a vault beside her parents and Chickie. "Fortunately, it's on the second level," Kim Lankford quipped to the magazine. "And there's nobody at the other side to annoy her."

It was a sorrowful affair. The mourners stood in stunned shock, hardly able to believe that Susan, with her over-the-top personality, her unflagging interest in their lives and loves, was dead, snuffed out by a cold-blooded murderer. If anything could have made the day worse, it was the certainty that most of them felt that she'd been killed by someone they all knew.

As his mother was laid to rest, Sareb was inconsolable. "He wept bitterly throughout her funeral and her memorial service too," remembers Sandy. "He had loved her from the moment he'd met her, and he'd lost the one person who never let him down. She was always on his side."

The kennels where she had boarded her "babies," her rambunctious terriers, found homes for them.

Susan's death reverberated on two coasts and although it took nearly a week before the news filtered across the country, her New York friends were as shocked as her pals in Los Angeles, and just as baffled. Why would anyone shoot Susan?

Stephen learned of her death while he was checking his computer for breaking celebrity items for PEOPLE.com.Daily. "It came over on the wires at 4:30 in the morning," he says, "and I cried. At that time, there was nobody I could call. In New York it was the middle of the night, and in Los Angeles it was still too early to wake anyone up. I thought about her and what kept going through my head was, that of all my friends, I realized, she was the one most likely to be murdered. You know the truly sad thing is, that all of this, the books, the movie scripts, the notoriety of being a gangster's daughter—she didn't want any of it. Susan would have settled for being a housewife. She played the game, oh, how she played it, but all she really wanted was a home and a family."

Sareb decided to have a memorial service for Susan in February. It was arranged that it would be at the Writers Guild in the screening theater. Press were to be banned so that Bobby Durst, his mother's longtime friend, would be able to grieve for her in peace. Sareb knew that the New York state police were back on the hunt for clues as to what happened to his wife, and that Bobby's every move was being scrutinized. He didn't want any hassles at the service for his mom.

Although Susan had not been officially contacted by the Westchester district attorney before her death, she had told friends that she was on their interview list, and the prospect of the meeting filled her with dread, says Sandy West. "She was very unhappy about it, and worried about Bobby. Susan was very private, she didn't like talking to strangers, and she didn't like people she didn't want to have around coming into her life. And she especially didn't like the police coming to talk to her about a good friend. She told me: 'Here we go again, they are trying to hang something on Bobby. He'll be dragged through the mud. It's so unfair.'

"When Kathie went missing she would say. 'The police suspect Bobby.' She liked Kathie, she told me she was a really nice woman. But she thought it horrible for Bobby because Kathie's family so totally suspected he'd killed her, and Susan didn't believe he had anything to do with her disappearance. I don't think she ever did. If she thought he'd done something to Kathie she would never have introduced him to her girlfriend, Kim Lankford," says Sandy. "She fixed them up—Susan was quite a matchmaker."

She had also agreed to talk to *The New York Times*, and Bobby knew that too.

Over 100 people attended the service. "Some of them were friends of her son's and a lot of people I hadn't seen in years showed up—old boyfriends for instance. Deni and I, Bede [Susan's friend Bede Roberts] and her cousin Tom Patton, Jr., spoke," says Sandy.

"Bede and Sandy, who'd both known her for thirty years, since they were in graduate school together, told all these whimsical, crazy things about her, like how she counseled them on how to snare the men they eventually married. It was girlfriend stuff," recalls Deni.

Bobby Durst, although he was in town and staying at the Shangri-La Hotel on Ocean Avenue in Santa Monica, stayed away, just as he'd avoided his own father's funeral five years before.

"He called Sareb and asked if he thought it would be okay to attend. Sareb told him, 'It's fine with me, do what you feel comfortable with,' and so he didn't come," says Sandy. "I guess at the time I didn't think it was odd because Susan had told me they were reopening Kathie's case and I knew he wouldn't want the publicity."

It was a matter, however, about which he'd given some thought, according to Julie Baumgold, who is also the wife of the New York *Daily News* editor Ed Kosner. After he was arrested on charges that he'd hacked Morris Black to pieces, she told the paper, "I read the stories about Susan to Bob, and we tried to figure it out together, as did all her friends. In February, when Bob and I were discussing Susan's murder and whether or not he should go to her memorial service, because, he was already notorious and suspect, he said to me: 'She was *my* witness.' "

His absence touched off a storm of whispering at the reception Sareb had arranged at the Guild after the service. "A lot of us were saying, it's obvious she was killed by . . . someone she knew. She knew he was coming over—she wasn't afraid of him. She locked doors on everything. She never showed me she was afraid of Bobby," says Sandy.

"She was a great friend. My children all loved her. When I would just show up she'd be dressed in her Auntie Mame outfit, as I called it. She'd have on her nice dress, the shoes with little bows. My kids always found that just fascinating. But when she was found dead, she was in jeans and a T-shirt, so this told me she was expecting someone, and that person had to be a really close friend. There was no break-in."

According to Sandy, as her devastated friends mulled over the horror of her Christmas Eve murder, they agreed that, unthinkable though it was, the killer had to be someone close to her. Bobby had been questioned by detectives who have also reportedly checked out Nyle to whom she left the rights to one of her books. But the L.A.P.D has never named anyone as a suspect.

Although she knew Susan had been besotted by Nyle, and had frequently discussed their relationship with her on the phone, Sandy disliked him intensely when he introduced himself to her at the Home of Peace Cemetery.

"Nyle and Susan were girlfriend and boyfriend for a long while—at least three years," says Sandy. "But I had never met him until the funeral, and he gave me the heebie-jeebies that day. Nobody had ever made me feel like that, it was real creepy. He was with his aunt and I thought that was really strange, because Susan detested her. She couldn't see him or go anywhere with him without this aunt tagging along. Then I shook hands with her and it was like shaking hands with someone who wasn't there."

"He said to me, 'Susan really loved you, I want you to know that,' and I said, 'Yeah, Nyle, she often spoke to me about you as well.' And he said, 'But Susan wove a web you couldn't escape.' I thought, whoa, somebody just died, that's not a suitable thing for him to say."

Hillary, who had learned of Susan's death in a chilling early morning phone call, says, "The sad thing was that none of her New York friends found out about her death until it appeared in *Variety*. . . . I flew out to the memorial service. I'd heard that Sareb banned the press because he wanted to accommodate Bobby Durst, but I think he was just heartily sick of reporters by then, and it was a private event. People were still in a state of shock and grief-stricken. And this was a month or so after her death, but they were having difficulty believing it was true. There seemed to be no reason for it, it was so insane, nobody could make any sense of it."

After the service, the mourners she talked to were also churning over possible suspects and dismissing some of them almost as quickly. "The idea that Bobby killed her was immediately ruled out by her closest friends," says Hillary. "What motive could he possibly have? Why would he help her and lend her money, then kill her?" Her friends knew that Susan's relationship with her landlady had deteriorated to the point where Susan said she was afraid of the woman who'd frequently appear on her doorstep unannounced. The feud had simmered below the surface for three years but in the months before Bobby had bailed her out, it had reached the boiling point over unpaid rent, repairs, and over Susan's exuberant wirehaired terriers.

"Susan was just waiting for that one hit to get out of there. She needed to find a place to rent where she could keep three dogs and that she could afford, and that's a challenge in Los Angeles. She was just hanging on, trying to get enough money to leave, and the landlady was someone she had to mollify. She tried to be as cordial as she could be to her, although she did trump her in court when the woman was trying to evict her, by proving she wasn't keeping the house up," says Hillary.

Despite the fragility of her domestic arrangements, a situation that "would have been debilitating to most writers, Susan not only continued to function under the circumstances, she wrote every single day," she adds.

According to *Talk* magazine, New Orleans mystery writer Julie Smith, to whom Susan had always vehemently denied that Bobby Durst was involved in his wife's disappearance, was dumbfounded by the revelation of another mourner after the service. She says the man, who was also a friend of Bobby's, confided to her that "Susan had told him she knew Bobby had killed his wife. Susan used to tell me it all the time. She would say, 'Bobby did it, but that doesn't mean we don't love him. Kathie's gone. There's nothing we can do, and we love Bob.' " The man added that when he'd asked Susan how she could be sure Bobby was the murderer, she'd replied: "Bobby told me." Julie Smith also claims that other people at the service insisted that "Bobby knew Susan knew, and they had this sort of implicit understanding."

The accusations, rumors and gossip swirled until late in the night in a nearby bar. But while Susan's friends were grappling with their own suspicions, the L.A.P.D. was encountering a spectacular lack of progress in finding her killer. They couldn't even say for sure when she was shot. It could have been, they said, a day or maybe two before her body was discovered. All they would confirm was that she didn't die in the course of a robbery.

"Nothing was disturbed or taken from the residence," said Detective Ronald Phillips. "It looks like the target of the murder was her. We are treating this as a homicide. Does this case have anything to do with the Mafia? I have no idea at this time. We have to look at every angle, of course. But the people her father dealt with are 80 or 100 right now. I don't think that's what this is about. I don't think it relates to the Mob thing."

The L.A. cops also seemed to rule out Bobby as a serious suspect. "He's someone who's certainly been looked at a little bit, and he's not completely off the list, but he's not front row center," admitted Detective Brad Roberts.

As the weeks passed with no arrest, Susan's family and friends grew increasingly dispirited. "It's been very frustrating to all of us," says Deni. "And all the speculation about Bobby—that also sounds insane, because if he had done it, surely they would have found out by now. The cops never contact me. For the first couple of months after Susan died, I'd call every couple of weeks and they'd just kind of put me off. Then they shifted the case over from the West Los Angeles Precinct to downtown and I think it just fell into an abyss of 'Who cares?' "

The uncanny parallel of the deaths of Susan Berman and Bobby's wife two decades apart is not lost on Deni. "It's like the Kathie Durst case. The police felt it was a failure. They were embarrassed because they couldn't solve it."

To Rhoda Weyr, it's no surprise there had been no arrest. "Jim Brady, who's been an investigative reporter for a very long time, told Hillary that whoever did it, if they got rid of the gun, it would be almost impossible to solve."

She too thought immediately of Robert Durst when she heard her friend had been killed. "I knew that he was still part of her life, because she talked about him. She told me once she was going to be seeing him, that she was worried because the case had been reopened and the only time she gave me pause was when, some months before she died, she said she was on to a really big story.

"It's just so ironic. This was a girl who lived on conspiracy theories. It was understandable, you never really knew whether her father was murdered or her mother, but there was no question in Susan's mind that they were. And there was also no question in Susan's mind that the people who killed them were after her and other members of her family. When she let me know that, I said, 'Well, why do you want to get into this book?' And she said, 'Oh, I'll be okay because I don't really know anything.' And that was true, she really didn't know anything. Jim Brady told me Susan never knew anything. She always thought she did, but she didn't.''

Sandy West was interviewed by the L.A. cops. She told them everything she knew about Susan's life, her friends and her suspicions. She said to one of the detectives, "I've read that she was killed execution-style."

"Don't believe everything you read in the papers," he cautioned her.

By April, they had stopped returning her calls too. "I tried to get a copy of the police report and the L.A. police said they would send it, but it never arrived," she says. "Since I work with the Oakland police I thought it might be easier. Susan was appalled at that too," she says about her eventual career choice. "We protested everything together at college. What a great about-face. But my sons have been hassled by the police. The police need to understand the community; most of them don't live in Oakland. And the community needs to understand that the cops are people too.

"But it makes me chuckle when I think about Susan. I was with her when she discovered what her dad did for a living, and she had a nervous breakdown. Susan was one of the most moral people I knew. We'd all be smoking dope and things, but she wouldn't touch it. She didn't swear, didn't use bad language. She'd drink a little, but that was the extent of it."

Sandy says her suspicions that Bobby Durst might have had something to do with Susan's death have begun to haunt her. "In the September before she died, the driver's-side window of my car was shot out, and we never did find out who did it. I thought it was so bizarre that she would be murdered right after that. I was very nervous because I thought he might think that Susan had said something to me about Kathie. Bobby had a place not far from Oakland, and it was very nerve-wracking to lose your good friend like that anyway. Every time I go in or out of the house I look at every man that seems halfway strange. Until he was arrested, I was pretty scared.

"I'm sure that Kim had some pretty sleepless nights too. He was supposed to be there that day, the day Susan was murdered, with Kim, in L.A."

Kim Lankford insists Sandy is mistaken. "I wasn't even in the country," she says. Thrown together by Susan, who told Bobby that Kim was "just perfect" for him, Bobby and Kim made a handsome couple. Although by this time he was 56, Bobby was in good shape. He still worked out every day, starting with a punishing round of push-ups and sit-ups, and hadn't put on so much as an ounce since his student days. He had a few more wrinkles, and his hair was thinner and grayer, but he was still a catch.

Along with the *Knots* series, which finished in 1983, 40-year-old Kim has appeared in a string of TV specials like 1997's "Get to the Heart: The Barbara Mandrell Story" and a slew of B movies like *The Octagon* (1980) with Chuck Norris, *Terror Among Us* (1981), *Cameron's Closet* (1989) with Mel Harris and Tab Hunter, and most recently, the 1996 clunker, *Street Corner Justice*. Forever Ginger to fans of the nighttime soap, you can buy her face on a mouse pad on the Internet. Although she and Bobby had known each other for fifteen years, they started dating in the spring of 2000 and were still an item when Morris Black washed up in Galveston Bay.

CHAPTER 13

WHERE'S BOBBY?

AFTER Susan's memorial service, Bobby dropped out of sight again. To the people who'd known him for years, he'd become a wealthy gypsy, crisscrossing the country, continuing the strange nomadic existence he'd led since quitting the Durst Organization. None of them had an inkling about the double life he was leading in Galveston and they were totally in the dark about his gender-bending activities.

In late March he drove up to Palm Springs with Kim Lankford, so the two of them could get away from headlines in Los Angeles, regroup and comfort each other after Susan's tragic death. They divided their days between the tennis courts and the spa, and spent the evenings lingering over leisurely dinners.

They returned to Los Angeles on April 1, and on the trip back they chatted about Susan. She was my best friend, Kim told him, and wondered aloud for the umpteenth time who could have wanted her dead. They talked about Debrah Lee, whom Kim had met several times; although she knew that Bobby had some sort of relationship with the New York realtor, it hadn't stopped their romance, which had blossomed since Susan had played matchmaker the previous year. Maybe it was Bobby's idea of an April Fool's joke, but when Kim asked, "How is Debrah?" Bobby replied, "She's fine." He didn't bother to add that they had married several months before. That night they went to dinner in Los Angeles with Rich Markey, the last person to see Susan alive, except for her killer.

According to *Talk* magazine, Markey, who had never met Durst before, couldn't resist twitting him about his

missing wife. "How do you deal with the whole world wondering if you did it?" Markey asked.

"Kathie was friends with a bunch of cokeheads," explained Bobby. They were dealing huge amounts of dope
and wanted him to bankroll their transactions. He refused
to have anything to do with them. That's who killed her,
he said, seemingly oblivious to his own skewed logic.

If a drug kingpin were looking for cash, it would hardly be in his best interests to bump off a woman whose only
access to serious money was through her husband, especially if they were, as all Kathie's friends knew, on the
brink of divorce. It would be doing him a huge favor by
getting rid of the wife and saving him a bundle at the same
time. Bobby's explanation only made sense if the dealer
had tried to blackmail him for Kathie's safe return, and he
didn't say a word about that.

"So if you had nothing to do with it, why don't you
fight back?" Markey asked. Bobby told him he would, just
wait until November, until "that bitch" Jeanine Pirro got
booted out of office by the Westchester voters.

A few days later, Bobby took Sareb to dinner in Los
Angeles. During the meal, Susan's 28-year-old son told him
that she had left Bobby something in her will, and handed
him a small box. Inside was a silver medallion, the size of
a dollar coin, on a silver chain. On one side it had a Star
of David and the word "Zion," the other was engraved with
the name "Davie Berman." It was supposedly given to Davie by Bugsy Siegel and was the necklace that Susan's Aunt
Lilian, Davie's ever-loyal big sister, had left to Susan when
she died in 1979. She'd worn it all the time.

The next week Bobby flew back to his Connecticut
estate to keep an appointment with his past. April 12, 2001,
was his 58th birthday; Kathie and he would also have been
married for twenty-eight years. On the morning of the an-
niversary, he got into his sporty metallic blue Saab and
drove to South Salem, to Truesdale Lake.

From the outside, the pretty stone house looked just
the same. It had been bought from the Garceaus six years

before by artist Gabrielle Colquitt. She had been blissfully ignorant about her new home's haunted past until little Sharon Mayer piped up. "My little daughter told her the first time she met her, 'There was a murder in your house,' " says Ruth Mayer. But just how notorious her new digs were didn't sink in until a few years later when the Westchester cops reopened the investigation. "One morning she was outside washing windows when a TV crew arrived, cameras rolling. And there she was, all over the news." Since then her home had been taken apart several times by state police, and she was heartily sick of the whole business.

Gabrielle has a large black labrador who, according to the Mayers, is normally hyper, but on this April morning, when she was leaving to go into town, he seemed unusually lethargic. As she pulled out onto Hoyt Street she noticed a car, which she knew didn't belong to any of her neighbors, parked a little farther down the road. She drove on for a few hundred yards, then stopped; the dog wasn't his usual feisty self, and there was something about the car that made her uneasy. She turned around and headed back to the house.

When she got there, the blue car was parked in her driveway. She went around the back of the house and saw a man standing on her dock, facing the water and staring into space.

"Gaby is a bit like Kathie was, gutsy," says Ruth. "She yelled at him, 'Get off my dock.' He didn't even look at her. So she yelled again, 'Hey, get off my property.' He turned around and began walking toward her and got into his car without saying a word. As he passed her she thought, 'Oh my gosh, that's him!'

"It must have been eerie for Bob when he saw Gaby," says Ruth. "She has long blonde hair and the same kind of angular face as Kathie had. She thought she'd better get the license plate, so she memorized it as the car was driving away, and went in and called the police. When she repeated the plate number, Joe Becerra said, 'Yup, that's him.' We had police coverage 24/7 on the block after that."

Becerra and Jeanine Pirro later learned that Bobby had called his sister Wendy Kreeger after this incident and told her he would be out of touch for a while. He didn't tell her that he was headed back to Galveston and his secret life as Dorothy Ciner. Every so often, he'd surface long enough to have lunch at restaurants like the prohibitively expensive Four Seasons with Durst family lawyer, former State Appellate Division Justice Theodore Kupferman, or stay for a few days at the Bridgehampton home of his secret wife Debrah Lee, or spend time at his apartment in New York, where every morning, according to the building superintendent, Kenneth Shane, he would jog along the promenade or the Hudson River.

"He told me that he spent most of his time in Florida, and when he was away, a housekeeping service took care of the place. I painted the apartment for him when he first moved in. It was decorated more like an office than a home," says Shane. "The man was a bit quirky, but pleasant. He didn't seem to have any friends in the building, he never had girlfriends at the apartment and nobody ever saw the wife here. And we never saw him dressed as a woman—at least if he did, we didn't know it was him. He was very low-key."

But after ABC-TV aired "Vanished: The Cold Case of Kathleen Durst" on the July 25 edition of *20/20*, tongues began to wag. "We knew about the thing in Westchester, but no one ever said anything about it to him, and he just went on as if nothing happened," he says. "When he was here we saw him go out in his jogging outfit. It was always 'Good morning, Mr. Durst, 'Good morning, Mr. Shane.' There's an elderly woman who lives on the same floor as him, and after he was arrested in Texas she said, 'I can't believe it, he was so very nice and polite.' I joked with her, 'Hey, it could have been you.'"

Battery Park City, like all of lower Manhattan, was dominated by the colossal twin towers of the World Trade

Center, and Rector Place is less than a third of a mile from where they stood until the unthinkable terrorist attack of September 11, 2001. Bobby's building suffered no structural damage, but it was covered in the acrid gray dust that shrouded the devastated neighborhood and assailed the lungs of everyone who lived or worked nearby for months.

Bobby was miles away in Galveston becoming more and more sucked into his bizarre double life when Al Qaeda's suicide pilots struck. Like most of the country he learned about the horror from the television. The friends he'd lost touch with and those he still talked to bombarded his cell phone numbers, anxious about his safety. He called back, assuring them that he was fine, and that all the property owned by his family was unscathed. Shane says that, to the best of his knowledge, Bobby never went back to Rector Place. "The only visitors have been the police. They wanted to open the apartment with a passkey. I didn't see what they took out."

At the end of the summer Bobby turned up at a family wedding in Houston, Texas. To everyone's delight, it looked like he was mending fences with the Dursts after over five years of bitter estrangement. He reportedly had a great time, dancing most of the night. He left promising to keep in touch, and returned to Galveston on Sunday, September 23. But whether he needed to make a mental adjustment after being with his wealthy family before going back to his seedy digs or whether he was reluctant to deal with his mad-at-the-world neighbor Morris Black, he didn't head over to Avenue K. Instead, he checked into the posh San Luis Resort and asked for a room overlooking the bay. He was given a key to room #1515.

According to *GQ* magazine, he spent the next week there, ordering up Caesar salads and Guinness stout from room service, strolling to the hotel bar for nightcaps. He also hit the phones, consulting a computer whiz in New York about his laptop, and calling both Debrah Lee and Kim Lankford.

On Friday, the 28th, he dropped by Chalmers Hardware

at 2004 Broadway with his shopping list, bought the bow-saw, drop cloths and plastic trash bags and went back to the hotel. The next day he had his hair cut at the hotel's barber shop and ate in his room. All day Saturday no one heard from him, or saw him. On Sunday afternoon, the body of Morris Black washed ashore.

When 13-year-old James Rutherford made the gruesome discovery that last day of September, Bobby had been secretly living on and off at the Avenue K apartment for nine months, moving easily between his life as the mute Dorothy Ciner and the millionaire, Robert Durst.

In the days after the headless corpse of Morris Black was laid out on a cold slab in Galveston's medical examiner's office, Detective Cody Cazalas doggedly continued with his investigation, searching for a link between the two men, and for a reason that would make sense of the old man's brutal murder.

There was plenty of forensic evidence gathered at the crime scene. The blood trail, the evidence he'd discovered inside Durst's apartment, in the trash and his car all pointed to him. And after Durst had been arrested, Cazalas and his team had searched room #208 in the Galveston Holiday Inn Express where Durst had stayed as Jim Turss after the murder. There, they had found another packet of Metamucil, two pairs of shoes, two bottles of pills and some clothing. If the numbers on the laxative packets matched the ones found with Morris Black's limbs in Galveston Bay, thought Cazalas, that would be difficult for Durst to explain away.

It looked like an open-and-shut case except for two things. One, there was no motive. Cazalas didn't buy the theory that Morris Black was killed over the volume of a TV set. Two, a background search of the two men had failed to provide a single clue as to where they'd met before. And he still hadn't figured out why a millionaire, who just a few years before had presided over a vast real estate empire, would move to a run-down Galveston apartment, then kill and chop up a total stranger.

He went back to talk to Rene Klaus Dillman. There was another thing about Mrs. Ciner, Dillman remembered, she must have something wrong with her hair too, because she always wore a blonde wig. In fact, he wasn't absolutely 100% sure that Mrs. Ciner was a woman at all. Cazalas asked Dillman to describe her. She was around 5'7" he was told, kind of flat-chested, well-dressed, usually in beigy pantsuits that fastened up to her neck, low heels and she always wore a scarf. She must have broken her eyeglasses recently because they were held together with tape. She suited her ash-blonde wig, Dillman added and although he had doubts, he couldn't swear Mrs. Ciner was a man either. "Her gestures, her movements—it was a good performance," he said.

She was very reclusive, he added. She kept her shades drawn when she was home, she never wrote checks, her rent was paid by money order, and she paid several months in advance. He'd asked her if she thought she'd ever get her voice back and she had written, 'No, I don't think so.' He'd felt so sorry for her, she seemed such a nice lady, he told Cazalas, that he skipped the usual background checks and let her have the place right away.

Then the landlord said something that rang alarm bells for the cop. On September 28, Durst had asked him if another friend of Mrs. Ciner could rent Black's apartment. This was before he could have known that Dillman was going to tear up Black's lease.

Neighbors told Cazalas that Durst sat on the steps outside the house smoking and that he yelled at noisy kids and barking dogs—he barked back—and that both Durst and Mrs. Ciner separately used the Rosenberg Library on Sealy Avenue. And if they thought Durst was weird, they were even less fond of Black.

The truth was, he was the neighbor from hell, they told him, a scrawny, wizened old guy with a bad leg who strode angrily around town wearing baggy khaki shorts, a red woolen fisherman's cap and a brown fishing satchel slung across his chest. He had a squeaky voice that was usually complaining or yelling at somebody. Lonely and paranoid, he trusted nobody and riled everyone who crossed his path. He'd start up conversations just to whine about the landlord, his neighbors, slamming doors, barking dogs—it didn't seem to matter, every petty little annoyance drove him crazy.

"Black was peculiar," Dillman told the cop. "He didn't run the air conditioner, he never turned on the gas. He must have been taking cold showers the whole time he was here."

With the nation's press descending on Galveston, A.D.A. Kurt Sistrunk knew he had the beginnings of a major headache, but publicly spouted his confidence that Durst, who had disappeared since making his bail, would be back for his October 16 arraignment.

"I think the fact that he has retained local counsel is a good sign that he isn't taking flight," he said, somewhat unconvincingly. "Our efforts are focused on the case and on the evidence we have yet to examine, not on where he goes."

A couple of days later, on Thursday, a detective traveled from Galveston to New Orleans with the dry-cleaning receipt Officer Jones had found in Bobby's silver Honda CRV. The store owner handed over a comforter. He remembered it, he told the cop, because it had been splattered with blood. The suspect had driven 370 miles to have the stains removed.

To Sistrunk's embarrassment, Bobby skipped the arraignment. Over in a grand jury room prosecutors were presenting evidence to get an indictment of their slippery suspect. That evening, his face was all over the evening news. Outside the Galveston courthouse, Westchester District Attorney Jeanine Pirro, who had made the trip south in the hopes of questioning Bobby about Kathie, was fuming: "The defendant has exhibited his contempt for the court," she said.

But for all the publicity surrounding Durst's arrest, the Galveston cops were no nearer to solving the puzzle of

Morris Black, who he was, or where he had come from. For twenty days his mutilated corpse lay in the mortuary, but no family had come forward to claim him. It wasn't that the story of his death and subsequent dismemberment had been kept quiet—the town was buzzing with the story. Murders didn't get much grislier, people agreed.

Morris's head had still not been found. He'd been identified by his fingerprints which came up on a police computer. He was in the system because on October 6, 1997, police in North Charleston Beach, South Carolina, had arrested him after he threatened to detonate a utility company in a dispute over his electric bill. The row—Morris claimed he'd been overcharged $50 by South Carolina Electric & Gas—had escalated into his yelling at the unfortunate manager who'd tried to placate him that he was "coming right over to blow the motherfucker up." After a night in jail, he was convicted of a misdemeanor, and ordered to perform 108 hours of community service.

Ted Streuli, an enterprising reporter who was covering the case for the Galveston *Daily News* and *Journal*, called Bobbi Bacha of Blue Moon Investigations. Her husband Lucas, co-owner of the private detective agency, is a former aerospace engineer who worked on the Presidential Commission which investigated the space shuttle *Challenger* disaster.

"You know how to find people," Streuli told her. 'If anyone can track down this man's family, you can."

"At first the Galveston police thought that Black and Durst were two old gay lovers who had a fight and the one killed the other," says Bobbi. This theory was quickly rejected. "They did nothing to locate the victim's family at all. It was ridiculous to have a body in the morgue for so long without anyone even trying to find them. By the time I was called in, the police had taken everything out of the apartment, so I had to start from scratch."

Bobbi, daughter of retired Police Chief Robert Trapani, who was on the Galveston force for thirty-seven years, began her search on AutoTrack, which cops use to track down people using their cars' Vehicle Identification Number.

From the information she a found a driver's license, along with a Social Security number and where it was issued, Massachusetts. Using the SS# she did a property check and established that Morris had owned property there in the eighties. Then she started looking for people with the same name living nearby in the hopes she could trace some relatives.

First she found a sister, Gladys Saslaw, in West Peabody, Massachusetts, and a sister-in-law, Trudy Black on Cape Cod. Gladys refused to talk to her, but Trudy gave her an address for her estranged husband Harry, Morris's brother. She found Harry in Green Cove Springs, Florida, and he filled her in on the family history. He'd had four siblings, he told her, Israel, Gladys, Beatrice and their brother Melvin, who had been committed to Worcester State Mental Institution and had died some years before. They'd had a tragic childhood: when they were tots, their Russian immigrant parents had been declared unfit by the local authorities who split them up and fostered them out.

"I broke the news about Morris as gently as I could," says Bobbi. "I told him there had been a terrible accident. When I first contacted Trudy, I told the Galveston police what I was doing and asked them to get someone from the local police to go over to her house and tell her officially. I was actually on the phone with her when a cop arrived at her door."

Harry hadn't seen or heard from his brother for over thirty years. He was able to tell Bobbi that Morris, who the family had known as Jack, had been a seaman in the 1940s. He thought he had worked also as a handyman and as a watch repairman.

For the oldest of the family, Israel (David) Black, who, for reasons about which he is still in the dark to this day, was removed from his parents' custody as an infant, the news of his brother's murder was mind-boggling. "Until last November I never knew I had any siblings. I first learned about them when Bobbi found us all," he says. "A police chief in Galveston and then the lawyer called me. I honestly thought it was an error. About ten years ago I had to get a birth certificate. I dug it out and the names of my parents matched the names my brothers and sisters had on their birth certificates.

"I was brought up in an orphanage near Boston. I can't remember anything before I was 10 or 11, I have some sort of mental block," says David, who made streetlights for GTE until he retired, and now works nights as a security guard. "When the war broke out I joined the U.S. Navy and thank God for that. WW II saved my life. The way we were treated in the orphanage, I thought if I got out of the Navy alive I was going back there and kill the people that ran the place. I'll be 77 in August and until this year I never knew I had a family.

"If Jack [Morris] was alive and I tripped over him, I wouldn't know him. I met my sister Gladys for the very first time this October, and now I have a picture of Harry, and outside that I have a little more hair than him, we look alike. They tell me we have the same voice. Gladys had a daughter and we all have the same color eyes. Gladys knew Jack [Morris] very well and she says he and I have the same mannerisms, so yeah, they are my family.

"They all knew Mother and Father except me," he says. "Harry told me our parents were mentally ill and we were taken away by the state. Gladys was fortunate, she went from one foster home to another, but they were all the same family and they treated her very well, put her through school and she became an accountant. Jack [Morris] was partly raised by his father. He was in the Merchant Marine and loved the sea. Maybe that's why he settled in Galveston."

Harry's ex-wife Trudy kept in occasional touch with Jack [Morris]. "The last time I saw him was 1995, when he came to visit me in Massachusetts. He would stay for a few days, then move on. He was very loving and kind-hearted, but he did have a short fuse. He'd just blow up," she recalls. Gladys also kept in contact with the brother she says wrote poems for her when she was in school. A couple of years before he died, he'd given her the numbers of his bank accounts and told her that if anything happened to him, the contents would be hers. Trudy says Morris had given her the same instructions.

The Blacks were appalled at what had happened to their brother. Harry and David called Bobbi and asked her to find out what she could about why he had been killed. The only thing was, they hesitated, they didn't have much money. "No matter," Bobbi told them. "I'll do it for nothing. I love mysteries."

Morris had died in such destitute surroundings, seemingly a penniless, lonely and angry old man. But just as they'd been stunned to discover that Bobby Durst was a millionaire, the Galveston authorities were flabbergasted to discover that their elderly victim had nine different accounts in BankFirst, in Sioux Falls, South Dakota, and that they totaled nearly $140,000—$139,597.52 to be exact.

To try to make sense of his death Bobbi began her investigation with a background check. "When I started, I got chills up the back of my neck," she says. "I've been doing this for nearly twenty years and you can tell, from looking at the background, what kind of life this person has lived." The life Morris Black had lived, she figured, was on the move, or on the run.

From 1994 until he died, for instance, he had at least five addresses. From 1988 until July 1994 he lived in Galena Park, Texas. In August he gave an address in Del Rio, Texas, yet another in Stockton, Texas, for July 1994 until May 1995, while from September 1994 until June 1995, he'd had a place in Long Beach, Mississippi. He next turned up in North Charleston, South Carolina, moved on to Brownsville, Texas, and stayed there until October 1998 when he relocated to Galveston, moving into an apartment on Broadway where he got his lease torn up after a year for harassing the other tenants. He arrived at 2213 Avenue K in November 1999.

She went back further. In 1981, he was in Norfolk, Massachusetts, and he bought a property in Dorchester for $6,500. Around October 1981 he moved to New York, scratching out a living on 45th Street as a watch repairman. A year later he was back in Massachusetts, where he opened a jewelry store. Where, asked one family member, did he get the money to open a store and buy a house, if he was as broke as he claimed to be? One thing was for sure. Morris had as good a head for a real estate deal as Bobby Durst. Seven years later, the three-bedroom home was sold for $137,800. Pronouncing himself retired, he told Trudy and Gladys that he was heading south to sunnier climes where the weather would be kinder to his leg—the left one was permanently damaged by childhood polio-myelitis. They assumed he was living comfortably off the profits from the sale of the house and his $700 monthly Social Security check.

To anyone who had the misfortune to live next door to him, Morris was a nightmare. Debbie Monogan lived upstairs from him in North Charleston, South Carolina, in 1996. Every morning, she says, he would get out of bed. By 6:00 A.M. he'd be stomping around his apartment ranting and raving at the top of his voice. She'd wake up or come out of the shower and he'd be screaming and yelling and slamming his door back and forth. After weeks of this, she told him: "If you don't stop, I'll call the cops." That made him yell even louder. "I don't want anyone arrested, I just want him to stop. I don't know what sets him off," Debbie told the cops. When the police arrived, Morris went ballistic: "You bitch, I'll get you!" When he wouldn't stop, he was cuffed and stuffed in the police cruiser and taken off to cool his heels in jail. When he got back the next day, he started up again. "I've been through your trash. I know all about you. I've got your credit cards. I'll get you!" he shouted.

He hung his laundry on the porch and on the bushes in the yard until the landlady told him he couldn't do that. He screamed abuse at her and from then on arranged it over the open doors of his car. He kept his rent money stuffed down in his socks. When his lunatic behavior worsened, the owner filed to evict him. "She asked me to give evidence, and while we were waiting for the judge, he was running up and down the street outside the court building screaming. He'd get so angry he'd vibrate," remembers Debbie. "The clerk came in and said: 'Does anyone know that crazy little man outside?'

"In the hearing he was allowed to interrogate me. 'Ms. Monogan, isn't it a fact that you snore?' he asked. 'Not that I know of, no boyfriend or family member has ever told me that,' I told him. That made him furious. 'Well, don't you drink?' he asked next. I don't wish what happened to him on anyone, but he was such a mean, miserable man I'm amazed nobody whacked him before."

Etelka Myers has worked for the city of Galena Park for thirty years. "Once you met Morris, you never forgot him," she says. "He could be sweet sometimes, you couldn't ask for anyone nicer, and fifteen minutes later you could kill him. He was always raging about something. I'm in the tax department, and he couldn't understand why he couldn't sell off one little piece of his property. It was a 100' by 150' lot someone had sneaked two real little houses on. He bought them and wanted to sell one, and when I told him 'no' he just went berserk. I told him, 'Go talk to my boss, I have no control over this.'

"Anything small he could fuss about, he did. Utility bills, trash pickup, we wouldn't let him junk up whatever he wanted to junk up on his property. It was his property, he'd do what he wanted, he'd scream. He came in once a month to pay his water bill. We knew when he hit the front door; everyone in the building knew it. He was a funny-looking little man, wore plaids, big old straw hats, tennis shoes and he even came in barefoot. One time he arrived cursing his head off. The mayor told him: 'I have women in this building. Walk out that front door right now and don't come back.' He turned up the next day as if nothing had happened.

"He was a very unhappy person. When we saw the papers we said to each other, 'Well, he finally got it.' He could irritate you to the point you wanted to kill him. But we were surprised he was in Galveston, because when he left here he went down to Brownsville. He came in specifically to tell us he was moving there because that was a nicer place, they were friendly, and talked to him, and we were all sons of bitches. Everybody laughed and said, 'Bye.' "

In Galveston he also berated anyone who was reckless enough to give him the time of day. His obscenity-laden rants got him thrown out of the library, and kicked off buses. Twice the staff at the library called the emergency services when he thought his heart was pegging out. Rage, blocked arteries and heart disease were killing him, doctors told him, and they prescribed medication.

Two things struck Bobbi: "Morris has lived like a man in hiding since the early eighties, and you ask why? My educated guess is that he was living this way either to hide from someone, or to keep a very low profile. Just because his address history showed low-rent districts doesn't mean he was broke; his bank account proved otherwise. Why did he live so poorly? We may never know the full extent of his possessions, or how many bank accounts he really had.

"And why would this man come to Galveston to kill him? Durst doesn't have a history of just killing anyone. This was not unmotivated—the way Morris Black was killed was angry, even the police psychiatrist said it was a death of rage—like the killer knew him. If this is true, how did they know each other?"

Intrigued, Bobbi drove down to Channelview Drive with its quaint old wooden beach houses. It was familiar territory to her, she'd grown up in the neighborhood and knew the area well. As a youngster she'd gone swimming in the same spot where the body floated up.

The H-shaped community has the bay on one side, a swamp, dunes and railroad tracks north and south, and at

the back there is a murky lagoon which is home to an
alligator that feasts on chickens. Not long ago the alligator
set off a heated local dispute which raged for months after
the owner of the birds accused his neighbors of pilfering,
and wasn't settled until the creature was spotted with
chicken feathers stuck to his mouth.

Bobbi started knocking on doors and the people she
talked to told her, "The police wouldn't listen to us. Durst
was down there the day the body was found." One resident,
later identified as Lorre Cusick, who works as a nurse in
Dallas, who lived at the corner of Channelview and 81st,
had even spoken to him. She'd watched him staring out
over the bay. When he caught her gaze he'd asked her, "Do
people fish here at night?"

"No one's allowed to fish here," she'd told him. Then
he was gone. She recognized him after his picture appeared
in the paper.

According to the neighbors a brown suitcase sat on the
shore all Saturday night and disappeared early the following
morning. They also saw the plastic bags bobbing in the
water, but thought they were debris, and they said they
heard dogs barking fiercely that night.

"When he put the bags and the torso in the water, they
probably did start floating out immediately," Bobbi says,
"but the wind changed and they washed right back. Durst
was not counting on the body and the parts being around
at all, never mind being traced back to him—that's what
caught him. He even stayed in town acting nonchalant."

Near where the suitcase had sat, Bobbi noticed scrape
marks in the mud, as if something had been dragged to the
edge of the water. When she got back to her office she
decided to run a background check on Robert Durst and
came up with another interesting wrinkle. Apart from the
one he'd been issued, he seemed to be using two other
Social Security numbers, both belonging to other men.

The first was issued in Michigan 1965/66 to a Robert
Jezowski. She found six addresses in four states where
Durst/Jezowski had lived at the same time between Feb-

ruary 1985 and March 2001. The matching addresses showed up in Coral Gables, Florida, Los Angeles and Pasadena, California, Maldenbridge, New York, and two in New York City. Jezowski bought a Mercedes in 1997, but the search didn't produce a driver's license. Durst's license turned up the second Social Security number. This one was issued in New York between 1962/63. The same number also belongs to a James F. Fleischman of Belmont, New York.

Did Durst use them as aliases? wondered Bobbi. With a Social Security number he could rent or buy property, set up bank accounts, get credit cards and driver's licenses. He could take on new identities whenever he liked.

The cops uncovered other aliases. Apart from calling himself Dorothy Ciner to rent the Avenue K apartment, and James Turss at the Holiday Inn Express in Galveston, he'd borrowed the ID of a Diane Winne to lease another low-rent apartment in New Orleans in January 2001. She turned out to be a New Yorker who'd moved to Rock Hill, South Carolina, and was down on her luck. Landlord Michael Ogden called the police after seeing Bobby's mugshot in a magazine. He told them that on October 10, the same day he posted bail in Galveston, he stuck a note for Ogden in his mailbox. "My plans have suddenly changed. I am leaving N.O. I will not be back," it read. After he'd gone, Ogden found an auburn wig sitting on a Styrofoam head, a videotape of the *20/20* program about Kathie and the Star of David medallion that Susan Berman had bequeathed him. The note said that Ogden could keep them.

Bobby had had his utility bills in New Orleans sent to James Cordes who police learned was a photographer he'd hired years before to take pictures of his properties. He also obtained a Wal-Mart card as Cordes and got himself an American Express card in the name of James Klosty, another former classmate at Scarsdale High School who now lives in Millbrook, New York.

How useful would a bunch of different identities be for a man who has been under a cloud of suspicion in the 1982 disappearance of his wife, had been named a "person of interest" in the shooting death of his friend Susan Berman, and who expected at some point in his life, maybe even for the rest of it, to be on the run? With Morris Black's ID, he could hide out in seedy neighborhoods and loot the old man's $140,000. But with some of his wealthy Scarsdale acquaintances, the stakes would be much higher. They would have almost unlimited credit available. If the fugitive Bobby hankered for finer surroundings, he could simply max out their cards before changing his alias once more.

With the exception of Morris Black, the aliases Bobby assumed were living persons. Police rarely track down people who steal identities and even when they do, it's often hard to prove who is the real McCoy.

CHAPTER 14

DEBRAH AND THE JESSE TREE

NOBODY had seen Bobby since the morning of October 10, when, wearing a smirk, he'd posted his bond and walked out the door of the Galveston jail, but his face was pasted on FBI wanted posters and had appeared on news telecasts across the country. His lawyer, Mark Kelly, who had assured police that his client would be at the October 16 arraignment hearing, hadn't heard from him either.

The speed by which he was able to scare up $300,000 overnight had left the authorities scratching their heads. They made inquiries and found that the money had been wired to him by a small, expensively dressed woman who had turned up at a New Jersey bank on October 15 and told the cashier that she wanted to withdraw $1.8 million from an account belonging to Robert A. Durst. For identification purposes, she showed them a power-of-attorney notice and a marriage certificate. "I am Mrs. Durst," she said.

Suspicious bank officials, who had seen the stories about the real estate heir wanted for murder plastered over the newspapers and on TV, called the cops. Texas investigators were tipped off and the account was frozen. "Mrs. Durst" had to go home empty-handed.

But the story that a "Mrs. Durst" even existed was a bombshell. At the same time he was writing a check for $25,000 to help his buddy Susan Berman offset her crushing debts, Bobby had picked up a marriage license. And less than three weeks after his longtime friend was found brutally murdered, he tied the knot for the second time.

His bride, 44-year-old Debrah Lee Charatan, was the

girlfriend with whom he had briefly lived at 975 Fifth Avenue eleven years before. She'd started in the real estate business as an ambitious teenager, learning about apartment management in a dreary basement office. "It was 8' by 8' and it was disgusting," she'd once complained. But she thought the address, 8 East 48th Street, just off Madison, sounded pretty good. In her early twenties, determined to shake up a business that was then still a middle-aged white man's club, she launched an all-women outfit she called Bach Realty. Whether it was a stroke of genius or a crass gimmick, the firm became a roaring success. By the time she was 29, the butcher's daughter from Borough Park, Brooklyn, found herself at the head of a $200 million company and was the poster girl for the industry. She took over a whole floor in the East 48th Street building where she'd labored in the dank basement, and ruled her thirty-five employees with an iron fist.

The aggressively feminist company attracted lots of attention. For a while Debrah Lee had it all: a soaring career, a successful attorney husband and Ben, an adorable 2-year-old boy who spent his mornings at Rockefeller University Children's School. She was on the boards of fifteen charitable organizations from the March of Dimes to the Metropolitan Museum of Art. She looked the part too; outfitted in designer suits, she posed for *Harper's Bazaar* and bragged she'd be "the next Harry Helmsley," an industry titan whose vast holdings included the Empire State Building.

She also appeared in the business bible of the 1980s, the now-defunct *Inc.*, under the banner headline, "Young Founders," She told the magazine she expected her staff to clock up 250 calls a day. "We keep track," she said. As profits shot through the roof, she put less wealthy friends and family on notice: "I prefer not to lend," she said. In another magazine piece called "Money Dearest" she was said to be so controlling as a boss that she inspected her employees' armpits—a charge she later scoffed at.

A former employee, broker Adam Weprin, who is now

president of Weprin Realty, told *The New York Times*, "She's as tough as nails. You have to be in the real estate business." But Debrah Lee's toughness didn't inspire the admiration of all her workers. She was sent a bunch of dead roses at an office party, and once got a dead fish in her mail.

"I worked for Debrah Lee Charatan for over thirteen years when she had the women-only company," says Manhattan broker Adelaide Pulsinelli. "It was brutal, a concentration camp—I wouldn't wish it on anyone. She chose naïve people who had no business experience because she knew she could get away with things with them. It was like a brothel. All I can say is that this woman is one of the only people I've met in my life who has no conscience and no soul. She stiffed people out of commissions. That's why a lot of people left, and several took out lawsuits."

When the novelty of lady realtors wore off, her profits plummeted. Her own lawyers took out an action against her in Queens Civil Court in December 1991 claiming she owed them $9,405. As creditors lined up against her, brokers left the firm complaining they'd been cheated. Some of them sued claiming she'd hidden assets to prevent them getting money owed them when the company folded. Bach Realty filed for bankruptcy on December 1, 1994.

In the early nineties, she relaunched herself as Debrah Lee Charatan Realty. "Debrah Lee looks like a blonde version of Heidi Fleiss, skinny with sandy blonde hair—obviously it's not her own color," says a colleague who requests anonymity because, she says, speaking out against the powerful Dursts would be to commit career suicide. "She wears Chanel suits, you know, the pink plaid ones with the gold trim, and six-inch stilettos. She's very petite. She's also as thin as a rail, I mean she must be ninety pounds dripping wet.

"She's also one of the most cutthroat people in the real estate business in the city," claims the colleague.

The reed-thin Debrah keeps her stamina up for the dog-eat-dog realty business—and her figure for those Chanel suits—by jogging. On June 9, 2001, she ran the Road Runners Club's 10K New York Minimarathon in Central Park in a respectable 59 minutes and 25 seconds.

And she's still a major player in society charity circles. In May 2001 she was on the committee that hosted a gala at the swank Plaza Hotel in Manhattan to benefit the Tenement Museum on the Lower East Side. The museum, the aim of which is to pay tribute to the struggles of immigrants to this country in the early 1900s, is currently engaged in an ugly battle to evict the latest wave of newcomers from their homes in an adjoining building to make space for a proposed expansion.

Bobby and Debrah Lee took their vows on January 11, 2001—less than three weeks after Susan's death, and seven weeks after Bobby learned that Jeanine Pirro had reopened the case of his missing wife—before Rabbi Robert I. Summers, whose name they had found in the phone book. They told him they had each been married and divorced once before. The fifteen-minute-long ceremony was held on the 25th floor of 1500 Broadway, directly across Times Square from the sparkling new Conde Nast Building, the award-winning tower erected by Douglas Durst.

It was a particularly joyless wedding, according to the cleric who married them. He told the New York *Daily News* that the couple both wore suits and looked as if they were agreeing to a business deal, rather than taking vows to become man and wife. The bride didn't beam with happiness, and her groom looked like he'd rather be in Philadelphia.

"Durst was rather taciturn," said Rabbi Summers. "He was not buoyant and didn't smile. They stood under the chuppah, they said 'Amen,' drank some wine and kissed, then went out the door," he added. "There was nothing to it."

They took no wedding pictures and told no one, not even the bride's mother. Their secret surfaced ten months later when Debrah Lee showed up at the bank to withdraw Durst's money. Pauline Charatan, who lives in the Howard Beach section of New York and was once fired by her es-

tranged high-flying daughter, was puzzled when reporters
turned up at her door asking for a comment on her new
son-in-law, and, at first, refused to believe they were married. Bobby was, she said, a stranger to her. "I only met
him once," she says, "and that was sixteen, maybe twenty
years ago."

The people Debrah Lee worked with were also surprised. "We knew she was dating him, but she never told
anyone she was getting married," said one. But no one was
more shocked than Kim Lankford, Bobby Durst's girlfriend
for the previous eighteen months. She'd known about his
relationship with Debrah Lee, and dismissed her as an op-
portunist. She also knew that Susan had loathed her and
that the feeling was mutual.

"Kim was stunned when she read a report in the newspaper that Bobby had married this woman," says Sandy
West. "It surprised me too, because I thought it odd that
Bobby, who always exhibited his lack of interest in real
estate and development, that this was the partner he chose.
He married her right after Susan died, and that was so bizarre, because he was still dating Kim at the time. Kim
never knew that he was married."

The bride still refuses to break her silence about her
wedding, or to defend her admitted killer husband. But during the days that followed Bobby's arrest, there was much
speculation as to whether the marriage was even valid,
since Kathie Durst was still listed as a missing person and
had never been declared legally dead. Detectives from the
New York state police immediately descended on Debrah
Lee and questioned her for hours. Her "husband" was missing, and they suspected she was helping him evade recap-
ture. They discovered that the new Mrs. Durst was as
slippery as her husband: "She provided a lot of information
but at the same time I think she provided information that
would not be sufficiently damaging," said Galveston Police
Lieutenant Mike Putnal, "and deliberately left out information about his whereabouts. I think she knows more than
she's willing to tell."

While police in three states were trying to sort out Bobby's tangled private life, the emergence of Debrah Lee was gratifying to Susan Berman's friend Hillary Johnson. "What's her story?" she asks. "Anyone who could hang out with Bobby Durst and marry him. . . . There was always something off about Bobby. Now it's obvious there has been a huge problem, which he'd always been able to keep under control. Susan was very sympathetic, she'd had a hard life and had overcome many, many things to emerge quite intact psychologically and emotionally, but she was understanding of anyone who'd been through any type of childhood trauma."

The marriage posed a problem for Jeanine Pirro. Had Bobby taken care of the two people who might have information about what had happened to Kathie? Susan Berman had been one; she was now dead. The other was Debrah Lee Charatan; she was now his wife and therefore not legally required to give evidence against him. There was no doubt in Pirro's mind that he was sly as a fox.

Whether or not the marriage was legal, Bobby was still on the lam. While they were still looking for him, the Galveston police got their first hint that Morris Black and Bobby Durst might not have been total strangers, and they could have known each other prior to Durst moving into the apartment across the hall from Black in November 2000.

The tip came from a Galveston social worker, Ted Hanley, who runs an outreach program for down-and-outs called Jesse Tree on a run-down stretch of Market Street, a few blocks from the harbor. Morris had turned up in January 2001 with an idea that fit perfectly with the philosophy of Hanley's agency, which uses technology and innovative solutions to relieve the chronic problems of homelessness.

"Morris had been on a computer in the local library and found a site on the Internet where he could buy eyeglasses in bulk. The kind of magnifying glasses that would normally cost ten to twelve dollars in stores, he could buy for as little as forty-six cents," he says. "His idea was that I would pony up $2,000, he'd pay the balance, and he, Morris, would give them away to candidates of his choosing." When Hanley explained that Jesse Tree couldn't afford to be a partner in the scheme no matter how worthy the cause, because it simply didn't have access to that sort of money, Morris had stomped off in disgust.

Three months later, Hanley spotted the old man outside the First Presbyterian Church on Church Street where dozens of homeless men and women were waiting for the soup kitchen to open. Morris was going down the line, holding eight plastic bags crammed full of eyeglasses, doling them out to outstretched hands, loudly berating anyone he saw smoking.

A few days later he turned up again at Jesse Tree with his glasses. "He wanted to dish them out himself and he did," says Hanley. "But he would get frazzled dealing with people. He'd get mad when someone would ask for two pairs, or he would see one of his recipients buying a beer in a convenience store down the street. But over the next few months he would show up with his glasses several times a week, and he always had plenty of takers.

"What he did was a wonderful thing, he gave away thousands of them. It was a great idea and he was a nice man. But he had to do everything on his terms," says Hanley. "He was not a warm and fuzzy guy. This was his idea and he would carry it out the way he wanted to. I frequently ran him home, but I never was inside his house. He was adamant that he didn't want anybody in his apartment. I never saw him with anyone, he never had a friend. He was lonely and needy, cantankerous and very eccentric, but I'm eccentric too, and I never thought that was a negative."

But although Hanley could appreciate Morris Black's goodheartedness and the clever simplicity of his scheme, dealing with him was a nightmare. "He'd come to Jesse Tree and demand to see me," says Hanley. "It didn't matter what I was doing, he wanted me to stop and talk to him. He had a very short fuse. He would become verbally abusive and shout and yell. He'd get very upset if he wasn't attended to immediately." Often, the agency's volunteers had to throw him out.

Hanley, who'd worked as a teacher and an architectural designer before starting to work with the homeless and people with chronic mental illness, designed the program about fifteen years ago. "We offer counseling, medical and addiction screening, mammograms for uninsured women. We have health and medical equipment we can give out to those who need it," he says.

"We do the work the churches used to do at their doors. Now they give us the money they used to spend and we run this service. We do things in new ways using technology, like the Internet, to help share ideas and services." The program has been so successful that in 2001 the Surgeon General's Office gave Galveston $1 million to replicate the work of Jesse Tree, which is a faith-based group, "supported," says Hanley, "by Christian, Jewish and Islamic churches in the region."

By early summer Morris was tiring of his glasses scheme. He was sick of dealing with what he considered the ungrateful beneficiaries of his largesse and stopped coming by. But he showed up again in July with a new plan. He'd heard that Jesse Tree had been looking to buy a vacant building across the street to expand its services. Morris barged into Hanley's office and told him that he knew someone "with a lot of money" who could help. Maybe this "someone," he said mysteriously, would provide an interest-free loan.

A few days later Robert Durst strolled into the Jesse Tree. He did not, says Hanley, look like a man who had millions in the bank.

"He looked quite poor. He was highly agitated. I didn't smell alcohol or see any behavior that would make me think he was on something, but he was very abrupt, and had a very demanding attitude that was almost like a challenge—How far can I push this guy?

"When he'd arrived at the reception area he motioned

to the receptionist and another female worker that he had to see me. He was writing down on the back of an envelope and banging the pen. The receptionist came in and told me, 'There's a man out there who is mute and wants to see you.' When I was a teacher I taught the deaf and so I can sign. If you are mute it's usually because of a laryngectomy or it is congenital. I didn't see any sign of a laryngectomy scar, so I said and signed to him, 'Are you deaf?'

"He said 'No' and motioned that he wanted to go to an adjoining room. I showed him into our resource center where we have the computers.

'I don't speak to women,' he growled. He said it in such a nasty guttural way, even though the women at the desk had been nice and polite to him.

"I asked, 'What can I do?'

"He sat on a chair and I sat at my desk. He had on huge glasses almost completely covered in white adhesive tape, leaving just a triangle on one lens to see out of. He kept one hand over his eyes as he talked. My feeling was that it was a gag, or a disguise.

" 'I want fifty dollars to go to Beaumont. I don't like Galveston, I'm sick and tired of it and I want to go to Beaumont,' he demanded.

"I tried to lighten the atmosphere. 'We're the Jesse Tree, not the money tree,' I told him.

" 'Is this one of those Goddamn places that give you the runaround?' he barked. " 'No, we are precisely not that,' I told him. 'If you are cold, I can give you a blanket, if you are homeless, I can give you a voucher to a shelter.'

" 'I want fifty dollars, and I want it in cash,' he said. Then he wanted to know what if he didn't like Beaumont and wanted to come back to Galveston? What would he do then?

" 'The same as you've done here,' I told him. 'Find an agency that can help and go talk to them.' "

Convinced that Durst was a phony, Hanley stalled for time, telling him he had to get permission before he could fork over the money, and suggesting he come back after lunch. He never reappeared.

A few days later, Hanley was driving past the Cotton Exchange building at 2102 Mechanic when he saw Black leaning against the building in obvious distress. He stopped his truck and got out.

" 'What's the matter, Morris? Are you all right?'

" 'No.' Morris spat out. 'I have terrible, terrible problems; very complicated, very serious problems.'

" 'Maybe I can help.'

" 'Nobody can help—ever,' he moaned. 'Nobody can understand the nature of my problems. Not you, not anybody.' "

It was the last time Hanley saw the troubled old man alive.

"I was out of town when his body was found, and was on the way back from the airport when I saw the newspaper. When I read the address I said to my wife, 'I know who that is. It has to be Morris Black.'

" 'How do you know?' she asked me.

" 'I've dropped him off at that house,' I told her.

"I called the paper, but still I couldn't remember where I'd seen the picture of Durst before. Then I heard that he'd been pretending he was a mute and dressing as a woman and it hit me, the Jesse Tree, that's where I've seen him."

Hanley talked to Morris's sister Gladys, told her what he could about her brother and she thanked him for saying nice things about him. "It was a wonderful thing he did. He gave away thousands of glasses. He never told me how they were paid for, but the police told me he had bought them all."

He told the cops about Morris. He also told them about his strange encounter with Durst which took place a few days after *20/20* aired the segment about Kathie's disappearance. That suggested two possibilities: Black recognized his across-the-hall neighbor from the TV show, or he knew him from before.

Hanley believes the latter. "I think it's highly coincidental that they ended up in the same place at the same time, renting apartments in the same building."

On October 12, Bobby tried to rent another luxury apartment in Dallas. He'd given up his previous posh Dallas digs in April. The broker, Shelley Cox, called the police, who figured he had to get a place there quickly since he'd given the court an address in Dallas, and if they found out he'd lied, his bail would have been revoked. Their suspect, they acknowledge, knew the law.

Three days later he checked into the Residence Inn, Mobile, Alabama, then walked into Rent-A-Wreck and asked the owner, John Foster, if he could use cash instead of a credit card to rent a car. Foster told him the deposit would be $2,500 plus $1,056 for a four-week lease. That same day Debrah Lee tried to withdraw money from his New Jersey account.

The day after he failed to show for his arraignment, October 17, Durst went back to Rent-A-Wreck, handed over $3,556 in bills and chose a red 1996 Chevrolet Corsica. As ID, he produced Morris Black's driver's license and Medicare card. Then he checked out the Residence Inn and moved across the street to the Marriott Courtyard Hotel for a two-night stay.

With Bobby on the run, his powerful family hired a private investigator, Houston-based Tim Wilson, who claimed he was being paid to look for him and help build a defense. His fee, he said, would come from a Durst trust fund.

Durst was spotted at a Northern California campground on October 22 by a former neighbor in Trinidad. Diane Bueche, who had sold the house there to Bobby in 1994, and had lived next door to him for the next six years, also owned a campsite, The Lazy Devil B Campground, fifty miles away in Eureka where he'd leased office space in 1997. The building manager says he'd never been there, but sent rent checks for months in advance. The camp manager recognized his picture from *People* magazine. Bobby had stayed there the week before and, ironically, his fellow campers included a bunch of retired cops.

"He [the camp manager] saw the picture, his face went pale and he says, 'That's him, that's the guy in the pup tent,'" says Diane Bueche, who told Bobby about The Lazy B just days before his October 9 arrest.

That same day, the top-notch Manhattan criminal defense lawyer, Michael Kennedy, who had been asked by the Dursts to help extricate Bobby from the mess he was in, appealed to his fugitive client to give himself up.

"We're here to say to Robert, 'Come in, please, because you will be treated fairly, you'll be treated justly, you will get a fair trial.'" Kennedy claimed his new client was fragile and running scared of trigger-happy cops. "Based on the family's knowledge of Robert, we believe he wants to come in, but he is isolated, apprehensive and troubled by prejudgments," was the spin the attorney threw on Bobby's flight from the law. Kennedy, who has previously represented a mixed bag of celebrities like LSD guru Timothy Leary, members of the Irish Republican Army, and Ivana Trump, the socialite ex-wife of New York real estate mogul Donald Trump, added that he'd sent an army of investigators to sift through evidence and talk to witnesses in Galveston, Los Angeles and New York.

"We think he's terribly frightened and driven more deeply into fugitivity by allegations that he's a suspect in the execution-style slaying of his best friend, and in the disappearance of his wife," Kennedy added. "He's being painted as a triple murderer by the police. But the only real charges that exist are in Galveston."

It was the pressure of those cases being revisited that caused Bobby to run, he contended. "That increased the weight and heat so significantly on Robert that his judgment caused him to flee. People don't just flee because of a sense of fear and guilt. People flee because of a sense of fear and a sense of hopelessness." The family also set up a twenty-four hour hot line for Bobby to call for help, also funding it from the trust his father had established for him forty years before.

This kinder, gentler approach to a man wanted for a heinous crime infuriated Jeanine Pirro. "Robert Durst is charged with a brutal and vicious murder," she pointedly reminded his lawyer, family and friends. "We would expect anyone with information regarding his whereabouts to be in touch with the authorities." Later her spokesman, David Herbert, ripped into Kennedy's theory that Pirro's revived investigation had forced Bobby to go on the lam.

"I've heard a lot of farfetched criticism and allegation and innuendo from defense attorneys in my day, but frankly, this one takes the cake," he scoffed.

Next Kennedy pulled out the old chestnut of blaming the victim. He said that Morris Black was a scary individual who was feared by his neighbors.

Back in Galveston, on October 25, the screws were being tightened. The case had landed in the lap of District Judge Susan Criss who threw out the original ruling that Bobby's bail be set at $300,000 and upped the ante to $1 million. And although the Durst family had hired Kennedy to represent him, she ordered that Mark Kelly remain his local attorney until she gave further notice. "I believe Robert Durst can still get a fair trial in Galveston County, and I encourage him to contact me so we can make arrangements to bring him in," she said.

Two days later, prosecutors in Galveston and Westchester were on the hunt for Bobby's other bank accounts. They left several unfrozen in the hope that he would try to access them and thereby leave a trail. That same day, a grand jury in Galveston indicted him on charges of the murder and dismemberment death of 71-year-old Morris Black.

The financial brakes were also being slammed on by the Black family. Gladys asked the New York Supreme Court on November 13 to block the sale of any assets that Durst has in the state. Her lawyer, Franklin Levy, told the judge: "Durst is in hiding and attempting to avoid a national manhunt seeking his arrest for murder in Texas. His known bank accounts have been frozen. It is likely that in order to obtain funds, Durst or third parties acting on Durst's behalf may attempt the liquidation or sequestration of the New York assets." Gladys's petition detailed a partial list of his holdings including five pieces of real estate, a trust fund and nine companies in which he is a partner or owns stock.

While the legal wrangling kicked into high gear, Bobby, whether frightened or feeling picked on or whatever his lawyer was claiming as his reason for this interstate chase, had no intention of surrendering. Nor did he care that the Galveston bail bond company he'd used would forfeit the balance of his $300,000 bail.

For the next nearly two months, he made a farewell tour of his life—visiting for the last time the places where he'd been happiest. His sentimental journey took him to Danbury, to the campus of Western Connecticut State University where Kathie had trained as a nurse in the seventies. He stopped off in Scarsdale, at the childhood home where his mother had thrown herself off the roof. He drove to the Katonah estate where he and Kathie had begun their married life sharing the family mansion with his younger brother and his wife.

And he made another visit to the cottage in South Salem where Ruth Mayer spotted him in the neighboring town. "I went into the dry cleaner's in Cross River on Saturday morning and there was a person with bleached blonde short hair and a turquoise sweater grinning at me," she says. "It was dressed like a woman but looked like a man. I hadn't seen him or a picture of him in a long time, but when I got back in the car and I said to Bill, 'There was this guy in there that looked like Bob Durst, but he was dressed as a woman.' Monday's *New York Times* published a picture of Bobby and I went, 'Oh, my God,' and called Joe Becerra. He was in Texas, but they punched the call through to him."

Bobby was in the Atlantic City area around November

18. On the way, police believe, he stopped at Frederick, near Baltimore, Maryland, where he took a license plate from a car parked outside the Moore Printing Company. The car was owned by retired Hagerstown Doctor Georgia McDaniel, whose daughter Michelle had driven it to work that day.

With the stolen plate installed he drove 135 miles north to the Staybridge Suites at Hanover Township, Pennsylvania, where he booked into a room on the fourth floor under the name Emilio Vignoni. His destination was Bethlehem, the home of Lehigh University, where he'd graduated with an economic degree in 1965. He'd "borrowed" the name from a handyman who once worked for him at his estate in Ridgefield, Connecticut.

He stayed there for the next twelve days, hanging around the campus and using the library, where he logged on to the computers to read about the manhunt he'd triggered, and told campus security that he was visiting his daughter. He was also spotted muttering to himself over a beer at the bar of C. L. Checker's across the parking lot from the hotel, but that's not what made the other customers stare. He was wearing a woman's brown wig and a white mustache at the time. He also turned up in the same garb mumbling to himself at The Golden View Family Restaurant.

CHAPTER 15

WHEN WERE YOU LAST IN TEXAS?

ON the morning of Friday, November 30, Bobby checked out of the Staybridge Suites. That afternoon, he caught the eye of a guard at Wegmans Market, a twenty-four-hour convenience store just off Route 512. He was an odd duck and no mistake, with a bald head and no eyebrows, wearing a black parka and sneakers. The guard watched him furtively removing a box of Band-Aids from a shelf, taking one out and sticking it over what looked like a shaving cut under his nose, then replacing the box. He lifted a $5.49 chicken and roasted pepper sandwich which he stuffed in the bag he had slung over his shoulder and slunk towards the door. On the way out he helped himself to a newspaper.

The security guard tipped off store manager Kevin Stickles, who cornered Bobby in the parking lot, asked him to go back inside and called the cops. When Officer Dean Benner from the Bath, Pennsylvania, station house arrived, he thought he was looking at an elderly cancer patient who had been on chemotherapy and lost all his body hair.

"He wasn't expecting me, and when I walked through the door he got really upset. More so than someone who'd just stolen a paper and a hoagie, eight dollars' worth of goods, would normally be upset. He was so antsy, so wired, that it raised red flags for me and I just didn't trust him," says Officer Benner. "I asked if he had ID. 'No,' he said, 'but I do have ID in the glove compartment of my car if you want to walk back with me and get it.' I was just totally unsettled with this whole thing and I told him, 'No, I'm not going back to your car, I'll figure out who you are later.' Later, when the detectives searched the vehicle, the only thing in the glove compartment was a .9-mm handgun. I don't know if that's what his intentions were, to take me back to the car and shoot me to get away or what.

"He said he was living in New York, relocating to the Baltimore area and was passing through Lehigh Valley. Since he had no address, our state policy is to arraign him, and I could have taken him straight to the magistrate, but I called my sergeant and said, 'This guy seems a little too weird. I'm gonna bring him back and process him now, and so we will have his prints, etc.' I brought him back to the station and started asking him questions. He gave me a different Social Security number than he had given Wegmans. I said, 'What's the deal here, which is the real one?' He looked at the floor and said, 'The one I gave you is the right one.' I called dispatch to run a check and thirty seconds later they came back. 'Are you sure you have this guy? Let's go through this, name, date of birth, SS number.' Everything checked out and they told me, 'Well, he's wanted in Texas for murder.'

"I went back and asked him, 'When was the last time you were in Texas?' And with that, all the blood rushed out of his face, his face went like pure white, and he got this stone-cold look. 'I'm not saying another word until I speak to an attorney,' he said and that was the last he spoke to us.

"The detective had put him in our interview room, which has a two-way mirror. I was on the phone running paperwork on him. Next thing we hear is a bang, almost like the sound of a gunshot. I looked at the detective and said, 'How the hell did he get a gun?' and we ran in. He'd banged his head hard off the mirror and kind of staggered back."

Bobby was searched. They found $500 in his back pocket.

"He had no ID on him," says Detective Gary Hammer of the Colonial Regional Police. "We had no idea he was wanted for murder, we were checking for previous shoplifting convictions—no matter the dollar amount, that would make it a more serious offense."

He was fingerprinted and photographed for another mugshot. It was the end of the line for the real estate heir, and he knew it as he stood in front of the police cameraman, his chin defiantly jutting upwards, his eyes refusing to make contact with the lens.

"We contacted the Galveston Police Department and they sent his mugshot over [by e-mail]. I could identify him from that," says Detective Hammer. He was so sure they'd got the same guy he told Texas not to bother sending fingerprints. At that very moment, Detective Cody Cazalas was on a plane to Washington to appear on a segment about Durst for *America's Most Wanted*. It aired the night Bobby was recaptured.

Later that afternoon, after the paperwork was processed, he stood before Judge Barbara Schlegel. During the ten-minute hearing, where he was arraigned on a fugitive warrant, he repeated only his name and New York address before telling her, "I'm not going to answer any questions until I speak to my lawyer."

Judge Schlegel didn't care for his attitude. "He was just angry that he was here," she said. "His demeanor was, I am not answering any of your questions."

This time there was no buying his way out. The judge wasn't interested in how much money he could raise. "In Texas they give more people the death sentence for murder but they give bail on a homicide charge. There's no bail for homicide in Pennsylvania," says Detective Hammer.

But Officer Benner, Detective Hammer and their colleagues in the Colonial Region Police Department weren't fully aware of how big a fish they'd caught until the press descended on Bath.

Shortly after, the New York state police called to confirm their interest in the fugitive millionaire. And Bobby didn't have to wait long for his lawyer. In fact, just how little time he had to wait had local police puzzled. "Less than an hour after he'd been taken into custody, we got calls from three lawyers," says Detective Hammer. "One was hired by Durst's new wife. Another identified himself as Durst's New York attorney, Michael Kennedy. Yet Durst hadn't made a phone call, and word of his capture had not yet been made public, says Detective Hammer, which meant he wasn't traveling alone, or had managed to make a call from inside the convenience store.

Prisoner #01-7537 was taken to Northampton Adult Correction Facility at Easton and tossed into a 12' by 12' cell, his home for the next few weeks as extradition proceedings to return him to Texas got under way.

For the first few days, like all other detainees, Bobby was put under suicide watch, wore a prison gown and was denied a pen.

As he languished in the lockup, police from Texas, Pennsylvania and New York were trying to piece together his odyssey, trying to figure out how he had eluded the F.B.I. and police agencies in half a dozen states for seven weeks and wondering why he hadn't used his money and connections to flee the country.

He had $500 in his pocket, yet he'd risked his liberty for a measly chicken sandwich. "It's not the first time Bobby has been caught shoplifting," says a police source. "He does it for the risk, he gets a kick out of it. What he didn't count on was the officer showing up so fast. Usually he throws some money at the store manager and gets away with it."

Bobby and the lawyers began to plot his defense. "To tell the truth, he was hardly in his cell," says Detective Hammer. "He had so many meetings with his lawyers that he was always out."

On Tuesday, December 4, the manager of the Staybridge Suites, Bruce Hoegg, told police his staff had seen Durst's picture in the local paper and identified him as having stayed there from November 18 until the 30th. The maids there remembered him, but only for his cheapness. He never tipped any of them.

The Westchester authorities, who were already in Pennsylvania, were interested in Emilio Vignoni, whose Visa card Durst had used to pay for his twelve-day stay at the Staybridge Suites. They'd discovered that Vignoni, who used to live in a Manhattan apartment building owned by the Durst family, was a former business partner of Bobby's in a land deal that netted a tidy $107,000 profit for the real estate heir. In 1982, Durst had paid $18,000 for seventy-nine acres in Lewisboro not far from the South Salem cottage. In February 1993 he deeded the lot to Vignoni. Vignoni then deeded it back to Bobby in September 1994. In June 1997, Bobby sold the land to a construction company for $125,000.

"We are looking into the possibility that someone was assisting him," said Jeanine Pirro.

Since a shoplifting bust didn't give the Colonial regional police the right to search his car, they had to wait until detectives from Galveston arrived the following Wednesday, December 5, before unlocking the trunk of the rented Chevy. The Galveston Police Department spokesman Lieutenant Mike Putnal had described the visit as a fishing trip. "We are looking for something that could connect Robert Durst to the murder of Morris Black," he said. The search turned up Black's South Carolina driver's license and two suitcases stuffed with clothes. It also uncovered a bag of marijuana, four joints, two more guns, a Taurus .38-caliber handgun and a Smith & Wesson .38 weapon, along with ammunition, the bill for the Staybridge Suites and several handwritten New York phone numbers and directions to various locations in New York.

The discovery of the maps gave Kathie's brother more sleepless nights. "The police said there were very detailed driving instructions—I'd like to see where he wanted to go. It scared my family. Bob allegedly came into New York during his flight and visited Scarsdale, Westchester County, Connecticut. To get to any of those places from Pennsylvania he had to be within ten miles of my home," he says.

The cops also found four Bank of America envelopes containing $36,200 in $100 bills, and an HSBC bank envelope with $2,400 in it. It was all evidence, according to Colonial Regional Police Chief Daniel Spang that was "germane to the investigation in Galveston and might also have implications in the investigation in Westchester."

Since the Bank of America has no branches in the New York area and 952 branches in California, investigators think that Bobby must have been in the Golden State for most of his seven-week-long game of hide-and-seek.

"We really don't have any idea of where he was," said Lieutenant Putnal, "He wasn't accessing bank accounts or using the credit cards we know of. So many of his activities were shrewd, he took elaborate measures to avoid capture."

Gradually a picture of Durst's bizarre life began to emerge as the investigators checked out his various disguises and aliases. Mrs. Dorothy (Ciner) Armstrong, who now lives in Grand Rapids, Michigan, told police that she hadn't seen Durst since high school and had never set foot in Galveston. They discovered that in the eleven months during which he'd rented the apartment on Avenue K, he'd floated between his life of luxury and a sleazy and lonely existence as a not very convincing transvestite. He was constantly on the move. One week he'd be strolling around the ritzy Hamptons with Debrah Lee, the next he'd be drawing sniggers with his blonde wig, women's clothes and pink lipstick, chowing down on breakfast at the Saltwater Grill in Galveston, sitting alone and mumbling to himself, just as he'd done in Pennsylvania. The owners of a liquor store where he occasionally bought booze remember him barking at dogs.

Yet Justice Theodore Kupferman, who had lunch with Bobby at the Four Seasons in New York a few months before Black's murder, noticed no hint of his client's weird, double existence during the couple of hours they spent together. "It sounds like he's schizophrenic at the very least, but at lunch he behaved like a completely normal person," he told the *Daily News*.

Police say he hung around New Orleans from October 12 through 17, making calls from a pay phone at the city's

Memorial Medical Center. During this time he rented the red Chevy in Mobile and on October 19, wearing one of his lady outfits, he drove to Plano, Texas, to say goodbye to a friend. By the time the police arrived, Bobby had left.

The landlord in New Orleans, Michael Ogden, had said that when Bobby rented the $650-a-month apartment he was dressed in a wig, a loose blouse and pink lipstick. Ogden had no doubt that "Diane" was a man in drag, and a pretty sorry excuse for one at that. "He looked like a sad transvestite who just didn't have the energy to do herself up right," he remembered.

At the time, Bobby's New York lawyer, Michael Kennedy, seemed more outraged at the accusations of Bobby's gender-bending than he was about the charge that he had killed and chopped up a 71-year-old man. "There were no women's clothes found in his apartment and there is no reason for anyone to think that," he railed. "I find it appalling."

Jeanine Pirro, Joe Becerra, and the authorities in Galveston are not convinced that Bobby is as crazy as he would like them to think. The cross-dressing, the babbling, posing as a deaf mute, pretending to be a botanist, are, they believe, just clever ploys to deflect attention from the barbaric murder of Morris Black, and to open the door for an insanity plea if charges are brought against him in the future in other jurisdictions.

"Don't be surprised if they find that all the bizarre behavior he has exhibited these past weeks is nothing more than a clever façade," warned Lieutenant Mike Putnal. "The calculated way he disposed of the body and tried to hide the weapon [a saw] was not the act of a crazy man."

Bobbi Bacha also shoots down the theory that Bobby was a mentally unstable, nomadic transvestite. His motives, she believes, were much more sinister.

"It was a disguise and nothing more," she says. "And a pitiful disguise at that. Anyone who knows about cross-dressers knows that they are going to look good as a woman. They have the nails down to a tee, the makeup just perfect. This guy was just flopping on a wig and a dress."

While Bobby kept mum about his secret past in his cell at the Northampton County Jail, where he was held in the maximum security wing, Ann McCormack went to court seeking to have Kathie declared dead and to wind up her daughter's estate now that her former son-in-law had been charged with murder. That put an end to a deal that had been on hold since the Westchester authorities reopened the investigation. In December, Judge Renee Roth of Manhattan Surrogate Court agreed. Kathleen Durst had been legally dead since February 1, 1987, she ruled, and Kathie's estate, which, with accumulated interest, had grown to nearly $127,000, could now be distributed. Kathie's mother would receive $36,000 just a few days before her 88th birthday on Christmas Day. Bobby Durst was entitled to the remaining $61,000. She also ruled that his share be held in escrow until the Westchester D.A. decided to charge or absolve him in the death of his wife.

"Kathie had never been declared dead by any court," says Jim McCormack. "It's a formality, but it had to be done."

A few days later Kathie's family and friends were furious to learn that Bobby was harboring another secret. He had quietly divorced her years before. The relief her family had felt at the surrogate judge's decision turned to anger at this latest revelation. "You can't trust Bob Durst," Jim lashed out. "This is just another extension of his deceptive personality. He never reached out or attempted to contact anyone in our family before doing this."

Once again, Bobby had slyly sidestepped the law. In New York, he had no legal responsibility to notify the McCormacks of his plans, and in the divorce papers he listed them as living in Manhattan, although he knew that Jim had lived in New Jersey for years. His only obligation was to use his best efforts to locate his missing wife.

The procedure he sneakily used is called divorce by

publication. He had to make a search for Kathie and did this by writing to government agencies such as the Post Office and the Department of Motor Vehicles, asking for a forwarding address for his missing wife. Since none of the agencies could provide one, he got court permission to publish a notice stating his intention to seek a divorce. The notice can appear in any rinky-dink publication; the only stipulation is it must be in English, appear three weeks running and be within the court's jurisdiction. The missing spouse has thirty days to reply. According to the court papers, Bobby filed for divorce in March 1990 after he had advertised his intentions in the obscure *Westchester Law Journal*. Bobby went back to court with copies of the advertisement and a notorized letter declaring he'd had no response. He was awarded an uncontested divorce on June 13, 1990, the same year he sold the Truesdale Lake cottage. To make it more hurtful to the McCormacks, Bobby was granted his divorce on the grounds of spousal abandonment, claiming that Kathie had deserted him.

Worse, he may have gotten the idea from Kathie's mother, who, at the direction from Surrogate Court, had posted notices of intent in the *New York Law Journal* in November 1982 when she first sought to become the temporary administrator of Kathie's estate.

While Jeanine Pirro's office was still investigating the legitimacy of Debrah Lee Charatan's claim to be Bobby Durst's legal second wife, Debrah began visiting him in jail.

She arrived in a gold-colored Lexus 6 on December 12 for her first hour-long visit. Her first glimpse of the 120-year-old Northampton County Prison must have been a daunting sight; it's perched like an armed fortress on top of a hill above the town of Easton. The couple, whose relationship had flourished in palatial homes, sat across a bare wooden table under the watchful eyes of prison guards and the curious stares of fellow inmates and their kin.

"They were hugging and kissing," commented one prison visitor. "He looked old." She also befriended Christina Fredericks, the girlfriend of another alleged murderer locked up behind bars with Bobby. Fredericks, a married mother of five, was visiting her boyfriend, 35-year-old former jeweler Alton Field, who was awaiting trial on charges that he'd killed his wife, Theresa, wrapped her body in a rug and hidden her in a basement.

He had told everyone that his wife had left him in May 1998, but police became suspicious after they discovered that he and Christina had been lovers for five years. When the landlord of Field's jewelry shop stumbled over her corpse, Field was arrested.

Christina was protective of her new friend, who obviously unaccustomed to prison visiting rules and regulations. She tipped her off to reporters lying in wait outside the jail, and shielded her from cameras.

While his new wife was ducking the press, Bobby was making the most of his celebrity status in jail. One guard griped that Bobby was getting special treatment, claiming that he and Debrah Lee were allowed to use a staff room for her visits, and that the other guards addressed him as "Mr. Durst." They were impressed, he claimed, by Bobby's tales about John Lennon and his romance with Prudence Farrow, who, since hitting the headlines with her affair with Bobby, has pursued a career of her own in the movies with limited success. Prudence never managed to ease herself out from her famous sister's shadow, and worked on several of Mia's films in various supporting roles. She was a production assistant on the 1984 movie, *The Muppets Take Manhattan*, art department coordinator on Woody Allen's *The Purple Rose of Cairo* (1985), a coproducer on *Widow's Peak* (1994), which featured Mia with Natasha Richardson and Adrian Dunbar, and finally won an acting part in the 1999 made-for-TV movie, "Andy Kaufman's Big Show."

Back in Galveston, Judge Criss put Durst and his lawyer on notice that once he was back in the grip of Texan justice, he wouldn't be leaving before his trial. He would be held, she said, without bond. She also ruled that he would face bail-jumping charges at a January 22 trial. Instantly, Bobby's new trial attorney, Dick DeGuerin, complained that Durst didn't jump bail, because no one had told him about the October 16th hearings.

"It would be manifestly unfair to arbitrarily set a court date, not notify the defendant and then file for bail-jumping," he argued.

The assistant district attorney was having none of it. He told the judge that his office had contacted Mark Kelly, the lawyer Durst had hired after his October 9 arrest, and also bondsman Troy McLehany with whom Durst had had to keep in regular contact as a condition of his release. McLehany said that Durst, who had told him he was a writer from Dallas, had spoken to him on the phone October 12 about the hearing on the 16th. "He told me he'd be there," he testified.

Ignoring DeGuerin's protests Judge Criss reiterated her October 25th order that the bond on the bail-jumping charges be hiked to $1 billion.

The high-powered Houston lawyer then demanded a gag order. Police and prosecutors in New York, California and Texas were talking too much, he complained. They were blabbing to the press details of allegedly incriminating evidence and sitting on information that pointed to his client's innocence. Jeanine Pirro particularly felt the brunt of his wrath. She was guilty of grandstanding, he said, and had made "egregious" and "outrageous" statements about Mr. Durst. And, added DeGuerin, "She refuses to make a direct statement, although by inference her statements say that Mr. Durst is a suspect in the disappearance of his wife, about which there is absolutely no evidence that Mr. Durst is responsible."

He also said that ballistic tests proved that the gun found in Bobby's car when he was arrested in Galveston on October 9 was not the murder weapon that killed Susan Berman. He was only telling half the truth; the L.A.P.D. didn't say the bullet that killed Susan had come from the .9-mm pistol, but they wouldn't confirm that it hadn't either. The preliminary tests, they said, had been "inconclusive."

Although Jeanine Pirro had told Judge Criss in a letter that she had said "virtually nothing" about the case, and added that it was essential for her to appeal to the public to come forward with information that might offer clues about Kathie Durst, she didn't bite.

Reluctantly, Judge Criss granted the defense's request. "I would never have imagined I would be issuing a gag order, because of my feelings about the First Amendment. But I have an obligation to make sure that not just Mr. Durst, but the state of Texas, the people of Galveston County, the district attorney's office and Morris Black's family all get a fair trial," she said in her December 17 ruling.

It was a master stroke by DeGuerin, the veteran lawyer who had represented Branch-Davidian sect leader David Koresh before his standoff against the F.B.I. and the A.T.F. at Waco. As soon as Judge Criss banged her gavel, the police and prosecutors were barred from refuting DeGuerin's claim about Bobby's .9-mm pistol. Her ruling applied to all police, prosecutors and potential witnesses in Galveston, as well as to authorities in other states. "I'm gagging them from talking about anything that applies to this case," she said.

Bobby's first public appearance since his arrest came on January 25, 2002, at an extradition hearing to determine whether he should be returned to Texas. He didn't look like a crazed killer as he was led into the Northampton County Court; his bald pate was now covered by a coating of gray hair and he had a stubbly gray beard. For his day in court, he'd opted for a thoughtful librarian garb, a charcoal gray blazer and slacks, a gray flannel shirt and black-and-white sneakers. He'd forgone the new contact lenses that had led to his arrest in Galveston, hiding behind oversize goggle-like eyeglasses.

Michael Kennedy told the court that Bobby would not fight his transfer to Texas. Indeed, he added, "Mr. Durst is anxious to get to Texas to defend himself. He has a viable defense and he wants to raise it."

Judge James Hogan then asked Bobby if he understood what was happening. "Yes," he said in a voice that was barely above a whisper. "Are you satisfied with your legal representation?" the judge then asked. "Yes," he replied just as softly.

Bobby's new wife didn't show up for the hearing, but directly behind him in the courtroom sat his nemesis, Jeanine Pirro, still waiting for her chance to interview him about Kathie's disappearance. She never took her eyes off him, studying his every move as if trying to commit it to memory. At one point, Bobby turned around and glared at her. She held his glance without a blink.

Another pair of eyes had been trained on him. As he was led from the court in handcuffs, a middle-aged, gray-haired woman stepped forward and confronted him. "Do the right thing, tell me what you did to Kathie," she demanded. Bobby looked at her, taken aback for a second until he recognized her. It was his old enemy, Gilberte Najamy. He turned away without a word and Gilberte, overcome with the drama, burst into tears.

The next morning, Bobby was driven from the Northampton jail to Philadelphia Airport under police escort, wearing the same subdued gray outfit he had worn the day before in court. His hands were cuffed in front of him. As he sat waiting for his flight to leave, he had his nose stuck in a book, *Once in a Lifetime.*

He was a slight figure, pale and ashen-faced, sandwiched between the two burly Texan detectives from the Galveston Fugitive Squad who had flown north the day before to pick up their murder suspect. They hustled him to the back row of a Continental Boeing 737 and sat him down in a window seat, 21-A. Throughout the three-hour flight to Houston, he muttered and hummed quietly to himself and stared bleakly out the window. He ignored most of his free airline lunch of a beef sandwich, a bag of Fritos and a chocolate cookie, settling for an apple and sipping a

Coke. One of the detectives removed his plastic knife, and Bobby peeled the apple with his fingers.

Whatever nervousness he felt about what lay ahead of him in Texas didn't show until the plane was buffeted by turbulence, about an hour into the flight. According to the *New York Post* reporter Brad Hunter, who traveled on the same plane, Bobby clapped his hands over his ears, folded them together as if in prayer and looked mightily relieved when the plane landed. "That was quite a bumpy ride," he remarked to his uncommunicative guards.

At Houston a police car was waiting. Bobby was unceremoniously bundled in by his two tough escorts and whisked off to Galveston County Jail, sixth miles south. When he arrived he asked for a copy of the Koran.

In the most horrible of ironies, Bobby Durst stood in a court in Galveston before Judge Criss on January 31st, twenty years to the day after his lovely young wife went missing. By his side was his heavy-hitting lawyer. The sight of DeGuerin, a tall, steely Texan with a handsomely craggy face and silvery gray hair, filled the prosecution with trepidation; he would, they feared, be a formidable opponent. Any case against Bobby would have to be watertight; since he had very deep pockets, money would be no object in worming out even the slightest bit of extenuating evidence.

"He is very good, one of the best," says Bobbi Bacha admiringly. "He's such a bulldog, when you hear his name, you want to run."

Bobby was asked how he intended to plead to the charges that he'd killed and dismembered Morris Black.

"I am not guilty, Your Honor," he answered firmly.

CHAPTER 16

AWAITING TRIAL

DeGuerin went into attack mode. He wanted Judge Criss to let him into Bobby's apartment on Avenue K, and produced a letter he had written to landlord Rene Klaus Dillman asking, in an almost unprecedented move, if he could rent the place. With a difficult court battle ahead of him and an unsympathetic client to defend, he needed every edge he could get. By moving a raft of experts into the murder scene and allowing them unlimited access to it, he hoped to uncover evidence that the cops had missed during their exhaustive search.

Despite his (to him) very reasonable request, and his offer to pick up the cost of repairing damage caused by the police investigators, he'd been turned down. "I can't take any money from him, and I can't give him the apartment. It wouldn't be right," Dillman told the Galveston *Daily News*. He also didn't want his property ransacked; he had his other tenants to consider. "I've just had it all fixed up, and I don't want anyone messing it up again," he said. The judge allowed the defense team entry to the premises, but only to take photographs and measurements.

DeGuerin next asked Judge Criss to bar any testimony or mention of Kathie's disappearance before the jury at the upcoming trial, and requested that subpoenas be dished out to Jeanine Pirro, Joe Becerra and Kathie's pit bull friend Gilberte Najamy to find out what they knew that he didn't at a pretrial hearing. He also stepped up his campaign against the Westchester D.A., accusing her again of using the case to boost her own career.

Pirro's executive assistant, David Herbert, slammed

back, "The only person who keeps bringing up the district attorney's name is the defense attorney himself. We have a job to do and we're not going to stop doing it just because a defense attorney seems to have a preoccupation with my boss."

While the legal experts bickered amongst themselves, Bobby was getting used to life in the harsh Texas justice system. After a routine first night stay in the medical wing, he was transferred to a solitary cell—for security reasons, said officials. For the first time in his colossally privileged life, Bobby found out that his money counted, not for nothing exactly, but not for very much. His bed was a hard cot without a pillow or a blanket, the menu consisted of the minimum slop necessary for survival and bore no resemblance to the gourmet fare he was accustomed to chowing down on at the Four Seasons; prisoners can expect a meat course, two vegetables and bread, and dessert, if there is one, says Correction Lieutenant Dan Carnley. All visitors had to be approved by his lawyer, and DeGuerin allowed just Debrah Lee, Sareb Kaufman and one of Bobby's brothers to drop by.

But Bobby's notoriety brought some perks behind bars. He was given a "suite" to himself, a two-man cell which consists of a 7' by 10' sleeping area and an adjoining 12' by 16' dayroom with its own shower, TV, table and chair. He didn't mingle with the general prison population because the one time he did, another inmate took a slug at him.

"He was not in solitary confinement, he was held in protective custody because he was assaulted," says Lieutenant Carnley. "Some of these guys resent high-profile cases. The one who attacked him is kind of mental, we don't know whether he attacked him because he was Robert Durst or just because he was just standing there." Bobby was allowed out to walk or shoot hoops by himself in the prison yard for a short period daily.

When he wasn't on the phone or in a meeting with his team of four attorneys, he'd bone up on his rights at the jail's law library. His lawyers, says Carnley, brought him stories from the Internet, newspapers and magazine articles about him. He'd asked for a copy of the Koran as soon as he arrived, and also had a Torah. A rabbi conducted Passover services for him in his cell.

He burned up the phone lines. If they behave themselves, the 600 inmates of Galveston County Jail have almost unlimited phone access, up to sixteen hours a day. All calls have to be collect and no incoming calls are allowed. Bobby's favorite phone pals were Debrah Lee and Kim Lankford.

He was also popular with the prison staff. "He was very polite, respectful, didn't seem like the picture everyone painted of him as a butcher. There have been no disciplinary problems with him at all." When asked if he had the impression that Bobby thought he'd walk out of jail after the trial, Carnley says emphatically, "Yes ma'am."

His arrest, coupled with the horrendous details of the murder, sent shock waves through the people he went to school with, men who, like Bobby, are counting down to their 60th birthdays.

James Klosty, whose name Durst had used as a reference to rent an apartment—he claimed Klosty was his boss at a California lumberyard and obtained an American Express card using his name—says he doesn't remember ever having spoken to him. "I never would have recognized him from his mugshot except they showed a profile view and he was unmistakable because his nose was very memorable. Then I remembered what he looked like. He wasn't one of my friends."

Another classmate, Frank Wilman says: "I thought it most interesting that he had all of this money—he had thousands of dollars in the car—and he's finally caught shoplifting. Maybe when you have so much, you don't really recognize what you actually have." What troubles Wilman is that Durst may be the most famous member of the class of '61.

"It was a school system where so much money is spent on education, which had a high percentage of high school graduates going on to college—they were children of over-achievers—and yet you look through that yearbook and it's very hard to see any great successes. There is one guy who writes for *The Washington Post*, then there's Durst."

On February 6, Bobby was back in court to hear Judge Criss rule on DeGuerin's motion to suppress any mention of Kathie or Susan Berman in front of the jury. DeGuerin told the judge that it was "time for Westchester County District Attorney Jeanine Pirro to put up or shut up" about her allegations against his client. She was grandstanding, he complained, hounding Bobby for her own gain, hoping to establish a foothold in a political career.

"Counsel believes Ms. Pirro will have to admit that there is no evidence that Robert Durst had anything to do with Kathie Durst's disappearance. The evidence in this case will be complicated enough without Ms. Pirro out there running for governor," he sniped.

She fought back. In an affidavit filed by her lawyer, Michael E. Weill, she accused DeGuerin of attacking her in an attempt to steer attention away from the killing of Morris Black. "It's obvious that DeGuerin's agenda is to switch the focus from the evidence against his client in the brutal murder, beheading and dismemberment of a senior citizen, to the bizarre claim that the district attorney made him do it," Weill said.

Anything Ms. Pirro had said or done was aimed at encouraging people to come forward with information and, to that end, she had been successful, said Weill. There were new witnesses who have volunteered relevant information and they were prompted to come forward by the publicity the case had engendered.

Galveston District Attorney Michael Guarino jumped into the fray. He moved quickly to squash the idea of forcing Pirro to reveal details about any evidence she had gathered while trying to build a case against Durst. "I can't imagine a crazier situation," he said.

Judge Criss agreed. She ruled that Jeanine Pirro would not have to testify. But she also agreed with DeGuerin that she was perilously close to violating the gag order. The Westchester D.A. has persistently maintained that a gag order issued in a Texas court has no standing in New York, but says she will obey it because she doesn't want to jeopardize the Texas case or cooperation with the authorities either in Texas or in California where the investigation into Susan Berman's death is also ongoing. "I do have concerns about Ms. Pirro continuing to make statements about this case. I don't want her investigation to interfere with Mr. Durst's right to a fair trial."

What she specifically didn't want was a repeat of the extradition hearing in Pennsylvania, where Pirro not only turned up, she sat directly behind Durst in the courtroom and announced that she "intended to get to the bottom of Kathie Durst's disappearance." Judge Criss also allowed the police to remove samples of walls and flooring at Black's and Durst's apartments and said that Bobby should be allowed to read newspaper accounts about himself.

One story he must have read with alarm surfaced in GQ magazine and suggested that Bobby may have been drawn to Galveston to be near the University of Texas Medical Branch and the Rosenberg Clinic's pioneering gender-treatment program. He'd contemplated seeking hormone treatment, said the magazine, but he couldn't bring himself to disclose his real name to the doctors. He allegedly spent his days on the hunt for crack cocaine and his nights in the company of an expertly gussied-up African-American "girl" called Frankie who interceded on his behalf with attractive young male prostitutes down at the seawall. According to Frankie, Bobby, who liked to be called Roberta, was such a pitiful sight in his ill-fitting blonde wig and black tube top, not to mention his usual surly demeanor, that he frightened even the most desperate crackheads away. He needed "her." She claims to have met him in a gay bar, the Kon Tiki Club, which features a penis-shaped dance floor, and to have acted as his pimp.

The Galveston police, who knew nothing of any of this, would like to talk to Frankie, especially since she'd offered up the helpful information in the article that Bobby had "cut that man up! First the head. . . ." Was this an eyewitness? they wondered. Frankie also said she knew what happened to Susan Berman, alleges the magazine. "That woman knew what kind of person he was! Why shouldn't she? I knew! And then she started asking for money!"

The day after the hearing, actor Bruce Willis jumped into the picture. It had already been rumored that the star of *The Sixth Sense* and the *Die Hard* movies was interested in playing the cross-dressing fugitive millionaire on screen. He'd been following the case avidly and pounced upon a *Vanity Fair* article which painted Gilberte Najamy as a dogged crusader and avenger of her friend's death, who'd devoted her life to bringing to justice Robert Durst, the man she was convinced not only killed Kathie, but had also slain Susan Berman and Morris Black to silence them.

Willis' production company, Cheyenne Enterprises, was said to be about to close a deal with Sony; *Vanity Fair* scribe Ned Zeman and his partner Daniel Bernstein were to write the script and share a $1 million payday.

Gilberte denied accusations that she was expecting a cut of the fee. "I know nothing about a movie deal," she protested. "My best friend has been missing for twenty years. The only thing that's important is finding out what happened to her. If everyone else wants to make money off the story, God bless them. The sad thing is that people aren't looking for Kathie," she added, "they are more focused on this kind of stuff." What she didn't add was that she already had a deal with another writer.

Jeanine Pirro didn't welcome this sudden surge of interest from the macho star and was worried that the credibility of one of her potential main witnesses, should she ever bring Bobby to trial, may be irretrievably compromised. "Even the discussion of profiting from knowledge of an investigation presents the possibility of obstacles to the prosecution," admitted her assistant.

A day later, the chances of Gilberte's campaign against Durst ever making it to Hollywood were dealt a blow from which it's unlikely they can recover. Bobbi Bacha, who'd been growing skeptical of some of Gilberte's allegations and claims, decided to look into her life a bit more closely.

What she found was shocking. The 50-year-old Gilberte, who now works as a domestic abuse counselor, had an extensive rap sheet of her own, with five arrests on drug possession charges, one for theft and another for violating probation. All in all, she'd been charged a total of eight times in her native Connecticut. She was arrested in March 1987 for possession of cocaine and writing a bad check; a year later, she was picked up for violating her probation. In 1988 she was nabbed again for drug possession and sentenced to two years in jail. In 1990, she was given three years after being convicted on another narcotics charge. In January 1991, she was arrested for larceny and fined $75. In March she was back in front of a judge, again on narcotics possession charges, and given another year in the slammer.

The revelation about Gilberte's past stunned Kathie's friends and family. "I just wanted to reach out to her," says Jim McCormack. "This case has been so traumatic to so many people for all sorts of reasons. I guess the issue would be her vulnerability on a witness stand. Lawyers can be so nasty. But the timeline doesn't change. I still don't know what happened to Kathie. I asked the investigators, and they said Gilberte's record would have turned up if it could have, would have been relevant. But it wasn't. Maybe it's better it surfaced now and it's out of the way.

"Her friends are mad with her. I've asked them to talk to Joe Becerra—maybe there's a name from that time they can remember which might help. Joe is following every single lead," he says.

Gilberte's fall from grace was greeted with glee by Bobby, who called Kim from jail to say he'd read the stories exposing her as a junkie who had done time. Her shame was also vindication for Hillary Johnson, who has complained bitterly that in her zeal to see Bobby Durst rot in hell, Gilberte had accused Susan of an unspeakable crime, conspiring with him to cover up the alleged murder of his wife.

"Maybe no one involved with the fictionalization of Gilberte as an Erin Brockovich–type heroine who spends twenty years bringing a killer to justice really cares about the truth," she says. "It was always going to be Hollywood fiction anyway, just like most of the rest of the coverage. They'll probably find a way to mess around with the facts and make it work anyway. It's a movie, right?"

Hillary is just as suspicious of the motives of the Westchester D.A. "I think that whole Westchester cabal, from Jeanine Pirro on down, is suspect. They have increasingly struck me as little more than a bunch of publicity hogs. If they had a shred of evidence on Durst, instead of the whine-a-minute Gilberte as their 'front man' out there working the press, they should have arrested him. I think they are trying him in the press, just as the Durst defense claims."

A couple of days after Judge Criss's ruling, Bobbi Bacha took a team of divers back to Galveston Bay in an attempt to keep her promise to the family of Morris Black, who asked her to find his still-missing head so they can bury it with the rest of his body. In a strange coincidence, it turns out that the judge is related to her; they have the same great-grandfather, says Bobbi. "He died mysteriously while working on an investigation on the Galveston Docks. We believe he was onto something illegal and was killed. He slipped off the docks one night and was found floating in Galveston Bay. Susan and I are second cousins or something like that."

"I wouldn't recognize her if I saw her," says Judge Criss.

The search was scheduled for Saturday, February 9, because of its exceptionally low tide. The morning dawned clear and calm as Bobbi, her husband Lucas, investigator

Jeff Moore and her father, retired cop Robert Trapani, and two divers started the grim hunt over a twenty-five-foot grid from the pier where teenager James Rutherford found the body.

The Galveston Police Department didn't sanction the search, but had an officer on hand just in case Bobbi's divers did retrieve the head, or any other evidence. The good-natured cop assigned to the task cracked jokes as the search went on. "Jerry Netherland is known around Galveston as "Officer Smurf," because he acts and looks like Joe Pesci, he's short and he wears blue," says Bobbi. "My dad used to have breakfast with him every morning, and he would tell the waitress, 'Get this man a booster chair!' "

The divers picked over every skull-sized rock on the seabed. The others waded into the waist-high water using their feet like brushes to sweep the bottom. After four months in the crab-infested waters of the Gulf, Bobbi expected the head to have been picked clean by sea creatures. Should they find Morris Black's skull, she was hoping that still lodged in the bone would be the bullet she believed had killed him. But after four hours in the chilly water, and with the tides swiftly rolling in, the divers had to give up.

Still, Bobbi was satisfied with the day's work. On the shore, northwest of the pier where the dismembered body had washed up on September 30, her team found two women's wigs, one blonde, the other red, a pinkish blouse, a lipstick and an unused eyeliner which were all turned over to Officer Netherland. "It looked like they had been tossed out of a car window," Bobbi says.

She may not have found Morris Black's head, but she was sure she was closer to unraveling what happened the night he was tossed into the bay. "X never marks the spot," she says, "but I really think we've found the place where the body was dumped. It was put into the water farther up the bay near where we found the clothing and the wigs. The police haven't searched there. The body floated back towards the shore, but the head is dense and will have sunk to the bottom like a rock."

Bobbi is convinced that Durst threw Black's remains into the water late at night, under the cover of darkness. "We'd been looking to the left of the pier, because that's where the witness saw him and talked to him when he asked her if people fish there. So everyone assumed that's where he dumped the body. That was wrong, he was just hunting for a spot to get rid of it.

"Instead he must have walked two streets farther along. On the next street there lives an old hermit man who is dead nosy, so he wouldn't have gone there, but the street after that leads to the Old Galveston Causeway. Few people know about that road, and he was looking for a safe place to dispose of the corpse. It should have floated out into the bay, but because of the cold front that came in that night, it washed back over to the piers."

The next suitable tide fell on February 24. A week before, the witness who'd answered Bobby's questions about fishing on Saturday, September 29, saw a black Lexus draw up by an empty lot near where he'd been found. An expensively dressed middle-aged man and woman got out and started nosing around.

"What are you doing here?" she'd asked.

"We've bought this lot and we are going to build our house here," the couple told her. The witness didn't buy that. She knew the owner and was certain he hadn't sold it. But before she could answer, they began plying her with questions about the body. They wanted to know where exactly it had washed up, and where the trash bags were found. She told her she didn't know and shut the door.

With an expanded team of fifteen investigators, two scuba divers, two boats, grid walkers and team leaders, nearly 100 people in all, Bobbi resumed the search over a much larger area. The divers slipped into the 50-degree water near the old three-arch railway bridge. Despite being roped to the boat, they had to battle the strong current, and one them was almost sucked under.

Meanwhile the waders found a 2 foot by 6 foot–wide section of rolled-up carpeting containing what appeared to be bloodstains and tissue, which Bobbi and her team suspect is cerebral (brain) matter. She believes the cool water temperature over the winter months and the tightly rolled carpet provided some protection for the tissue from the weather and sea life. "It did test positive for blood," says Bobbi, "but we don't know what type of blood, however. If the carpet can be tested for gunpowder residue and the tissue is cerebral, and the tissue matches Morris Black's DNA, then I believe that the police could conclude from this that the cause of death was a gunshot to the head."

Officer Netherlander took the carpet into custody, but not before some of the tissue floated away in the rising tide. Bobbi began scouring the causeway. About a quarter of the way along, where the water is deeper, she found what looked like a bloodstain. On closer inspection, she saw what looked to be a gray hair stuck to some moss. The area also tested positive for trace blood. All in all, her team found and identified over 120 pieces of possible evidence on the shore and even more on the causeway. She believes they may have belonged to the victim, but since Black had no friends or close family living near him to identify them, and, the cops think, Durst cleaned the old man's apartment out of all his personal effects, it might be impossible to prove that any of the items that floated up were his.

"I do believe we found the correct dump site of the body," says Bobbi. "And I believe the head is on the bottom, rolling back and forth with the super-strong currents, but I don't think we'll ever recover it." Because of the gag order, the Galveston police will not comment on Bobbi's findings, but a source told her that they were "significant."

Morris Black's ghoulish death seemed to breathe some life into the Los Angeles Police Department, whose investigation into the shooting of Susan Berman had yielded not a single suspect in fifteen months of inquiry, and left her friends and family heartsick with frustration. Both Sareb and Deni say they haven't been contacted by the Los Angeles investigators in well over a year.

At the end of February, it was suddenly announced that

just after her death, the Beverly Hills police had received an anonymous note on which was written Susan's address and the single word "cadaver," sent to them with "Beverly" spelled "Beverley." The L.A.P.D. were interested in Bobby, they said, because his arrest on murder charges indicate that he was capable of great violence. "His criminal behavior has made us take another look at him," said Lieutenant Clay Farrell, one of the detectives working the case.

They wanted Bobby to submit a sample of his handwriting so they could compare it with the letter. His lawyer instantly dismissed handwriting analysis as a "pseudoscientific" practice which was just about as accurate as tealeaf reading, and said the L.A. cops could use any letters that Bobby had written to Susan that already were in their possession. He didn't deny his friendship with Susan, or having given her money.

The emergence of the note after fifteen months of silence seemed to upset Bobby as he languished in his Galveston cell. What was unbearable to him was that Susan's beloved children would now think—if they didn't already—that he had killed her. According to *New York* magazine, he called Sareb to tell him that he didn't kill Susan, and that he hadn't sent the macabre note: "It's absolutely ridiculous, I didn't write it," Bobby assured him. Then at the beginning of March, he called Susan's son again. He wanted to meet with him, talk to him about Susan and explain what had happened with Morris Black. If he paid for the trip, would Sareb come?

"How could I not go? This was a person my mother trusted more than anyone," Sareb told the magazine. For two hours, separated by a glass screen, he listened intently as Bobby swore again that he was not Susan's killer. Once more, his charm worked its magic.

"I went not knowing what to think, but I came out feeling that this was one of Susan's dearest friends, and I wanted to give him the benefit of the doubt," says Sareb. He says that Bobby asked him what his mother would have thought about the murder of Morris Black.

"She'd be standing by you, like she always did," he told him.

By the end of the month, Dick DeGuerin had soured on Bobby's plain old "Not Guilty" plea. With the mountain of evidence that linked Bobby to the murder, there was almost no likelihood he would be acquitted. And while the veteran attorney had flirted with the possibility of entering an insanity plea, it seems he shied away from that option after the jury in the shocking Andrea Yates case returned a "Guilty" verdict. He knew that if the chronically depressed young Texas mom who systematically drowned her five children in a bathtub "to save them from Satan" couldn't convince a jury she was temporarily insane, then there wasn't a snowball's chance in hell that his cross-dressing millionaire client would.

Perhaps DeGuerin had an early tip that DNA had been found on Morris Black's body. Whatever had prompted the switch of tactics, he asked the judge to speed up the DNA testing at a March 28 hearing in which he complained that the prosecution was dragging its feet at bringing the case to trial: "The testing isn't really necessary because Mr. Durst's plea is Not Guilty by reason of self-defense and accident," he said. Everyone in the courtroom sat bolt upright in their seats, wondering if they had heard correctly.

Without giving any more details, DeGuerin outlined his new strategy. Bobby was admitting that he had killed Morris Black during a violent scuffle, and therefore any DNA evidence that the prosecution had was no longer relevant. By his side, in his first public appearance as an acknowledged killer, Bobby, in his dark green prison scrubs, looked oddly unconcerned as his lawyer assured the court: "Mr. Durst is anxious to get to the truth and get to trial."

The defense attorney's strategy took a blow to the solar plexus when the results of the old man's autopsy were released a week later on April 4. In his damning report Galveston's Chief Medical Examiner Dr. Charles M. Harvey put the cause of death as "homicide of unknown means."

But Morris's body was covered in bruises; they were on his chest, shoulders, upper, mid- and lower back, left leg and elbows. His right arm was broken in four places, and it looked like Bobby had tried to slice off his fingertips and given up mid-attempt.

Bobby also knew enough not to try to sever the limbs at the joints; instead he'd sawn them off just below. The arms were chopped off cleanly, and the legs had been hacked at, leaving "jagged and irregular" cuts. The report also showed blood in the lungs, and indicated that Morris had choked and suffocated.

The blood in the lungs could have been caused by a heavy blow to the head or from a major slash to the throat. Or if Morris Black had been shot in the head and the bullet went near the trachea, that also could have caused bleeding into the lungs. The old man was in poor health, said the coroner. He had severe chronic heart disease, clogged arteries, high blood pressure and a degenerating liver. There was no evidence that he used drugs or alcohol.

Dr. Harvey sent blood, bone marrow, muscle and other tissue samples to the University of North Texas Health Science Center where DNA testing was carried out. In five instances, the DNA found on the body—the report did not specify where—was from the "highest probability a Caucasian individual." It seems that the Galveston cops had the DNA of Morris Black's murderer.

DeGuerin now faced the uphill battle of explaining to a jury that the man Bobby Durst killed, accidentally, in self-defense, because he was afraid for his own life, was pounded black-and-blue to the point where his arm suffered multiple breaks, while Durst suffered no visible injury. He had to convince them why, if the murder was not premeditated, Bobby went out and bought the tools to dismember and wrap the corpse four days before. And the DNA that was found on the body—if it belonged to Bobby—how could that ever be explained away?

It was never a fair fight. Morris Black was, by all accounts, plain crazy. He was an insufferable, tightfisted, ornery, unsightly old man given to uncontrollable rages, hounding his neighbors and riling everyone he met to the point where sweet old ladies in city halls and kindly librarians admit they could have killed him themselves. Hardly anyone had a good word to say about him; no one was surprised when they read about his death in the papers. Most of them wondered why nobody had silenced him long before.

But Morris, who had no record of physical violence, couldn't stand up in court to defend himself, and it isn't a crime to just be crazy. Bobby didn't have to stand up in court and defend himself either; he had a squad of high-priced attorneys to do that for him. All that the Texan jury had to believe—and the master courtroom showman Dick DeGuerin talked their language—was that Bobby Durst, a quiet and simple man, provoked beyond endurance and physically attacked, lashed out in self-defense, accidentally killed Morris Black and, in his blind panic, disposed of the body by hacking it to pieces, stuffing it into trash bags and throwing it into the Gulf of Mexico.

CHAPTER 17

AFTERMATH

WITH a blood trail that led straight back to Bobby, coupled with the incriminating evidence investigators discovered in his Galveston apartment, in his silver Honda and in the rented Chevy, even the tenacious DeGuerin knew that claiming Bobby had nothing to do with the fate of Morris Black would be asking even the most gullible jury to suspend belief.

Yet his new defense, that Bobby lashed out in a fit of rage stoked by the old man's constant badgering, had holes big enough to drive a bus through. The week before Black's mutilated torso floated ashore, Bobby wasn't anywhere near Morris, he was living high on the hog at the posh $125-a-night San Luis Resort, washing down delicacies from the hotel kitchen with glasses of Irish beer. Bobby Durst had enough money to live there, or anywhere else he fancied, for the rest of his life. If his elderly neighbor was driving him nuts, why not just move away?

DeGuerin apparently had thought of arguing that Morris had died of cardiac arrest before Bobby chopped him up. It looked like that might be the plan when the attorney obtained Black's medical records from Mainland Medical Center, where he was treated for a bad heart. But just hacking off a dead man's head and limbs for the hell of it is too sick to win any sympathy from a jury.

Why did Morris have to die? Did he know something that Bobby didn't want anyone to find out, ever? Ted Hanley of Jesse Tree is convinced that they knew each other. Carmen Sedgewick, who worked across the street from 2213 Avenue K said she saw Morris open Bobby's silver

CRV and put a shopping bag in it. Another neighbor said that Morris used to yell "Shut up! I don't want to hear it," at someone with such a low-pitched voice, she couldn't tell whether it was a man or a woman.

Did Morris watch the *20/20* show and figure out who Bobby, aka Mrs. Ciner, really was and torment him about his seedy double life as a transvestite? If he was a genuine cross-dresser who hung around the Kon Tiki Club picking up boys and trolled the seawall for transvestite whores down at the harbor as was claimed in the *GQ* article, the idea that someone knew his real identity, and was threatening to expose him, might gnaw at the core of his being. According to his friends, Bobby had suffered such an unbearable loss of face when he was passed over for the top job as the head of the Durst Organization in favor of his brother, that he cut himself off from his family and even his most steadfast friends. The humiliation he would endure and the ensuing scandal it would cause if word of his gender-bending proclivities secret was made public, could be too much for the intensely private Bobby to bear. Keeping his secret from his powerful, wealthy family, not to mention his new wife, might be a convincing motive to kill.

Or was the cross-dressing just a ruse as private detective Bobbi Bacha and Michael Ogden, his New Orleans landlord, think? Ogden said that Bobby, aka Diane Winne, was a hopeless transvestite, and he didn't have a clue how to look convincing. If it was just a disguise, and they did have some sinister link from the past, the timing and location is interesting: Morris was living on West 45th Street, New York, "Durst territory," when Kathie went missing. His brother Harry had a successful construction business in Massachusetts. The Dursts had connections there, Bobby and Kathie made dozens of trips to the state, trips that she wrote about in a diary. And if somewhere, those worlds collided, could Morris have known something about Kathie's disappearance that would have put Bobby behind bars?

When Bobby had been nabbed in Pennsylvania, his New York attorney, Michael Kennedy, speculated that the reopened investigation into Kathie's disappearance, and the presumption that somehow he was responsible for it, had driven Bobby to desperation. Kennedy claimed that fear had driven Bobby to flee, but had it also driven him to do the unthinkable, dispose of Morris Black? When Jeanine Pirro and Joe Becerra started nosing into the case of his missing wife, did they awaken a slumbering monster that had lain untouched for nearly twenty years? Kennedy said that Bobby began to feel hunted and paranoid. Is that why he traveled to Galveston, having tracked down Morris, and used his lady disguises to watch the old man at close range for a few months to figure out if he was a threat? What he found was someone he could neither reason with nor buy off; Morris in his twilight years was a babbling, rabid geriatric, who could, at any moment, blurt out a story, as he came so close to doing to Ted Hanley. After Morris told Hanley that he knew someone with a lot of money, did Bobby reckon it was only a matter of time until he disclosed a secret they shared? Or was Morris simply bumped off because he would have made the perfect alias if the case against Kathie wouldn't die? No family or friends ever came near Morris; there was nobody to miss him when he was gone.

Over the last few years Bobby had stolen the identities of at least a dozen people to provide himself with access to the credit cards and bank accounts of his victims if he were ever to be cut off from the family money tree and needed ready cash. Using these aliases he had assembled a network of safe houses. Was this a man who was sure that, sooner or later, the far-reaching tentacles of the law would close around him?

And why on earth did Bobby's lawyer want to rent his apartment when Bobby was in jail awaiting trial?

Then there is Susan. In the last phone call they shared, just before she left on her Christmas vacation, when Susan

told her she had "big news, something that's going to blow
the lid off everything," Kim Lankford was only half listening. She'd just assumed that her friend was working on
another story about Davie Berman and Bugsy Siegel and
she hadn't been interested enough to prod for more information. But since Bobby's arrest, she's been racked with
doubt and guilt that she didn't attempt to coax Susan's secret from her. Was the "big news" about Bobby and Kathie?
Was that why Susan had to die too?

Everyone knew that the case had been reopened. It had
been plastered all over *People* magazine. And although the
Westchester police hadn't contacted Susan directly, a *New
York Times* reporter had and she had agreed to talk to him.
Bobby knew that too. Did he jump to the conclusion that
she was going to reveal that he had confessed to her about
killing his wife, as the mourner at Susan's memorial service
had claimed?

And then there was the money. Bobby, despite living
frugally, could be extraordinarily generous. He'd bailed Susan out time and time again, to the tune of $50,000 in the
last weeks before her death. He'd told Julie Baumgold, "Susan was my witness." If Susan was convinced that Bobby
had murdered Kathie, had she made a deadly miscalculation
in asking him for money? Perhaps in his heightened para-
noia he saw it as an implied threat. Even if he had intended
the $50,000 as hush money, Susan, who friends insist was
honest to a fault, would never had viewed it as such. If he
had persuaded her to make the phone call to the dean on
February 1, 1982 pretending to be Kathie, did she tell him
twenty years later that despite the gifts, she no longer believed him to be innocent and would have to tell the truth
to the Westchester district attorney? Or maybe she said
nothing of the sort, maybe she just called him and said,
"The police want to re-interview me about Kathie, let's go
over what happened again," and he, frightened she'd make
a slip, decided he couldn't take that risk.

Who was the real Bobby? The sweet guy Kim Lankford had known for 15 years and dated for 18 months or the killer of an old man who was found hacked to pieces? How could she not have suspected something? Maybe what all Kathie Durst's friends had been saying for years was true, that he did have something to do with his wife's disappearance. If he had confessed as much to Susan, why hadn't she warned Kim? Intead she'd played matchmaker for them. And after everything they'd meant to each other, was it Bobby, God help him, who pulled the trigger and snuffed out the life of Susan, his most loyal supporter?

If Bobby did blow Susan's brains out to stop her breaking her twenty-year silence, did he think that Kim was a threat to him too? Is that why he took her to Palm Springs that last week in March, not to console her grief over Susan's death, but to worm out what Susan had told her? If that was also true, would Kim have been his next victim? The fear and confusion as she tried to sort it all out made it difficult to get on with her normal life. If the cops think Bobby killed Susan why didn't they arrest him?, she reasoned. If he's innocent, why won't they clear him?

If Bobby did shoot Susan to silence her, she died in vain. Susan was not going to blow Bobby's cover. She'd told a friend that she loved him unconditionally, just like she'd loved her dad. Even if they both had killed people, she couldn't turn her back on Bobby any more than she could on Davie.

Just before her death, she'd told friends she was working on another book about the Mob—it's what she knew and what paid the rent. She'd discovered that Galveston was the model for its Las Vegas empire. In the forties and fifties, the island was a gambler's paradise, a regular den of vice rife with corruption and violence.

Bugsy Siegel visited Galveston and when he saw how wide open gaming was in the port city, he got the idea of replicating it in Vegas. When, in the mid-fifties, the state of Texas finally soured on drug dealing, prostitution and the other low-life activities that accompanied gambling, all the casinos in Galveston were closed. Many of the owners, not to mention the dealers and whores, relocated to Las Vegas to ply their trades in the more sympathetic environment found by her father and his partners.

Susan had already interviewed some owners of Las Vegas casinos about the old days when they had operated in Galveston. She'd talked to New Orleans writer Dick Odessky, author of a book on the Las Vegas Mob called *Fly on the Wall*. Susan's big breaking news was probably as Kim had guessed correctly at the time, everything to do with new Mafia secrets and nothing to do with Bobby Durst.

A Hollywood producer and Susan's cowriter on *Las Vegas Diaries* believes his friend was shot by a professional who wanted it to look like a Mob hit. "Normal people don't kill each other that way," said Jonas McCord. "They go crazy, they shoot five or six times. They use really big caliber guns." Is it feasible that she was the victim of Mob revenge?

And finally, there is poor Kathie. Did she, as many of her friends suspect, dig her own grave when she got hold of Durst's financial documents? She was smart enough to know her way around a balance sheet—her friend Eleanor Schwank said she was interested in the market. "She followed the financial news and read *The New York Times* business pages every day. She would tell me, 'Eleanor, you should buy this,' and everything she steered me to turned out to be good investments. She did the same with Bob. She had a lot of know-how."

Why did a young, intelligent woman raised in a loving home stay with an abusive husband? Was it because of her solid upbringing like Dr. Marion Watlington says? "She was really young when she met him and had been raised in a big Catholic family and she knew he was a troubled soul. His mother committed suicide when he was just a young kid and he was in trouble as a youngster—Kathie was determined to be the one to make him happy."

Kathie also thought she could handle Bobby and his

demons. She was so near independence. In four months she would have started work as a doctor and could have told him to get lost and keep his precious money, or sued him for her rightful share of their marital assets at her leisure. Instead, when Bobby wouldn't budge from his arbitrary and miserly sum of $100,000 as a divorce settlement, cut off her credit cards and refused to pay her last tuition bills forcing her to borrow money from friends, she put the confidential documents in an envelope and mailed them to a U.S. senator. It never occurred to her that the politician, who had taken large financial contributions from the powerful and influential Seymour Durst, would make sure they found their way back into her father-in-law's hands. Enraged, Seymour had reportedly told Bobby to "take care of his wife." Did Bobby think this meant silence her forever?

For twenty years, Kathie's anguished family has had no peace. Now her memory is being blackened by the revelations about Najamy's drug use which may also bolster Bobby's claim that Kathie was a user and had been killed by drug dealers. It may also have investigators questioning what was going on at Najamy's party on the last day she was seen.

With her marital troubles at the boiling point, Kathie was spoiling for a fight with Bobby when she got home. They'd flown at each other verbally, that's for sure. She had said they couldn't be in the same room without fighting. Was there a push, a shove or a punch? Did Kathie fall heavily, cracking her head on the stone fireplace or tumbling downstairs to the stone floor in the downstairs room? Is that what happened? Did Bobby, realizing he'd killed her and knowing that there were plenty of people who would swear he'd beaten her in the past, panic?

If there had been an accident, did he think that nobody would believe him? He ran out of the house into the sleety blackness. Somewhere, he made a call. Did he call Susan Berman, and did Susan, who was still in touch with one of the "uncles" who'd guarded her as a child, ask one of them to help Bobby get rid of Kathie's body? Or did he call some rough contacts of his own? It was an open secret that the Mafia controlled the construction industry in New York; there was simply no one else to deal with if you wanted to build in the city. Did someone help him dispose of Kathie? Is that when, if the Galveston police are right about him having sawn up Morris Black with chilling expertise, he learned how to dismember a body?

The next day, did he get his "witness" Susan to make the call to the medical school dean posing as Kathie and saying she was sick and wouldn't be in class? Or maybe since he later displayed a penchant for posing as a woman, did he raise his guttural voice an octave and make the call himself pretending to be his wife? If Susan had nothing to do with any of it as many of her friends swear, maybe Bobby confessed his guilty secret one of the nights when he was high as a kite, and Susan was sickeningly sober. And so when the case was reopened and the fear of capture he had suppressed for nearly two decades began to unhinge him, did he freak out when Susan didn't get the message of his "gift" of $50,000 and in a fury over her willingness to talk to *The New York Times*, did he shoot her?

And what role, if any, does his new wife, Debrah Lee, play in his fractured life? Why did he marry her? They had a relationship that spanned twelve years, but it was never so passionate they couldn't bear to be apart; they'd only lived together for a few months and that was over a decade ago. While he was parading around as a woman in Galveston, she was clobbering business rivals with her multi-million-dollar real estate deals in New York. He was also dating Kim Lankford at the time of their wedding. Like everyone else, she knew he was a suspect in Kathie's disappearance. Did he fear Debrah Lee might uncover all the family skeletons? Was it a cynical ploy on his part; did he persuade her to marry him to neutralize her, to make sure she wouldn't give evidence against him? If so, it all might have worked—except for the sudden storm.

Jim McCormack, a gentle man whose pain is evident in his eyes when he talks about the baby sister he loved and couldn't protect, is tormented by these questions.

"She sent the financial documents to the politician, and they showed back up on Seymour's desk. He was a huge power in politics and gave money to both parties, essentially buying business favors.

"Seymour told Bob: 'You have to take care of this situation" or words to that effect. How do you interpret that? What does it mean? Does it mean you have to do something drastic, or just get your wife under control.' Seymour's not here to tell us what he meant, Bob will never tell us what it meant and Kathie can't tell us either.

"Because of the Durst name and financial clout, Kathie and Bob got into lots of places the ordinary person would never get into. But she was young and naïve to trust people with a public image and not realize they had a darker side behind it.

"She told her friends and some of the family she was afraid. The more the abuse escalated, the more she poured out her heart to other people. She arrived on Gilberte's doorstep, on Eleanor's—they all tell the same stories. Things got so bad that just a month before she went missing, she opened up to perfect strangers. (The police won't give out their names because it could be corroborating evidence of her state of mind.) We trusted the authorities to pursue leads and investigate and to visit all the appropriate locations. Quite frankly, they didn't do as good a job as they should have.

"I just want an answer," says Jim. "It's such a hard thing to carry. And you have to get on with the rest of your life, for your wife and family, your kids have to have a life. But underneath it all, especially in the eighties, I couldn't stop crying. My father-in-law who's been wonderful, told me, 'It's the not knowing, lack of closure and the denial in the face of accumulating information and evidence.' I want to know what happened to her, and give her a memorial service.

"Somebody somewhere knows what happened to Kathie. Now that Bob is in jail, maybe someone who was afraid to talk, or was under his influence, will come forward and help the police find out what happened to my sister."